1995

Change in the Contemporary South

Change in the Contemporary South

edited by *Allan P. Sindler*

Duke University Press   Durham, N. C.   1963

© 1963, Duke University Press
Library of Congress Catalogue Card number 63-21317
Second printing, 1964
Third printing, 1969

Printed in the United States of America
by Halliday Lithograph Corporation

Foreword

Although it is evident to all that the postwar South is undergoing important change, the specifics of the changes are considerably more difficult to determine and to assess. In the belief that the time was ripe to analyze certain of those changes, the Department of Political Science at Duke University initiated a conference held on the campus of Duke University in Durham, North Carolina, from July 12 to 14, 1962. The conference theme was "The Impact of Political and Legal Change in the Postwar South." Eight invited papers on specified aspects of the contemporary South comprised the core materials for the conference. Each of the writers understood that, after the opportunity to revise his conference draft had been provided, the papers would then be submitted for joint publication as a book. The present volume is the end product of that mid-1962 conference.

When presented at the conference, each paper was commented on by several discussants. Their observations made the conference more effective and were of use in the revising and editing phase as well. Accordingly, we are pleased to record our thanks to all the discussants: Richard Bardolph (Woman's College of the University of North Carolina), Fred V. Cahill, Jr. (North Carolina State College), Robert H. Connery (Duke University), Paul T. David (University of Virginia), C. Aubrey Gasque (Administrative Office of the United States Courts), Douglas H. Gatlin (Wake Forest College), Hugh M. Hall (Duke University), Alexander Heard (University of North Carolina), Abraham Holtzman (North Carolina State College), Richard H. Leach (Duke University), I. Gregory Newton (Peace Corps), George W. Spicer (University of Virginia), and Robert H. Woody (Duke University).

Both the holding of the conference and the publication of this volume were made possible by a Grant in Public Affairs awarded to the Duke University Department of Political Science by the Ford

Foundation. We gratefully acknowledge that financial assistance, at the same time making clear that the Ford Foundation bears no responsibility for the conference or the contents of this book.

ROBERT S. RANKIN *and* ALLAN P. SINDLER
Conference Co-Chairmen
Duke University

Editor's Preface

As noted in the Foreword, this volume has evolved from a mid-1962 conference at Duke University on "The Impact of Political and Legal Change in the Postwar South." The conference co-chairmen determined in broad terms the topics of the eight papers and extended the invitations to the authors whose essays comprise this book. Each contributor prepared his conference draft with knowledge of all the topics to be treated by the other papers, but without awareness of their actual content. Subsequently all papers were revised, in several instances substantially. In undertaking revision, each author was familiar with the substance of all conference papers and the comments by discussants on them, and with the suggestions of the editor in regard to his own chapter.

Since the form of the conference determined the initial structure of the papers, it was not considered feasible to have each contributor attempt, when revising his paper, to refer to the content of other papers in any continuing or explicit manner. Rather, each author was encouraged to concentrate on developing his own topic, leaving it to the editor to add a concluding section in which areas of agreement and disagreement among the essayists would be highlighted. The responsibility of each contributor, therefore, extends essentially only to his own essay, while that for all matters relating to the volume as a collection of essays on selected aspects of a common broad theme is assignable solely to the conference sponsors, including the editor.

The content of footnotes, in nearly all cases, consists of reference citations and not of substantive additions to the text. The footnotes, accordingly, have been located at the end of each chapter.

No group of eight papers could hope to do justice, of course, to the variegated patterns of ongoing change in the South. This volume, like the conference, has focused on some facets of change, with a special though far from exclusive stress on political trends. No uniformity of view has been sought other than to accept, if the materials permitted, a common definition of the South as the eleven former Confederate states. By design, a variety of disciplines—history, economics, law, sociology, and political science—and of analytic approaches has been tapped. Some chapters attempt a broad and systematic overview of the subject, others apply original empirical research to more specialized inquiries. If these several essays, in sum, clarify some of the directions, old and new, of Southern response to the forces of change, their purpose will have been well served.

ALLAN P. SINDLER
Duke University
March, 1963

Contents

Change in the Contemporary South

Thomas D. Clark

The South in Cultural Change

An Overview

Since 1920 the South has undergone profound and sometimes revolutionary changes in most areas of its agrarian way of life. Mechanization, plant breeding, the eradication of insects, parasites, and animal diseases, the expansion of the livestock industry, the organization of market facilities, and the shifting emphases on staple crops have revolutionized the Southern economy. Reconversion of land use from row to non-row crops and timber production has reformed the face of the region. Expansion of facilities for the generation and transmission of electric current has wrought deep change in the mode of Southern home life. The central fact of Southern history in the past half century has been the struggle to revise the regional economy. The older ways of Southern life linger on only in isolated fringe areas where facilities for producing change are lacking.

Though change has been so dominant a fact in modern Southern life there is a great paradox in recent Southern history. There is remarkably little evidence at the moment that controlling political forces have undergone significant modifications of past attitudes and philosophy toward the conduct of politics in the South. The outlook of the so-called conservative Southern bloc both in Washington and the state capitals is more nearly akin to that of the bourbons or readjusters of the last quarter of the nineteenth century than to that of the Democratic party since 1920. There is still a feeling that the vote should be kept small, that responsible management of political affairs should remain in the hands of the few, and that white supremacy should be maintained.

In a second area, the Southern churches, there is much resistance to change. Of course there have been acceptances of the fact that a rise of industrialism and an ever-expanding urban South have generated new problems and challenges. Individual congregations and groups of ministers and church leaders have revealed an awareness of the fact that religious organizations are called upon to accept new conditions of the times. Yet barely under the surface there is a restiveness caused by more modern views of the Scriptures, the problems of the social community, politics, and the place of the economic and urban man in the pattern of the old and conservative orthodoxy. There appears to be little danger that the region, which thirty-five years ago was rocked by the storm of fundamentalism, is likely to repeat the unhappy chapter of the anti-evolution fight. The South has not, however, advanced intellectually or philosophically to the point where the conservative forces of organized religion cannot stir the winds of bitter controversy. Whatever issues help to formulate attitudes toward religious orthodoxy also help to shape the South's political reactions.[1]

Forces and influences which shape political history in the South are subtle and sometimes remote. Thus the political development of the South must be considered against a background of culture, social conflict, crisis, and history. Since 1876 too many Southerners have excused their region's shortcomings as resulting from the Civil War and Reconstruction. More informed scholars of regional history have considered the vacuous years from the end of Reconstruction to the great depression as formative ones for many current Southern problems. In these years there began the devitalizing outflow of capable Southern youth in search of better educational and economic opportunities. They sought to escape the peonage of staple agriculture, and to forego the boredom of life in a static society. With these eager young expatriates went thousands of white and black laborers in search of rewarding employment. They were fugitives from cotton, sugar cane, and tobacco fields.[2]

There can be little doubt that where a vindictive demagoguery has prevailed it has discouraged more timid but progressive Southerners in all fields of regional activity during the last century. From 1880 to 1920 Southern weekly newspapers published a dreary running narrative of life in the region.[3] Collectively they recorded a history of political limitation, social betterment, race relations, and improved public institutions on the one hand, and of a stifled economy on the other. Editors persistently scolded their neighbors for a variety of failures. Public officials were deemed inefficient, venal, self-seeking, and blundering. In most Southern counties in this period the editorial voice was one of doom.

There prevailed in the New South a nagging consciousness of social frictions. Such travesties as lynching, abuses of convict labor, acts of capital violence, and indifferent law enforcement gave the region an unenviable reputation. The controlling forces in Southern political history have been labeled "bourbon," "readjuster," "redeemer," "oligarchy," "aristocracy," and "special interests." Whatever the label, there has ever been an awareness that political controls in most Southern states rested in the hands of relatively few wilful men as leaders, together with a remarkably small minority of participating voters.[4] In time, from Virginia to Texas, common men lashed out at oppressive exploitation and at embedded sources of regional control. In South Carolina Pitchfork Ben Tillman shattered the aristocratic-bourbon hold on that state. Thomas Watson stormed the ramparts of privilege and entrenched management in Georgia. James K. Vardaman of Mississippi, William Goebel of Kentucky, and James Hogg of Texas raised voices in behalf of embattled masses.[5] These were dreary years of shifting political patterns in which Southern politics were being cast in new molds of agrarian control.

Prior to 1930 Southern culture and economy suffered from numerous handicaps. Three of these at least can be easily identified. There was the enormous problem of making adjustments between the races, a problem made more difficult because whites had been antagonized on two counts: the freeing of the slaves and the elevation of the free Negro to voter and officeholder at the outset. There was lack of sufficient capital to reduce dependence upon staple agriculture, and thereby to lessen fears of exploitative special interests. Finally, the standard of comparison used to estimate progress made by the postwar South was backward looking. Repeatedly, Southern recovery was discussed by both European and American observers in terms of how nearly the region had come to restoring conditions of the ante-bellum period.[6] Though many Southerners of this earlier age may have dreamed by the images of the Old South, the New South was forced to live hard by standards of mediocrity as compared with national attainments.[7]

Political and social realignments of the New South produced different social cleavages in the region from those of the Old South. Poor whites became "Red Necks," and these multiplied with the recurring economic and social declinations of the passing decades. This era of Alliance and Populist outcry produced a kind of political protest which brought the South close to its only real threat of radicalism.[8]

This radicalism, however, was to be assessed more in terms of the shifting sands of political leadership than of an enduring upheaval of the agrarian ranks.[9] Constitutional revisions made in this period bound the South more tightly than ever to a course of rigid conservative political control.[10] These revisions restricted corporations, the Negro, the ability of legislatures to make available adequate funds for education, industry, and public welfare, and clamped down on the region a political status quo by their highly circumscribed provisions for representation and amendment.

The era of change ushered in by agricultural reversals of the early 1920's further amplified the conflicts and failures of the Southern agrarian system. The rising stream of out-migration, away from the farm and the South itself, set in action new impulses in Southern society. The rise of the new urbanization stirred afresh political and social restlessness. Mechanization of farming, application of new scientific techniques, and reversal of land usage went far to redirect the course of Southern history.[11] No doubt the development of a modern industrial society, along with increased urbanization, promises a new regional political posture. Clearly, political leadership at all levels has become conscious of and concerned with the meaning of industrialization and urbanization to Southern politics. The facts that there are Republican candidates for many offices in the South and that there is even more talk of two parties are reflective of new attitudes. Certainly the reshaping of the Southern agrarian pattern contains the germ of long-range political restiveness and change. Again, the current and localized political revolts are within the framework of a rugged conservatism which encompasses farmer, industrial and white-collar worker, management, and capitalist.

One region within the South reflects a different economic and political pattern. No study of Southern culture, politics, or economy is adequate without giving some attention to the Appalachian South. Too often Southern social and political studies tend to ignore this area. It not only embraces a large block of Southern geography but comprises one of the tightest states of mind in the region. The standards of cultural growth of the South have been almost as much depressed by social and economic retardation in the highlands as by the wavering fortunes of the more cultivable staple crop areas.[12]

The Appalachian highlander, along with his white and Negro farm neighbors elsewhere in the South to 1940, operated on such slender economic margins that even a slight decline in national economy threatened disaster. For the broader Southern agricultural belt cotton as an economic mainstay was weakening by 1910, and by 1920 it was threatened with ruin because of soil exhaustion, international competition, and, paradoxically, by overproduction, a fact arising largely from the expansion of the cotton belt onto new lands in the valley South and in the Far West.

It is enormously important in considering the social and economic progress of the South to be reminded that only since 1930 have many parts of the region broken the bondage of physical isolation. Not until 1950 did the South as a whole establish really effective communication with all its areas, and, in turn, with the rest of the nation. Highways are just now breaking barriers which have kept many sections in a state of backwardness, if not primitiveness. Since the end of World War I and the advent of the interstate highway system the South has faced a social and cultural revolution. The Federal-Aid Highway Act of 1956 promises to have the most enduring effect on the South politically and economically of any single piece of national legislation in American history. The effects of this era of change are yet to be meaningfully reflected in the political reactions of Southerners in attitudes toward current issues and partisan behavior. This is equally as true in every other aspect of Southern life. There is evidence on every hand that the last vestiges, not only of the Old South, but of what Henry W. Grady called the New South are being destroyed.

Some of the areas of social change that should concern both historians and political scientists are public health, utilization of natural resources, and the applications of mechanization. Since 1930 phenomenal advances have been made in the eradication of those peculiarly regional diseases that sapped vast pools of human energy. Part of this advance reflects an improved world-wide knowledge of medical care, but a good part of it is due more to improved utilization of natural resources such as water power, the use of machines and chemicals to destroy the old cesspools of malarial infections, and the development of new processes of food preservation.[13] Active campaigns of early disease detection and hospitalization have gone far toward preserving human health and energies. The impact of these changes is no doubt to be felt in Southern political reactions of the future in every phase of regional political expression.

No single cultural impact, however, has been greater in the South than that of education. To say that the South has an adequate system of schools and colleges as compared with other sections of the nation no doubt would be folly. To say even that the present South is making the necessary responses to its educational needs would be equally fallacious.[14] As compared with even its immediate past of the 1920's, however, it has made appreciable advances. However inadequate Southern effort in the field of higher education may be for purposes of developing colleges that will meet standards of modern education, the impelling effect of improved education upon Southern life is already an established fact.[15]

In 1888 Lord James Bryce with prophetic insight viewed the Southern Negro's future in Southern society:

> If the Negro shares in the prosperity of the South, if he grows richer and enters the professions more largely, he will become more "uppish," will be quicker to claim social equality and more resentful of its denial. What the whites deem his insolence will provoke reprisals from them. This will increase the tension between the two colours. And as the upper section of the negroes find that all their advances in knowledge and material well-being brings [*sic*] them socially no nearer the whites, their feelings will grow more bitter and the relations of the races more strained.[16]

The perceptiveness of these observations needs no underscoring in the light of contemporary racial strains in the South.

The Image of the South

Hundreds of books have been written about the South. Every regional crisis has produced its full quota of comment. Outsider and native alike have fed this rising stream. Native sons have mixed personal confessions and apologies in their explanations of why the South is like it is. This outpouring of regional books is exceeded in America only by those which deal with the West. The West, however, has been viewed largely through a gossamer of romance, but the South has been presented from many viewpoints. Romanticists have created a myth, while historians, sociologists, statisticians, and travelers have given mixed interpretations.

For more than a century Southerners have battled the statistician. In the 1850's Hinton Rowan Helper compiled his *Impending Crisis* from the tables of the 1850 census. This was not just another comment on Southern social and economic conditions, but a disturbing analysis in a moment of approaching crisis. Almost a century later, in 1936, Howard Odum and a corps of fellow sociologists and statisticians prepared a searching social and cultural analysis of the South defined in broad regional terms. Their book, *Southern Regions*, was a monumental study of conditions in the decade and a half following World War I. Two years before Odum's voluminous study appeared, W. T. Couch of the University of North Carolina Press persuaded thirty-one regional writers to define the South in more literary terms. The resulting *Culture in the South* was a forthright appraisal of factors which set the region apart from the rest of the nation.[17] Earlier a group of scholars at Vanderbilt University had published a provocative collection of essays under the title *I'll Take My Stand* (1931). Already their colleague Edward Mims had published his *Advancing South* (1926), in which he discussed Southern culture in terms of an expanding educational system and a rising industrialism. He was positive that the South could not stand still, and that it must not slip backward. These books showed little concern with the statistical technicalities of regionalism or especially with empirical social analysis. Primarily they sought to explain Southern culture in terms of its relationship to that of the rest of the country. This still remains a theme of Southern interpretation. With something approaching desperation, Southerners generally have clung to a tradition of distinctive regional culture, and they have hoped the tradition was valid. For some "the Southern way of life" has no deeper meaning than segregation of the races, but for those of sharper perception and maturity it has meant a way of life which has held to certain dependable standards of human and social values.

For three hundred years the South has boasted of its cultural heritage without fully defining it. Few people from Hinton Rowan Helper to the Vanderbilt essayists have stated their concepts in enduring terms. Contributors to *Culture in the South*, such as J. Den Hollander on the poor whites, Josephine Pinckney on the literary tradition, and Charles W. Ramsdell on the historical background came closer than any of the essayists.

Historians have viewed the Southern heritage largely in terms of its beginnings, and its economic, political, and social forces which have led to sectional conflict, and, subsequently, in light of changes within the nation. Some have regarded the South as a colonial region subordinated to a domineering Eastern industrial and capital control.[18] William H. Skaggs portrayed in his *Southern Oligarchy* (1924) a South struggling under the heel of an ideological and exploitative system which enslaved a good part of the population. Dealing more fundamentally with culture, W. J. Cash in a provocative chapter in *The Mind of the South* (1941) drew a sharp and realistic conclusion. Both Skaggs and Cash demonstrated that social immaturity, a dual racial system, and extra-regional economic pressures have at most produced a spotty cultural history. Isolation has accounted for the retention of many frontier attitudes. Thus any scholar finds evaluation of regional cultural attainments difficult largely because little of the Southern tradition has a common meaning to all the people.

Odum's composite picture of the South in the 1930's, composed of 273 parts, is a cultural jigsaw pattern encompassing all phases of Southern society. A majority of the parts of his picture contain a predominant element of failure. Collectively, his broad propositions cast the editor in the role of a Southern Martin Luther nailing both the South's shortcomings and its potentialities to a broad statistical door.

Whatever facts or appraisals have confronted the South in the past, Southerners have clung steadfastly to their belief in the region's cultural heritage. In large measure this heritage has been as difficult of definition as any tradition or folk belief. So far as it has realistic meaning, it has been largely an aspiration and a dream. Predominantly rural, the South of glorious memory was the Old South. Land was virginal and plentiful, life was assumed to have been zestful, whether lived in plantation house or backwoods hovel. Agriculture promised the fruits of good living. Abundant rainfall, good soils and forests, a moderate climate, and an unhurried approach to life developed a social system that was devoid of many complexities.[19]

Any re-evaluation of the system of labor in the Old South must be made in light of new evidence. Further mature historical research in this area might modify much of the Southern myth, especially as to the positions of yeoman and free labor and slavery. If a modern historian presented the austerities of slavery he might be accused of harshness. Modern probing of ante-bellum conditions of life might undermine the foundations of a tradition, or present a contrary picture to that held in the popular mind. Frank L. Owsley dealt a good part of the "moonlight and roses" myth a telling blow in his stimulating *Plain Folk of the Old South* (1949).[20] Like Odum, he resorted to the statistical record to pigment his factual portrait of an important segment of the ante-bellum South. Frontier yeomanry and agrarianism were basic themes of his study. The yeoman was far more numerous and economically more independent than the slavery-oriented studies have indicated him to be.

The modern South is shifting its foundations. Southerners moving to urban and suburban communities are being forced to leave many of their traditions behind with their abandoned plow tools and exhausted fields. Industrial community environment tends to submerge regional traditions and distinctions. New social and economic demands cause present-day Southerners to make responses well this side of the region's past.

Southern Literary Activity

In the field of literary merchandising the South was and still is a poor market for its authors' books. Painters have found it difficult to secure commissions, or to sell original works. Sculptors who depended upon political handouts to create commemorative statuary faced starvation as artists. The most profitable business a sculptor could engage in was carving tombstones to mark the final resting places of more prosperous local sons.

Despite the limited Southern market for books, Southern authorship since 1865 has thrived. Few or no purely cultural activities have made greater appeal than writing. Local colorists found the South and its way of life fertile sources for their stories. Even the very negativeness which suspended life in a cultural thraldom proved colorful subject matter. Old sentimentalities and even romantic frustrations have inspired authors to present their native South in varying hues and emotions. Southern political behavior also has been the theme of many books.[21]

Why has the South produced so many writers? The answer is complicated. Fundamentally, Southerners are highly reminiscent people. They have frequently recalled the days of pioneering, ante-bellum life, and the woes of Civil War and Reconstruction. Slavery and subsequent discrimination against the free Negro have been subjects for many books about the South. The existence of slavery within the world's most dramatic experiment in democratic government gave it the appearance of being a great paradox. The peculiarities of Southern social and economic systems have more often provoked than inspired regional authors. During those years when the South was caught in a stifling economic squeeze there was abundant material for social protest writers.[22]

The Southern system, 1865–1930, was productive of the stock characters of an agrarian society. There were storekeepers, moneylenders, landlords, decaying families, pious political frauds and demagogues, rear-guard hate peddlers, and a vast horde of faceless poor people. Under similar conditions England nurtured writers like Charles Dickens and George Eliot. In the South there was also a certain residual romance which led writers to escape present realities to take refuge in a gilded past.

In this long period economic advancement was slow and arduous for large numbers of Southerners. Professional and business opportunities were limited for ambitious men without capital. Industrialism was only a marginal part of much of the Southern heritage, and there was almost no turning to this field in a popular way before 1920. Too, for almost two centuries the South has supported a highly active newspaper press, and from editorial offices have come many of the South's ablest authors.[23]

The limited educational accomplishments of an agrarian society made writing as a profession by which to support oneself little better than a gambler's choice. It was, however, an avenue which could be opened with limited capital resources. Mississippi, for instance, has produced a far larger crop of writers than either its economic or educational history would seem to justify. William Faulkner, Stark Young, Eudora Welty, James Street, Hubert Creekmore, Richard Wright, David Cohn, William A. Percy, and Hodding Carter comprise an impressive list of literary people. Much of the contents of their books derive from the local scene. Few have ventured into the larger world of abstract ideas or have departed geographically from the theme of a romantic past or of social distress. This is true for the South in general. What changes will the new industrialism bring? Will the traditional Southern themes be discarded? Will there continue to be a productive Southern authorship which will follow laborers in from the cotton fields to the new urban homes and industrial plants? Will there be a modern interpreter of industrialism as Faulkner was for rural "Yoknapatawpha"?

The roll of Southern authors in the last half century is impressive when cast against a national backdrop. Subjects of their books and short stories have been as varied as life in the region. There are many Southerners who deplore rising industrialism as a possible blight to native literary creativity. They maintain that it will destroy the leisure and stimulus brought by the old society. Talents which in the past were devoted to creative writing will seek the more certain rewards of scientific industrialism. It may be true that rising urbanism and better communication will also drain the pool of provincialism which inspired so deeply the local colorists. At the same time there may be in the brackish change from staple agriculture to a balance with industry a leveling influence that will destroy an inclination to write. But industrialism elsewhere in the country has had no such deleterious effects, as is demonstrated annually by publishers' lists of books.

Three purely literary periodicals have survived the ravages of flagging interest. These are the *Sewanee Review*, the *South Atlantic Quarterly*, and *American Literature*. All three have institutional support and they have achieved creditable maturity. The *Sewanee Review* has been more specifically a journal of criticism than have the other two. Except for restrictions implied in the titles of two of these periodicals their contents cover a broad range of interests. The most disappointing incident in Southern literary history was the discontinuance of the publication of the *Southern Review* in 1942. This periodical, first published in 1935, had established a sound reputation for its mature articles, and was rapidly becoming a major publication in its field, but withdrawal of institutional support by Louisiana State University left it stranded. Its talented editorial board was lost to the South, and the *Review*'s fine reputation was ended.

Much of the literary interpretation of the South is largely in the vein of history. Many works, such as those of William Gilmore Simms, failed to attract a large number of readers in the South of their day, but now are given a creditable place in regional literary history. But literary people in the South have not escaped abusive criticism. Recent public letters have bitterly criticized William Faulkner, Robert Penn Warren, and Hodding Carter. In private conversations individuals can be most caustic toward views expressed by these authors. In fact it is doubtful that any Southern writers ever incurred so much widespread wrath as have these. They have dared discuss a contemporary problem and suggest that much regional leadership is heading the South into chaos. They are dangerous people because they have widely dispersed reading audiences, and their words carry more popular weight even than those of many a United States Senator.[24]

The adverse reaction of many Southerners to Southern self-criticism feeds on an underlying strand of anti-intellectualism. That strand is most evident in controversies sparked by opinion on the race issue. In recent years some Southern communities have gone so far as to prune the public library shelves of all books, including children's pre-school books, which remotely might be construed to bear on race relations and to imply support for racial integration.[25] Since witch hunting among books will hardly resolve social unrest in the South, it is to be hoped that changes wrought by industrialism will help to erode this anti-intellectual barrier in the region. As a supporting force, there still prevails in many areas of the South a latent but timid liberal spirit which can be counted on ultimately to help the South adjust to new ways of life.

In one fundamental respect Southern authors have brought about an important change. They have all but destroyed the last vestige of the genteel tradition. A romanticist of the James Lane Allen–Thomas Nelson Page "local colorist" generation would hardly be compatible with William Faulkner, Lillian Smith, Thomas Wolfe, Robert Penn Warren, and Eudora Welty. This modern generation of authors has brought to the South an enormous amount of favorable notice. But, again, one of the great unanswered questions facing the new industrial region is whether or not it can continue to produce writers of the caliber of its present crop of mature authors. Will a new generation of writers take the place of those now living? Are there new authors in apprenticeship to replace Eudora Welty, Carson McCullers, Truman Capote, Tennessee Williams, and Peter Taylor? Too, can the South appeal to its authors to remain in the region during their productive years? Many of the essayists who so stoutly defended the Southern tradition in *I'll Take My Stand* now live outside the South. Robert Penn Warren now lives in Connecticut, John Crowe Ransom is at Kenyon College in Ohio, and Allen Tate is at the University of Minnesota. Stark Young, apostle of the Southern romantic tradition, has long lived in New York City. Native sons, however, have not in the past always enjoyed the warm affections of their neighbors. No doubt this has accounted for the fact that so many have gone out of the South to live.

Less happily for the South's literary tradition there is a numerous authorship producing an extremist type of protest material which is devoid of both literary and scientific merit. Some writings on social anthropology and theology, for instance, reflect neither scientific understanding nor honesty of purpose. Other materials of a similar nature tend to dull Southern literary luster both as to a creation of fundamental understanding of the South's major problems, or willingness to seek the truth.[26]

Theodore G. Bilbo set a pattern for this type of writing in his book *Take Your Choice* (1947). The emotional and puerile tone of most of the current racial comment hardly portrays the South as a region of capable or rational authorship. Much extremist literature does genuine violence to the Southern cultural tradition, particularly when it provokes violence and anti-Semitism. A travesty of the present upheaval in the South is the involvement of so many talented people in writing about the race issue when they might enjoy peace of mind to apply their energies to more creative literary production.

The image of the South is further publicized in another literary medium which is highly significant because it fixes in the minds of people throughout the world a picture of the South's political and social behavior. Whether or not that picture is true is immaterial. For several centuries foreign travelers and observers have visited the South and gone home to publish their impressions. Today this great body of travel material constitutes an important body of contemporary viewpoint of the South. Earlier, slavery was a sore point of contention in this literature. Later, the period between two world wars saw scores of visitors come from Europe and South America to view the process of democracy in the United States, and almost all of these came South. Farm tenantry stifled agriculture, and there was definite need for social and economic readjustment in all areas of life. Southerners might have been highly disturbed if they had known that German and Italian fascist travelers viewed their society and went home to publish harsh comment on what they saw. It may be assumed that some of the bad guesses which Hitler and Mussolini made about the United States stemmed partly from these materials. But of greater importance was the adverse image of the Southern political system presented in this material.

Again, in the middle of the twentieth century the American democratic system and the South are on international display. Already a new body of travel literature is accumulating abroad. Once again the South is appearing in this literature in a highly controversial and confused light. The race issue with its recurring emotional outbreaks, especially since the Supreme Court decision of 1954, not only colors the great body of foreign travel literature, but attracts the travelers to the South in the first place.[27]

The Historian and the South

Along with the creative writers, historians have been faithful annalists of the Southern system, with some of them playing the role of apologists. Political theorists, demagogues, and liberal statesmen all have created sufficient obliqueness in their approach to the Southern processes of applied government to make interpretation of the past an uncertain thing. There is just enough uncertainty about the foundations of Southern politics to keep historians searching for fresh regional meaning in Southern history. The great Virginians, and Clay, Jackson, and Calhoun, plus an army of lesser figures, have kept the official records of Congress, the newspaper, pamphlet, and periodical presses filled with attacks, arguments, and regional defenses. It is not insignificant that of the eight major projects to collect, edit, and publish the personal papers of major Americans, six relate to Southerners.[28]

Despite the great national collections of papers, the South has been essentially a collectivization of local political neighborhoods. The history of these tiny molecules of Southern life is possibly regarded by many historians as of more importance than that of the nation or of the world. This local history combined color and frustration. Limited institutional facilities, lack of support for the individual historian, absence of vital source materials, and limited local pride and perspective have kept much Southern historical writing at a provincial level. The institutional historians, especially, have too often found themselves confined to local fields in their research and writings, unable to give even a broader regional implication to their works. The omnivorous subject, the Civil War, has taken a gluttonous share of the historian's energies. Like some intense light drawing moths to it, the war has been a near fatal attraction for each succeeding generation of scholars. Every new crop of historians contains an eager company who dredge diligently old materials in search of new facts, or who review and revise old and established interpretations of the struggle. For some time many Southern scholars have been working on centennial Civil War books, and publishers are crowding the shelves of bookshops with their works. Emotions stirred by the current integration arguments will doubtless greatly accelerate Southern interest in books about the war.

In some respects many contemporary Southern historians bear a kinship to those current European scholars who spend enormous intellectual energies on comprehending the medieval period. An investigation of the events of this century would yield them a richer return in understanding, and perhaps give clearer direction into the future. So it is with many Southern scholars who prefer to be preoccupied with the ante-bellum past rather than with the present, a past which has fewer complexities of social, racial, and economic conditions and in which there is some suggestion of romance and of predictable human nature. Emotions are calmer, and there is less likelihood of an individual stirring up unreasoning attackers in his account of human behavior and the course of public events.

Consideration of Southern history of necessity involves the presentation of many personalities. History of the region has always been a highly personal matter, and individuals who have had an impact on it invariably have been many-sided in personality and mixed in motives. Since 1876 the objects of historical inquiry also have included attitudes toward race, labor, religion, regional economics, and politics. Historians frequently have responded to such sensitive subjects by being cautious in their approaches, if not obscure in developing the full meaning of their published studies.

A penetrating history of the modern South must recognize that both national and international forces have exerted themselves on the region in the areas of international trade, federal taxation, labor laws, social legislation, economic development, and national security. A focus on these trends, to be sure, bears the most ephemeral relationship to the ante-bellum past, but surely the meaning of regional history for the Southerner during most of this century must be found largely in his efforts to choose an approach to the future in an era of staggering changes.

If all Southern historical scholarship concentrated on the ante-bellum, Civil War, and Reconstruction periods there would be just reason to question its perspective. Southerners, however, have matured since the days when attacking historians for expressing objective points of view about the South was almost a moral imperative. Since 1935 the *Journal of Southern History* has carried numerous articles which reached beyond narrow regional boundaries and which have been deeply critical of the South. Unlike the earlier publication of an organized group of Southerners interested in history, the present Southern Historical Association has no emotional cause to plead, supports no established point of view beyond objectivity, and makes no apology for regional prejudices. The *Journal* lives above the storms which beset Southern historical comment and publication in the past. No appreciable number of defenders of Southern faith even know of its existence, and such public support as it receives is beyond reach of legislator and extremist.

State historical journals in the South run the scale of like historical publications elsewhere in the country. Some are of high quality while others are little more than genealogical catalogues doing maid-service for people who wish to call more heavily upon the past than contribute to the present. Naturally, the local magazines of history are provincial in scope, but much of their good materials are basic to a broader interpretation of American history. The South and its history are important. Unhappily, vast numbers of Southerners have assumed that mere birth in the region has endowed them with special knowledge of its history. No regional people in the United States are more conscious of their history, or generally less well informed about it. This perhaps would not be too important except that major social and political decisions are often made in its name.

Southern University Presses

In a more mature way Southern writers have enjoyed considerable national prestige since 1900. Organization of university presses has made a solid contribution to Southern cultural development. The three older presses are those of Duke University, the University of Texas, and the University of North Carolina. In subsequent years presses in the state universities of Louisiana, South Carolina, Georgia, Florida, and Kentucky, together with Southern Methodist University, have produced highly creditable lists of books, including much Southern scholarly material too local or specialized in appeal to attract commercial press support. The North Carolina and Louisiana State university presses were the first to promote the writing and publication of serious studies which have made lasting contributions in the field of American scholarship. To the credit of the university presses they have avoided political and bigoted religious pressures. They have fought off regional apologists, genealogists, and hatemongers. Many university books have been both objective and liberal, a combination which defies a part of the nostalgic Southern tradition. These presses have not always escaped bitter criticism, and timid university administrations have sometimes shown fright in the face of objective truth. This occasional fear of objectivity has no doubt caused a reticence on the part of some university presidents to be more generous with the necessary funds to permit press growth. Use of public moneys with all the attendant bureaucratic red tape of the expenditure of such funds has been a further handicap. Lack of dependable sources of public income from regular university appropriations has also caused Southern university press history to be most erratic.

Library Facilities

Southern authorship and publication would have limited meaning at home except for the existence of libraries. The South has never approached an adequacy of library service at any time in its history; however, there are now better libraries than ever before. Whether or not the region can statistically compare favorably with the East, the Middle West, and the Pacific Coast means little. It may be true that Harvard and Yale have more books in their libraries than the combined Southern colleges and universities, except for Duke and Texas. More significant, however, is the fact that in 1920 not a single Southern university library topped a quarter of a million books, but today ten Southern universities have passed the half million mark, and four have exceeded a million volumes.[29] There were fewer volumes in the entire South in 1920 than are now contained in the Duke and University of Texas libraries.

Never in the most prosperous days of the Old South did any part of the population have access to a minimum fraction of so large a storehouse of literary materials as do modern Southerners. Even where relatively small numbers of people have had access to books in the past their range of selection was severely circumscribed. Antebellum Southerners were able to create a semblance of literary culture because they read carefully a few classics. In recent years in older parts of the South family libraries have come to second-hand bookdealers for sale. These have appeared in impressive bindings, and in uniform sets. Because of this fact, modern Southerners often conclude that these books were read by many people. A close physical examination of the books themselves, however, seems to indicate that many sets were little more than decorative properties in "gentlemen's libraries."

Early public library records and the sad experience of regional authors hardly present the Old South as yearning for widespread literary culture. The agrarian spirit of much of the region fostered a non-reading culture. A rural society has never been noted for its patronage of the arts, and reading was a highly dispensable pastime. Libraries in many Southern towns were as unused as the beautifully bound books found on the shelves in personal collections. They often sheltered lady-keepers of books, and were frequented by ancestor worshipers and children. Often the only practical use a man of affairs made of the library was to point it out to visitors as a cultural landmark.[30]

Indifference to library facilities is no longer true in many parts of the South. The practical man in present-day industrialism may be vitally interested in books. Scientists, public planners, prospective industrialists, businessmen, and even politicians all concern themselves with local libraries. The Jaycees have embarked upon a campaign to improve library services in the smaller towns. Often a local inducement offered industrial management is the availability of library resources. How much those executives would make use of public libraries is beside the point—local promoters are convinced that management feels more comfortable with this civilizing influence in a community.

Public library service in the South has become much broader than the mere existence of a library in a town. Library commissions, school book services, bookmobiles, and extension agencies all supply books to Southerners in many parts of the region. Statistically, the South was, and still is, at the bottom of the income scale. It had only a fraction of a book per person in public libraries, and poor roads prevented use of portable libraries.[31] In 1934 the Southern states were lowest in volume library holdings per capita of all the states. School libraries were limited in resources and unduly dependent on textbooks. Some religious groups frowned upon reading books other than the Bible and religious literature; to them libraries were both unnecessary and depositories of the devil's works.

The period from 1880 to 1930 was culturally a static one. Progress was hardly possible when the rate of farm tenantry was climbing, and personal income was at a minimum subsistence level. The shackles of illiteracy were clamped upon the South during the decades 1870–1920 and any broad cultural advance would have been little short of an anachronism. It is a paradox of Southern cultural history that the great depression of the early 1930's was to awaken parts of the South to the importance of library services. One of the first regional library projects organized by the Works Progress Administration was located in Athens, Georgia, and served Clarke, Oconee, and

Oglethorpe counties. Thomas County introduced the bookmobile to the state, and in 1955 fifty-two of these rolling libraries carried books to a majority of the state's rural people.[32] Elsewhere in the South library commissions, regional libraries, and bookmobile projects have helped to overcome leadership failure, lack of funds, and local prejudices to make books available.

Industrialism and Regionalism

In other social and cultural areas the South has made almost as much progress as in industrialization. Unlike those travelers who crossed the region in the ante-bellum period, the modern visitors see a tremendous change in the physical appearances of homes, business structures, and the new industrial plants. The change-over from Greek revival emphases to the modern and functional is as reflective of the social and political changes occurring in the region as are the statistics of the New South. No sharper break with the past has occurred in any phase of the South than in the field of architecture. In fact, architectural changes have often occurred in recent years in good part because of political and economic pressures. This was especially so in the field of public school building after 1948 when it seemed clear the United States Supreme Court would rule adversely in the *Brown v. Topeka* case. The new school buildings, the construction of new libraries and public coliseums, and the rise of modern buildings on Southern university and college campuses reflect the deep-seated impulses of the new age.

The South feels the heavy hand of cultural change in every field. It is not insignificant that disciples of the humanities have to exercise extraordinary vigilance to protect their fields of interest. This has come to be so in a land which in the past has all but made a fetish of liberal education. For the first time in Southern educational history the sciences have assumed a leadership in colleges and universities. Chemists, physicists, medical doctors, and engineers are rising aristocrats among the professionals. Traditional professions such as law, the ministry, teaching, and banking never offered such golden challenges as do the scientific callings.

New industrialism has brought the South other stubborn demands. Traditions, established patterns of culture, and even history mean little in the face of the demands of this leviathan. People do not build factories, manage labor, and produce goods by old-fashioned ideals. Likewise it is impossible to produce petroleum, light bulbs, chemicals, automobile tires, paper, and synthetic fabrics of a distinctly Southern type.

The time has come to re-examine the whole concept of regionalism as it might be applied to the present South. Will regional culture survive change? Can the South absorb a tremendous industrial impact without undergoing an institutional and cultural revolt? Already changes are clearly evident in public health, communication and transportation, wages, housing, farming, urbanization, and education. Clearly there can be no return to the agrarian past. Anyone who attempts this is no wiser than Lot's wife who stared back at burning Gomorrah. The agrarians of 1930 would have been horrified if they could have known that thirty years later the Commission on Goals for Higher Education in the South would say in its report that:

> If this region fails to cultivate its intellectual resources, it must abandon hope of directing its own economic destiny. Leading scientists and industrialists have made it abundantly clear that a region can expect to be economically healthy only if it has the technical training and intellectual development required to exploit the potential of the new science and technology.
> Our goals demand a partnership of southern higher education, business, industry and government to promote the growth of professional and technical manpower, to provide research necessary for full development of resources and to speed the economic progress of the region.[33]

Nowhere does this commission mention agrarianism, or an agrarian society as a goal "within our reach."

Inevitably Southern politics will feel the effects of change. Because of the deeply ingrained and reactionary nature of much political leadership, of ambiguous and extremist approaches to regional problems, the new forces now loose in the South have been slow to revolt against the past. The uprising of the urban Southerner could well be the opening of a new political era. Internally it will matter little whether the South goes Democratic or Republican in its national political expressions; the contest between urban and agrarian elements in the region will no doubt shape the dawning era of Southern politics. Where there are revolts against the traditional political alignments of the past, as in South Carolina with its mild flurry of Republicanism, the fury arises against the forces which are shaping a new South rather than in favor of a new and vibrant political philosophy of either larger regional or national meaning.

It is quite possible that as Southern industry matures it will patronize the arts as well as the sciences, and the South's cultural past will form a solid foundation on which to make many adjustments to the new age. However this may be, one thing is clear: the modern South cannot accept the advantages offered by industrialism without adapting many of its social and political ideas and forms.

1. *Annual of the Southern Baptist Convention* (Nashville, 1954), pp. 400–404; Brooks Hays, "President's Address," *ibid.*, pp. 85–89; Bishop William Watkins, *Episcopal Message* (Southeastern Jurisdictional Conference) (Junaluska, N. C., July, 1956); George W. Cornell, "Baptists Seek a New Concept," *Louisville Courier-Journal*, Sept. 8, 1962; *Southern School News* (Aug., 1957), p. 13, and (Oct., 1957), p. 13.

2. Howard W. Odum, *Southern Regions of the United States* (Chapel Hill: University of North Carolina Press, 1936), p. 51.

3. Thomas D. Clark, *The Southern Country Editor* (Indianapolis: Bobbs-Merrill Co., 1948), pp. 264–282.

4. V. O. Key, Jr., *Southern Politics* (New York: Alfred A. Knopf, 1949); C. Vann Woodward, *Origins of the New South, 1877–1913* (Baton Rouge: Louisiana State University Press, 1951), pp. 1–22; Albert D. Kirwan, *Revolt of the Rednecks* (Lexington: University of Kentucky Press, 1950), pp. 40–49; Francis Butler Simkins, *Pitchfork Ben Tillman* (Baton Rouge: Louisiana State University Press, 1944), pp. 106–119.

5. Woodward, *op. cit.*, pp. 175–204; Kirwan, *op. cit.*, pp. 99, 118–120, 148–161; Thomas D. Clark, "The People, William Goebel, and the Kentucky Railroads," *Journal of Southern History*, V (Feb., 1939), 34–48.

6. Examples of these observations are Horace Greeley, *Mr. Greeley's Letters from Texas and the Lower Mississippi; to which are added His Address to the Farmers of Texas, and His Speech on His Return to New York* (New York: The New York Tribune Office, 1871); Sir George Campbell, *White and Black: The Outcome of a Visit to the United States* (New York: Worthington, 1879); George Sala, *America Revisited* (London: Vizetelly and Co., 1882).

7. Charles H. Otken, *Ills of the South, or Related Causes Hostile to the General Prosperity of the Southern People* (New York: G. P. Putnam's Son, 1894), pp. 97–120; Woodward, *op. cit.*, pp. 175–204.

8. John D. Hicks, *The Populist Revolt* (Minneapolis: University of Minnesota Press, 1931); John B. Clark, *Populism in Alabama* (Auburn: Auburn Printing Co., 1927); A. M. Arnett, *The Populist Movement in Georgia* (New York: Columbia University Press, 1922).

9. Kirwan, *op. cit.*, pp. 93–121; John B. Clark, *op. cit.*; Rebecca L. Felton, *My Memoirs of Georgia Politics* (Atlanta: Index Printing Co., 1911); C. Vann Woodward, *Thomas E. Watson, Agrarian Rebel* (New York: Macmillan Co., 1938).

10. Good examples are the Mississippi Constitution drafted in 1890; Kirwan, *op. cit.*, pp. 58–64; the Kentucky Constitution was drafted in the same year. The Alabama Constitution was revised in 1894.

11. David E. Lilienthal, *T.V.A.—Democracy on the March* (New York: Harper, 1944), pp. 100–101; Rupert B. Vance, *Human Geography of the South* (Chapel Hill: University of North Carolina Press, 1932), pp. 497–498. A clear picture of regional change is contained in James Dahir, *Region Building Community Development Lessons from the Tennessee Valley* (New York: Harper, 1955), pp. 20–54.

12. Rupert B. Vance, "The Region, a New Survey," pp. 1–8, Thomas R. Ford, "The Passing of Provincialism," pp. 9–34, John C. Belcher, "Population Growth and Characteristics," pp. 37–53, James S. Brown and George Hillerey, Jr., "The Great Migration, 1940–1960," pp. 54–78, in Thomas R. Ford, ed., *The Southern Appalachian Region: A Survey* (Lexington: University of Kentucky Press, 1962).

13. Thomas Franklin Abercrombie, *History of Public Health in Georgia, 1733–1950* (Atlanta: Georgia Department of Public Health, 1950); M. Rice *et al.*, *Life Tables for Mississippi, 1930, 1940, 1950* (Starkville: Mississippi Department of Public Health, 1954); Thomas S. Hosty *et al.*, *Hookworm in Alabama* (Montgomery: Alabama Department of Public Health, n.d.); *History of Public Health in Texas* (Austin: Texas Department of

Public Health, 1950); W. T. Sowder, "A Survey of Progress in the General Field of Health in Florida for the Period from 1940 to 1949," *Journal of the Florida Medical Association* (Sept., 1951), pp. 3–7; "Progress in Public Health in Florida," *Journal of the Florida Medical Association* (April, 1949), pp. 3–7.

14. *Within Our Reach* (Atlanta: Southern Regional Education Board, Report of the Commission on Goals for Higher Education in the South, 1961), pp. 35–41.

15. Odum, *op. cit.*, pp. 99–125; Ernest W. Swanson and John A. Griffith, *Public Education in the South Today and Tomorrow* (Chapel Hill: University of North Carolina Press, 1955).

16. James Bryce, *The American Commonwealth* (New York: Macmillan Co., 1910), II, 562.

17. W. T. Couch, ed., *Culture in the South* (Chapel Hill: University of North Carolina Press, 1934), p. viii.

18. Benjamin B. Kendrick, "The Colonial Status of the South," *Journal of Southern History*, VIII (Feb., 1942), 3–22; B. B. Kendrick and A. M. Arnett, *The South Looks at Its Past* (Chapel Hill: University of North Carolina Press, 1935). Henry W. Grady dealt with this subject in most of his speeches. His story of the Pickens County corpse was an example. Henry W. Grady, *The New South* (New York: Robert Bonner's Sons, 1890), pp. 188–207.

19. Ulrich B. Phillips, "The Central Theme in Southern History," *American Historical Review*, XXXIV (Oct., 1928), 30–43, and *Life and Labor in the Old South* (Boston: Little, Brown and Co., 1929); Clement Eaton, *The Growth of Southern Civilization, 1790–1860* (New York: Harper, 1961).

20. Frank L. Owsley, *Plain Folk of the Old South* (Baton Rouge: Louisiana State University Press, 1949).

21. Key, *op. cit.*; Kirwan, *op. cit.* Especially pertinent to the background of Southern politics is Allan P. Sindler, *Huey Long's Louisiana: State Politics, 1920–1952* (Baltimore: The Johns Hopkins Press, 1956), pp. 1–67.

22. Thomas Stribling based his trilogy, *The Forge* (Garden City: Doubleday, Doran and Co., 1931), *The Store* (Garden City: Doubleday, Doran and Co., 1932), and *The Unfinished Cathedral* (Garden City: Doubleday, Doran and Co., 1934), on the economic and social unrest in the South. No books reflected more on the plight of parts of the South than Erskine Caldwell's *God's Little Acre* (New York: The Viking Press, 1933), and *Tobacco Road* (New York: C. Scribner's Sons, 1932). Louis D. Rubin, Jr., and Robert D. Jacobs, eds., *South: Modern Literature in Its Cultural Setting* (Garden City: Doubleday, 1961). This is a good anthology with carefully selected excerpts, accompanied by adequate historical notes.

23. Among these were Irvin Cobb, George W. Cable, James Lane Allen, Henry Watterson, and Joel Chandler Harris.

24. William Faulkner's views were publicized in many places. See his "Letter to the North," *Life*, XXXX (March 5, 1956), 51–52, and (March 26, 1956), 19; William Faulkner, Benjamin E. Mays, and Cecil Sims, *Three Views of the Segregation Decision* (Atlanta: Southern Regional Council, 1956); Robert Penn Warren, *Segregation: The Inner Conflict in the South* (New York: Random House, 1956).

25. Note, for example, South Carolina's House Resolution 2289, "Requesting the State Library Board to remove from circulation certain books antagonistic and inimical to the traditions of South Carolina and further request that said Library Board screen more carefully certain publications before circulating same." *Southern School News* (April, 1956), p. 12. This attempted witch hunt was sparked by Jerrold Beim's *Swimming Hole* (New York: Morrow, 1950), which had been selected from a bookmobile by the librarian of a small municipal library. The book represented white and colored boys playing together. *South Carolina Library Bulletin*, X (May, 1956), 2.

26. Examples of this voluminous literature are: F. R. Ackley, *The Bible Answers the Race Problems* (Denver, 1945); Tom P. Brady, *Segregation and the South: A Speech Delivered to the Commonwealth Club of California* (San Francisco, 1957); Joseph P. Kamp, *Trickery, Treachery, Tyranny and Treason in Washington* (Westport, Conn., 1957); R. Carter Pittman, *The Supreme Court, the Broken Constitution, and the Shattered Bill of Rights* (Dalton, Ga., 1956); G. T. Gillespie, *A Christian View of Segregation* (Jackson,

Miss., 1954); *Arkansas Faith* (Little Rock, 1955); and Theodore Bilbo, *Take Your Choice, Separation or Mongrelization* (Poplarville, Miss.: Dream House Publishing Co., 1947).

27. Rupert B. Vance, "The Twentieth-Century South as Viewed by English-Speaking Travelers, 1900–1955," pp. 3–106, and Lawrence S. Thompson, "Foreign Language Accounts by Travelers in the Southern States, 1900–1955," pp. 109–283, in Thomas D. Clark, ed., *Travels in the New South* (Norman: University of Oklahoma Press, 1962), II.

28. Thomas Jefferson's papers are being edited by Julian Boyd, James Madison's by William T. Hutchinson and William M. E. Rachal, Henry Clay's by James F. Hopkins, Andrew Johnson's by LeRoy Graf, John C. Calhoun's by Edwin Hemphill, and Andrew Jackson's by Daniel Robison.

29. *College and University Library Statistics* (1947) and *Statistics for College and University Libraries for the Fiscal Year, 1960–1961*, both published by the Princeton University Library.

30. Odum, *op. cit.*, p. 119.

31. Louis Round Wilson, *The Geography of Reading* (Chicago: University of Chicago Press, 1938), p. 72.

32. Lucille Nix, statement of the history of the Georgia Library Extension Service to author, 1955.

33. *Within Our Reach*, p. 12.

Joseph J. Spengler*

Demographic and Economic Change in the South, 1940–1960

Few Southerners have yet faced up to the question of whether they want industrialization badly enough to give up firmly held Southern traditions which are inconsistent with it.—W. H. NICHOLLS, Southern Tradition and Regional Progress (1960), p. 155.

While the South has made considerable economic progress since 1940, both absolutely and relatively, its rate of progress remains too low. This paper reviews that progress, identifies retardative and favorable conditions, and indicates steps essential to the acceleration of progress in the South (hereinafter usually defined as including the eleven states of the Confederacy plus Kentucky).

I. *Population Movements*

The movement of population through time, though a force bearing upon the course of economic events, is primarily an indicator of underlying conditions and changes. In and before the 1930's the South's economically depressive high fertility reflected the fact that as late as 1940 about two-fifths of the South's population lived on farms, usually under somewhat traditional arrangements. The heavy migration of the South's people away from farms reflects the inelasticity of its agricultural economy even as the migration of Southerners to the North and the West reflects the incapacity of the South's economy to absorb its growing population on terms as satisfactory to potential migrants as they expect to find outside the South.

* This paper was written while I held a John Simon Guggenheim Memorial Fellowship. I am grateful to the officers of the Foundation for having made possible the research involved in the preparation of this paper which complements a larger project on which I am engaged.

Table 1. Population and Population Change, 1940–1960

State	Population in 1960 (millions)			Per cent change						Per cent Non-white		
				1950–1960			1940–1950					
	Total	White	Non-white	T[a]	W	NW	T[a]	W	NW	1960	1950	1940
Virginia	3.97	3.14	0.83	1.8	21.7	11.9	2.4	28.0	11.3	20.8	22.2	24.7
North Carolina	4.56	3.40	1.16	1.2	14.0	7.2	1.4	16.2	7.9	25.4	26.6	28.1
South Carolina	2.38	1.55	0.83	1.2	19.9	1.0	1.1	19.3	1.1	34.9	38.9	42.9
Georgia	3.94	2.82	1.13	1.4	18.3	5.8	1.0	16.6	−2.4	28.6	30.9	34.7
Florida	4.95	4.06	0.89	6.0	87.6	46.7	4.6	57.2	17.5	17.9	21.8	27.2
Tennessee	3.57	2.98	0.59	0.8	7.9	10.9	1.3	14.5	4.3	16.5	16.1	17.5
Alabama	3.27	2.28	0.98	0.7	9.8	0.1	0.8	12.4	c	30.1	32.1	34.7
Mississippi	2.18	1.26	0.92	0	5.8	−7.0	b	7.1	−8.1	42.3	45.4	49.3
Arkansas	1.79	1.40	0.39	−0.6	−5.8	−8.7	−0.2	1.1	−11.4	21.9	22.4	24.8
Louisiana	3.26	2.21	1.05	2.0	23.1	17.9	1.4	18.9	4.1	32.1	33.0	36.0
Texas	9.58	8.78	1.21	2.2	24.5	22.4	2.0	29.9	6.3	12.6	12.8	14.5
Kentucky	3.04	2.82	0.22	0.3	2.8	7.6	0.4	4.2	−5.2	7.2	6.9	7.5
United States	179.32	158.83	20.49	1.8	17.5	26.7	1.47	13.3	17.0	11.4	10.5	10.2

Source: *Statistical Bulletin* (Metropolitan Life Insurance Co.) (April, 1953, Jan., 1961, Oct., 1961); Bogue, *op. cit.*, p. 133; *U. S. Census, 1950*, Vol. 2 (1950), "state returns."

[a] Annual rate.   [b] −0.02.   [c] negligible.

1. *Population aggregates.* Data in Table I indicate a continuation of tendencies manifested earlier in this century. The population of the South continues to grow somewhat more slowly than that of the nation as a whole, though faster than that of New England and the Plains states; indeed, of the twenty-eight states whose share of the population declined in the past two decades, eight are in the South. Individual Southern states differ greatly, however, in respect to rate of growth. Between 1900 and 1960 the rate of population growth of the United States (136 per cent) was exceeded markedly by that of Florida and Texas, and slightly by that of Louisiana and North Carolina; it was approximated by that of Virginia (114 per cent). In the other seven Southern states the population grew less than 80 per cent. In but two states, Florida and Texas, has population grown faster each post-1900 decade than in the nation; and in but two others, North Carolina and Louisiana, has the rate of growth exceeded the national rate in any decade between 1900 and 1930. Only in the 1930's when depression slowed outmigration did population grow more slowly in the nation than in most Southern states (i.e., in all but

Alabama and Arkansas). In both the 1940's and the 1950's only the populations of Florida, Texas, and Virginia grew faster than that of the nation, as did that of Louisiana in the 1950's. The slowness with which the South's population has been growing is associated with the slowness (attributable to outmigration) with which the Negro population has been growing. In the 1950's the Negro population grew less rapidly than the white in every state but Tennessee, thus continuing the growth pattern of the 1940's. The fraction which Negroes form of the Southern population has been moving slowly downward.

Within the South even more than in the nation population has grown unevenly; and numbers have become much more concentrated than in 1900, when the Southeast and the Southwest were only about one-third as urban as the rest of the nation and when less than 9 per cent of the South's population (as compared with 26 per cent of the nation's) lived in places of 25,000 or more. By 1960 this percentage had risen to 33 (as compared with the nation's 45), ranging from 14 in Arkansas to 52 in Texas. Much of this city growth was at the expense of the rural population, interior rural counties (e.g., those situated in the Appalachian region) having predominated among those losing population through migration in the 1950's and earlier. Thus in 1950–1960 only 45 per cent of the South's counties experienced any population growth at all, and only 18 per cent gained 20 per cent or more; the corresponding percentages outside the South were 55 and 21. Most Southern counties experiencing marked growth in the 1940's and 1950's were situated on or near the Atlantic or the Gulf coast. Within the South the counties growing in 1950–1960 ranged from only six of Arkansas's seventy-five, but two of which grew 20 per cent or more, to fifty-five of Florida's sixty-seven, forty-five of which grew 20 per cent or more. Growth by county in the 1950's was generally most significant in counties with 50,000 or more population in 1950, while only in counties of over 100,000 population was the rate of growth generally more than double that of the South as a whole.

It was particularly in Standard Metropolitan Statistical Areas (hereinafter designated SMSA) that the gap between population concentration in the South and that in the nation narrowed notably; their population grew 26.4 per cent in the nation and 36.2 per cent in the South (where the rate ranged by SMSA from −3.1 per cent in Texarkana to 298 in Fort Lauderdale-Hollywood), thus continuing a differential manifest already in the 1940's. In the South, moreover, population both within and outside central cities grew appreciably whereas elsewhere (other than in the rapidly growing West) most growth in metropolitan areas took place outside central cities.[1]

2. Natural increase. The slowness with which the South's population has grown is not attributable to the relative lowness of its fertility and natural increase, though the decline in its comparative rate of increase reflects in part its failure to participate fully in the post-1940 upsurge in American natality, net reproduction, and natural increase. Fertility was higher in the South than elsewhere during the first third of this century; indeed, in the Appalachian and similar regions the value system came to support a small family only in or after the 1940's. About 1910 gross reproduction was 44–59 per cent higher in the South than in other regions, largely because a much larger fraction of the Southern population lived on farms and because gross reproduction was 34–73 per cent higher in the Southern than in the non-Southern farm population. For like reasons as late as 1940 gross reproduction remained much higher in the South than elsewhere,[2] with the result that natural increase was higher. In 1940, of the eighteen states ranking highest in crude natality twelve were situated in the South, whose over-all natality (about 24.5 births per 1,000 inhabitants) exceeded that of the nation at large (19.4) by about one-fourth. Moreover, crude mortality was slightly lower in the South than elsewhere because the South's population included relatively more persons in age groups with below-average death rates.[3]

After 1940 the spread between Southern and non-Southern natural increase diminished appreciably, largely because the South did not participate fully in the significant increase in natality and natural increase that took place in the United States. Between 1940 and 1959 natality rose only about 5 per cent in the South to approximately 25.5, whereas in the nation it increased about 25 per cent to 24.3. In the United States between 1940 and 1950 the number of children under 5 per 1,000 women 15–49 years old, standardized for age of woman, increased 40.7 per cent, of which 35 per cent is attributable to higher fertility; in the South the number increased only about three-fourths as much. Between 1950 and 1960 the differential between Southern and non-Southern rates was further reduced; in 1960 the average number of children under 5 per 1,000 women 15–49 years old in the nation was only about 4 per cent below the unweighted average of the Southern state rates, whereas in 1950 it was about 12 per cent lower.[4]

Various conditions affect Southern fertility. The average level of fertility, by state, depends in marked degree upon the relative number of people who live on farms. Hence it is of significance that in 1960 the three Southern divisions included 47 per cent (almost 50 per cent by the old definition of farm population) of the nation's farm population but only 31 per cent of its total population. Moreover, in the South rural fertility is as high as it is in part because in the rural South Negro fertility has been about one-fourth higher than white fertility. Furthermore, fertility is inversely correlated with size of place, and there is some tendency for fertility to be lower in "central cities" in metropolitan areas than in areas outside these cities.[5] Even though fertility still varies considerably from county to county, fertility and natural increase will fall as the composition of the South's population changes, and particularly as the Negro and rural-farm fractions of the population decline. Indeed, in the near future decline through change in population composition is likely to be more important than decline in the fertility of specific categories of the population.[6] Should the rate of increase of the non-white population, now about three-fifths above that of the whites, persist along with recent levels of white fertility, then forty years from now 54 of the nation's 375 millions will be non-white and 140 years from now, 614 of the nation's 2,350 millions.[7]

3. *Net migration.* Net migration has been primarily responsible for the slowness with which population has grown in most Southern states. Outmigration of native whites first became heavy in the 1880's, rising to a peak in the 1920's, only to move to a lower level in seven states in the 1930's when the rate of expansion of the non-Southern economy was low; it rose again in the 1940's but fell off in the 1950's. Negro outmigration began later than the white, first becoming heavy in 1910–1920 when foreign immigration was interrupted; its rate moved higher in the 1920's; it continued in the 1930's but at a much lower rate, and then rose again in the 1940's and 1950's.[8] Between 1940 and 1950 net emigration from the three Southern divisions numbered 2,135,000, of whom 1,597,000 were non-white. Between 1950 and 1960, while non-white emigration totaled 1,457,000, 52,000 more whites immigrated than emigrated, as a result of the tremendous pull of Florida which drew 1,516,000 white migrants on balance. The numbers and rates, by state and color, for the past two decades are

Table 2. Net Migration, By Color, 1940–1960

State	Net migration (in thousands)						Net migration (in per cent)				
	1950–1960			1940–1950			1950–1960[a]			1940–1950[b]	
	Total	White	Non-white	Total	White	Non-white	Total	White	Non-white	White	Non-white
Virginia	15	84	−70	168	194	−26	0.4	3.3	−9.5	9.6	−3.9
North Carolina	−328	−121	−207	−257	−95	−162	−8.1	−4.0	−19.2	−3.7	−16.2
South Carolina	−222	−4	−218	−231	−24	−207	−10.5	−0.3	−26.5	−2.2	−25.3
Georgia	−214	−9	−204	−289	−49	−240	−6.2	−0.4	−19.2	−2.4	−22.2
Florida	1617	1516	101	578	564	14	58.3	70.0	16.6	40.8	2.7
Tennessee	−273	−216	−57	−144	−97	−47	−8.3	−7.8	−10.7	−4.0	−9.2
Alabama	−368	−144	−224	−342	−140	−202	−12.0	−6.9	−22.8	−7.6	−20.5
Mississippi	−434	−110	−323	−434	−108	−326	−19.9	−9.3	−32.7	−9.7	−30.2
Arkansas	−433	−283	−150	−416	−259	−157	−22.7	−19.1	−35.0	−17.6	−32.4
Louisiana	−50	42	−92	−147	−2	−145	−1.9	2.4	10.4	−0.2	−17.0
Texas	114	141	−27	72	173	−101	1.5	2.1	−2.7	3.2	−10.9
Kentucky	−390	−374	−15	−366	−349	−17	−13.2	−13.7	−7.6	−13.3	−7.9

SOURCE: *Current Population Reports*, Series P-25, No. 247, (April 2, 1962).
Net migration comprises net immigration from abroad and net interstate migration.
Movements of persons in the Armed Forces are included.
[a] Base is 1950 population. [b] Base is 1940 population.

reported in Table II. Only Florida has attracted white and non-white migrants each decade. Every other Southern state has experienced net non-white emigration each decade, and all lost white migrants except Texas and Virginia, which attracted whites in both decades, and Louisiana, which attracted whites in the 1950's. The Southern Appalachian region (exclusive of West Virginia) gave up on balance 512,000 migrants in the 1940's and 691,000 in the 1950's, but over half of these remained in the South.[9]

This net outward movement had its origin, as has the movement of population into Southern and other cities, in net migration from the farms, which became heavy after World War I. Net migration removed 6.1 million of the nation's rural-farm population in 1920–1930, 3.5 million in 1930–1940, and 8.6 million, or 30.9 per cent, in 1940–1950. The corresponding figures for the three Southern divisions were 3.6, 2.3, and 5.5 millions. Net migration on the part of the Southern farm population in 1940–1950 thus amounted to about 68 per cent of all such migration and about 36.1 per cent of the South's farm population. Every Southern state, even Florida, gave up farm population each decade, and generally in large numbers approximated in magnitude only in East and West North Central states.[10] Non-agricultural employment on satisfactory terms was not (and probably could not be) expanded fast enough in the South to absorb both the natural growth of the non-agricultural population and all the migrants from the farms. In consequence the equivalent of a large fraction (i.e., about 39 per cent) of these rural migrants left the South in 1940–1950; in contrast, the expanding industrial East North Central states absorbed the equivalent of all their 938,000 rural-farm migrants, together with 669,000 net migrants from other regions. The 1950's witnessed a continuation of net migration from farms, the nation's farm population (as formerly defined) declining 18 per cent from about 25.1 millions in 1950 to about 20.5 millions in 1960. Between 1960 and 1961 the white farm population (as newly defined) declined 645,000, or about 5 per cent, and the non-white, 231,000, or about 9 per cent.[11] Presumably, when final estimates become available, they will indicate that much of the migration from rural farms in the 1950's was from Southern farms, for the South's farm population decreased about 14 per cent in 1950–1956.[12]

Migration from Southern farms will continue, but whether it will continue to generate net emigration from Southern states depends upon whether suitable non-agricultural employment can be expanded rapidly enough in the South, and upon whether the comparative disabilities under which potential Negro migrants live diminish enough. It was recently estimated that in the South (exclusive of Virginia, Florida, Kentucky, and Texas) by 1975 the 875,000 farms and 4.4 million commercial farm population reported in 1954 will have declined to not more than 500,000 farms and 2.5 million people, but without greatly narrowing the gap between per capita income in agriculture and that outside agriculture.[13] The persistence of this gap would stimulate further migration from farms. Even so, the experience of the 1940's and 1950's shows that, so long as the rate of growth of the population of working age is large in the absence of migration, the capacity of migration to reduce the size of the rural-farm population is quite limited. Moreover, while some farm programs may have slightly retarded the transfer of labor out of Southern agriculture, and while migration-facilitating programs have exercised little influence, the government's failure to use its subsidy payments to finance migration from economically inadequate farms has held down the rate of migration from rural areas.[14]

Outmigration from low-income situations and states constitutes a response to population pressure and to income differentials in that potential migrants are attracted to places where they believe they can secure higher incomes and better economic conditions than they are enjoying.[15] Such migration serves to reduce income differentials, by making possible higher incomes in areas of emigration and perhaps also by slowing down growth of per capita incomes in areas of im- migration. Migration cannot be counted upon, however, to eliminate income differentials: it is affected by many conditions, some of which retard it; it does not reduce natural increase sufficiently, and it tends to be too small in volume to correct income differences unless power- ful investment and investment-related policies complement the out- movement.[16]

II. *Per Capita Personal Income*

Per capita personal income is lower in the South than elsewhere. In 1960 it was only 72 per cent as high in the South (exclusive of Texas but inclusive of West Virginia) as in the United States and even in the southwestern state of Texas it was only 87 per cent as high; and the spread continued to be greater between Southern and non-Southern Negro incomes than between corresponding white in- comes.[17] The three Southern divisions of states include about 39 per cent of the nation's families with less than $2,000 income because, though only 31 per cent of the nation's population live there, dis- proportionately large fractions of this population are non-white and/ or live on farms.[18] The distribution of money income is somewhat more concentrated in the South than in the non-South; and this condition (partly associated with the color and the occupational and industrial composition of the population) may be relatively favorable to capital formation.[19]

Immediately underlying the comparative lowness of per capita in- come in the South is the occupational and industrial composition of the labor force, together with the relative lowness of the labor-force/ population ratio and the rates of remuneration of workers in given occupations. Beneath these immediate conditions lie yet more ulti- mate income determinants, some of which have been shaped by the past industrial and social history of the South; among them are pro- ductive equipment per worker, supply of enterprise and managerial skill, education, race in the event racial discrimination makes for misuse of labor, and so on. This section examines the immediate conditions and in the next section the less immediate conditions will be discussed.

1. *Income trends.* The relative income position of the South has improved in the past thirty years. Per capita personal income (expressed in current dollars) increased 344 per cent in the Southeast and 303 per cent in Texas between 1929 and 1960 whilst increasing only 216 per cent in the nation at large. In the Southeast, therefore, per capita personal income, expressed as a percentage of the corresponding national average, has risen, from 52 in 1929 to 57 in 1940, 67 in 1948, 68 in 1950, and 72 in 1960. Meanwhile the corresponding Texas percentage rose from 68 in 1929 to 73 in 1940, 84 in 1948, and 90 and 87, respectively, in 1950 and 1960. Evidently much of this advance took place between the early 1930's and the late 1940's; for the incomes and relatives reported in Table III, though cyclically sensitive, indicate that improvement, which began with recovery from depression in the early 1930's,[20] proceeded quite rapidly in the late 1930's and early 1940's and then more slowly.[21] By 1960 personal per capita income, still only about half the national average in Mississippi, was over four-fifths of this average in three Southern states and 60–72 per cent of it in the remaining eight states.

2. *Immediate determinants.* In the past per capita personal in-

Table 3. Per Capita Personal Income, Absolute and Relative, by State, 1929–1960

State	1929	1940	1947	1950	1954	1957	1960
Virginia	435 (62)	466 (78)	1,002 (76)	1,215 (82)	1,480 (84)	1,671 (82)	1,848 (83)
N. Carolina	334 (48)	328 (55)	894 (68)	1,011 (68)	1,190 (67)	1,345 (66)	1,574 (71)
S. Carolina	270 (38)	307 (52)	779 (59)	877 (59)	1,063 (60)	1,210 (59)	1,397 (63)
Georgia	350 (50)	340 (57)	884 (67)	1,017 (68)	1,237 (70)	1,418 (69)	1,608 (72)
Florida	521 (74)	513 (86)	1,143 (87)	1,305 (88)	1,610 (91)	1,829 (89)	1,988 (89)
Tennessee	377 (54)	339 (57)	876 (67)	997 (67)	1,212 (69)	1,401 (68)	1,545 (70)
Alabama	324 (46)	282 (47)	794 (60)	868 (58)	1,091 (62)	1,325 (65)	1,462 (66)
Mississippi	285 (41)	218 (37)	662 (50)	729 (49)	873 (49)	992 (48)	1,173 (53)
Arkansas	305 (43)	256 (43)	719 (55)	802 (54)	979 (55)	1,148 (56)	1,341 (60)
Louisiana	415 (59)	363 (61)	881 (67)	1,089 (73)	1,302 (74)	1,565 (76)	1,604 (72)
Texas	478 (68)	432 (73)	1,128 (86)	1,341 (90)	1,574 (89)	1,815 (89)	1,924 (87)
Kentucky	391 (56)	320 (54)	850 (65)	960 (64)	1,216 (69)	1,429 (70)	1,543 (69)
U. S.	703 (100)	592 (100)	1,313 (100)	1,487 (100)	1,768 (100)	2,048 (100)	2,223 (100)

Source: Hanna, *State Income Differentials, 1919–1954,* pp. 28–30, 38–41; *Survey of Current Business,* XLI (Aug., 1961), 10, 13.

come has been lower in the South than elsewhere because a smaller fraction of the population was in the labor force, principally because a smaller fraction of the population was of working age. In 1950 about 58 per cent of the nation's population was 20 to 64 years old whereas the corresponding fraction in seven of the twelve Southern states was at or below 53.5 per cent. In 1960, 55 per cent of the nation's population was 18–64 years old. The corresponding fraction ranged, by Southern state, from 49.7 in Mississippi to 55.8 in Virginia, and remained below 54 in four states. In 1950, 40 per cent of the nation's and 37 per cent of the South's population was in the labor force. By 1960, however, both averages had declined slightly. Hanna's finding in his study of the impact of interstate differences in age composition and labor-force participation is relevant to the South-non-South differential. He concludes:

in 1950 some 13–23 per cent of the relative interstate variation in per capita personal income is accounted for by differences in the relative numbers of children below productive ages, of persons 65 years old or older, or of persons who are in the labor force and thus contribute directly to income production. . . . By substituting total labor force for total population as the denominator in per capita income computation, the relative interstate personal income differentials are reduced by 14 to 23 per cent.[22]

Per capita personal income in the South is lower also because the industrial and occupational composition of the Southern labor force is less favorable than the non-Southern in that it includes a relatively large number of workers attached to industries and occupations in which remuneration rates are relatively low. Thus per capita income is negatively correlated with activities (agriculture, raw-material-oriented manufacturing, and mining) which are relatively important in the South and positively correlated with activities (fabricating industry, business services, professional undertakings) which are relatively unimportant in the South.[23] Hanna's analysis of the impact of interstate differences in industrial composition and the source of wages and salaries upon interstate differences in earnings leads him to conclude that:

industrial composition, together with the forces correlated with it, appears to explain up to 70 per cent of the reported interstate earning differentials in the areas, other than governments, covered by the industrial series.[24]

Perloff and his associates find furthermore that relative increase in per capita income by state has been correlated with relative decrease in agricultural activity and relative increase in manufacturing activity.[25] Respecting the effects of interstate differences in occupational composition, Hanna concludes:

When both the independent and correlated effects of occupational composition are taken into account, interstate compositional differences are capable of statistically accounting for about six-sevenths of the interstate variation in reported earnings.[26]

Borts has interpreted Hanna's earlier estimate (of 80 per cent) of the influence of occupational composition to mean that "11 per cent of state income variation is due to the independent influence of occupation mix" while 69 per cent "is due to the joint influence of occupation mix and earnings levels changing simultaneously."[27] Hanna's analysis thus suggests that a large fraction of the margin by which average earnings in the United States exceed those in the South is immediately traceable to direct and indirect effects of interstate differences in industrial and occupational composition. It also suggests that, were the occupational and industrial structure of the South to approximate that of the nation, the over-all difference between average earnings in the South and that in the non-South would be greatly reduced and might almost disappear.

Southern average income is relatively low because often income in given occupations is lower in many Southern states than elsewhere. In the late 1940's when the ratio of farm population to total population was about twice as high in the South as elsewhere, cash receipts per farm worker were only half as high in the South as elsewhere, in part because the average size of the farm was only 44 per cent as great. An essentially similar relationship still obtains; in 1959 median white and non-white farm incomes were much lower in Southern than in non-Southern divisions of states, and median earnings too were lower in the South than elsewhere, especially among the less skilled.[28] Furthermore, about 1948 average salary-wage per employee was only about four-fifths as high in trade, construction, public utilities, and services in the South as elsewhere.[29] In manufacturing about 1947 average annual production worker wages were lower in the South than in any other region in each of three categories of manufacture, high-wage, medium-wage, and low-wage industries. At the same time the South's share of low-wage-industry workers (65.8 per cent) was more than double that of the nation (29 per cent) while its share (15.8 per cent) of high-wage-industry workers was less than half the national average (38 per cent). A parallel interregional comparison based on value added by manufacture per production worker yielded similar results; over-all average value added was only about 80 per cent as high.[30] Even so, by 1948 the South's comparative position was much better than in 1939, when the ratio of Southern to non-Southern averages was appreciably lower, the incidence of war and postwar changes having been particularly favorable to the South.[31]

Wage data also indicate that rates of remuneration are often lower in the South than elsewhere in essentially similar occupations, and particularly in industries and occupations requiring little skill and training and hence prone to be flooded by the large annual increments of unskilled persons to the South's labor force. Perloff and his associates present data which indicate that Southern wages were 10–30 per cent "below the national average in the majority of industries."[32] In 1960 average straight-time hourly earnings were 8–20 per cent higher in quite similar occupations in North-Central than in Southern non-metropolitan areas.[33] Because wages vary appreciably both within the South and outside the South it is not easy to compare Southern and non-Southern wages in simple terms. If, however, wages by occupation and community are arrayed within the South and outside the South, much of a given Southern array will lie below the corresponding non-Southern array even though some points in the latter array lie below the highest points in the Southern array. Of course, if wages in given occupations tend to be higher within than outside manufacturing, and if manufacturing engages a smaller fraction of those pursuing an occupation within than outside the South, the relation of the two arrays may be affected by interregional differences in manufacturing as well as by other differences.[34] Whatever the differential, a portion of it presumably would remain even if allowance could be made for differences in city size with which median income seems to be positively associated.[35]

III. *General Sources of Lowness of Southern Earnings*

It has been shown that the relative lowness of Southern earnings is closely associated with the comparatively unfavorable industrial and occupational composition of the South's labor force. This factor is responsible too for much of the heavy net outmigration from the South. It has been shown that incomes are relatively low in the South also because incomes in given occupations are often lower there than

elsewhere as well as because labor-force participation rates are somewhat lower. Underlying the composition of Southern economic activities and the comparative lowness of earnings in given occupations
one finds both a comparative scarcity of agents of production complementary to labor and an inadequate provision for schooling and access thereto. Since these conditions are remediable, it should be possible gradually to reduce the gap between Southern and non-Southern
incomes and thus to permit the Southern states to participate fully
in that convergence of state per capita incomes which has been going
on since the turn of the century.[36]

1. *Scarcity of complementary agents of production.* With technology given, output per worker is positively associated with the average amount of complementary agents of production—let us call them
"capital"—utilized per worker; thus an increase of 1 per cent in the
capital-worker ratio may increase output per worker by (say) 0.2 to
0.4 per cent. When technology is changing, capital is essential also to
generate further technological change and to permit the incorpora-
tion of technological improvements into equipment, and it may be
essential to introduce improvements in technical knowledge into the
content of technical education as well as to increase the per capita
level of technical education. In sum, in a technologically changing
economy, a great deal of capital is required, even when inventions
are capital-saving, to implement technology, increase productive capital per head, augment investment per capita in the improvement of
individuals, and make provision for growth of population and various
forms of public capital. Furthermore, given the importance of capital, much of the lowness of Southern earnings is likely to be traceable to dearth of capital.

Data respecting capital formation in the South are lacking. The
absolute rate of capital formation has probably been lower there than
in the nation at large, given that Kuznets is correct in inferring that
capital formation is usually limited on the supply-of-savings side; for
incomes, and particularly property incomes, have been lower in the
South than elsewhere, and the composition of income apparently has
not been appreciably (if at all) more favorable to saving.[37] It is quite
possible, however, that capital per head has been increasing relatively
more rapidly in the South than in some parts of the country. For
property income per capita, an important indicator of changes in
capital stock, has been rising more rapidly in the South than else-

where for the past half century.[38] Furthermore, the South has imported capital in slightly greater measure than have other regions; between 1880 and 1900 about one-fourth of the increase in its non-agricultural capital stock was imported from other regions, and between 1900 and 1919–1921, nearly three-tenths.[39] Comparable estimates are not available for more recent decades. It is believed, however, that more capital has been flowing into the South than has been flowing out. Yet, as will be indicated, the South remains relatively less well equipped with capital than other regions. Furthermore, the inflow of capital from outside the South is more or less offset by resources invested in the production of population which migrates to other regions.

2. **Capital per head.** Both interregional wage and interregional output differences in agriculture are closely associated with differences in capital per worker. R. J. Wolfson has found a high correlation between true interregional differences in agricultural wages and differences in the marginal productivity of farm labor.[40] Perloff concluded, on the basis of 1950 data, that "interstate variations in the labor incomes of agricultural workers are significantly associated with variations in marginal labor productivity reflecting variations in capital per worker used in agricultural production"; most of the explainable variation in output per worker is accounted for in terms of variation in the value of land and buildings per farm worker.[41] The Southeast is much less well equipped with land and buildings per agricultural worker than any other region; the unweighted average of the eleven Southern-state values—that for Texas is omitted—is only about half that reported for the United States, though the latter is exceeded by that for Texas as well as by those for all other regions. Incomes in Southern agriculture were relatively low about 1950, therefore, because Southern agriculturalists were poorly equipped with land and capital. The response of these incomes to increases over time in the value of land and buildings has been less marked than had been expected on the basis of these 1950 relationships, presumably because other forces also were operative, among them a relative increase in the importance of other kinds of capital.[42]

While relevant capital estimates are less satisfactory for manufacturing than for agriculture, indirect estimates indicate that in manufacturing, as in agriculture, differences in labor income are closely associated with differences in the marginal productivity of labor, and these are associated in turn with differences in capital per worker. For example, in 1950, 49 per cent of employment in manufacturing in the nation at large was in activities marked by a high ratio of capital to labor, but the corresponding percentage for the Southeast was only 38.6 per cent. Furthermore, indirect measures of capital per worker as of 1950 indicate, as do direct measures based upon 1919 census data, that capital per worker has tended to be low in low-income states; and correlation of these indicators with manufacturing-labor-income data by state reveals that interstate differences in labor incomes in manufacturing are explainable in considerable measure by differences in capital per worker. It may be inferred, therefore, that output and income per worker in manufacturing are lower in the South than in the United States in considerable part because the ratio of capital to labor is lower.[43] This explanation, if applied to all manufacturing, is not independent of explanations running in terms of industrial composition, since the over-all ratio is low in part because labor-oriented manufacturing is more common in the South than elsewhere; only when the industries compared are identical except for interregional differences in capital-labor ratio do we have an explanation independent of differences in industrial composition. In either instance, however, attention is focused upon the need of the South to augment its stock of capital if it would push up its average income.

3. *Qualitative composition of population.* The qualitative composition of the South's population remains inferior to that of much of the remainder of the nation's population. This inferiority is associated with inferiority in attained level of education; it may therefore be described as another manifestation of capital shortage, since education is essentially the result of investment in the formation of *personal* as distinguished from *extra-personal* capital, and since increase in level of education is the result of increase in investment per head in personal capital. As will be indicated, however, this form of investment has encountered two obstacles which are more powerful in the South than elsewhere: (*a*) a relatively large fraction of the South's white population has been spending its youth in rural areas where making provision for effective education has been difficult; (*b*) the South's population includes a relatively large number of Negroes, many of whom have been confronted by the disadvantage described

under (a) and most of whom have had less easy access to educational facilities than have whites in comparable circumstances.

It is here possible only to suggest the extent of differences in educational attainment. In 1957 the median number of school years completed was 12 and 8.7 among urban white males 18 years old and over, respectively, in and not in the labor force of the United States; the corresponding numbers among whites in the South were 12 and 10.6. Comparable figures for non-white urban males were 8.8 and 5.2 in the United States as a whole and 7.5 and 4.2 in the South. In the rural-farm population the parallel figures for white males were: in the United States, 8.8 and 8; in the South, 8.4 and 6.7. The corresponding figure for non-white males in the labor force was 5.1 in the United States and 3.9 in the South. It is because of the diluting impact of the South's less well-educated Negro and farm population, therefore, that the over-all medians for the United States are higher than those for the South; in the United States, 11.1 and 8.5 years for those in and not in the labor force; in the South, 9.7 and 8.1.[44]

Within the South, furthermore, school attainment has varied widely, even among younger persons (here aged 25–29 years) who have benefited from the marked improvement that has taken place in schooling since 1940.[45] For example, in 1960 according to the census of that year the median number of school years completed by white males 25 or more years old still ranged from 8.7 in Kentucky to 11.6 in Florida; in Ohio the number was 11. Among non-whites the corresponding median ranged from 5.9 in South Carolina to 8.2 in Kentucky; it was 9.1 in Ohio. It is now not until after the age of 17 is passed that non-white school attendance begins to fall appreciably below white school attendance and that rural white school attendance begins to lag appreciably behind urban white school attendance.[46] Even so, in the future, as medians by race and rural-urban composition for persons 25–29 or younger suggest, the spread between Southern and non-Southern averages will be narrower than at present.

It is not easy to assess the impact of interregional differences in education upon interregional differences in per capita income. Correlation methods may be employed to yield estimates. For example, J. L. Fulmer has estimated that with a one-year interstate difference in median years of schooling there was associated in 1940 a $56 interstate difference in per capita income, and in 1950, a $74 difference. These differences were roughly equal to those associated with an 11 per cent interstate difference in the fraction of the labor force employed in agriculture, forestry, and fisheries; or to those associated, in 1940 and 1950, respectively, with a 24 and a 13 per cent interstate difference in the fraction of the total population that was Negro; or to those associated, in 1940 and 1950, respectively, with a 3 and a 1.3 per cent interstate difference in the fraction of the total population employed.[47] In 1940 interstate differences in urbanization, with which most of the described differences were highly correlated, accounted statistically for about seven-tenths of the interstate differences in per capita income.[48]

Other studies merely indicate the importance of education. For example, in 1957, of the low-income population 20 per cent were non-white and 67 per cent had no more than eight years of schooling whereas the corresponding percentages for the relevant population at large approximated 11 and 39 per cent;[49] the differences between the observed and the expected incidence of low incomes thus exceed what could be attributed to chance. Again, both years of schooling and incomes are relatively high among craftsmen and managerial and professional people, of whom there are relatively fewer in the South than elsewhere, and relatively low among agriculturalists and laborers, of whom there are relatively many in the South. Yet this type of relation does not hold universally in that operatives, though less well educated than farmers and service workers, are much better paid.[50] Furthermore, as Becker finds, the rate of return on investment in college education is not higher than that on tangible capital, though it might be improved somewhat, and probably more in the South than in the nation at large. It would improve if good colleges enrolled all or most high-school graduates with I. Q.'s over 120; at present many such high-school graduates who are living in low-income and low-education families do not attend college at all or attend colleges that are too poorly equipped to develop the potential of very promising students.[51]

Increase in education in the South could affect Southern incomes indirectly by reducing the amount of discrimination to which Negroes are subject. The comparative lack of educational opportunities open to Negroes is associated with *political* discrimination, a condition associated in turn with their relative numerousness.[52] The adverse effect of this form of discrimination has probably been accentuated by the relatively low aspiration levels often characteristic of Negro populations as well as by the *market* discrimination to which

Negroes are subject. It is likely, of course, that increase in the educational attainments of Negroes would reduce somewhat Negro-white income differences of the sort reported earlier, at least insofar as these differences are associated with differences in skill and productivity arising out of differences in education, training, etc.[53] Yet, even if all educational differences were eliminated, market discrimination against Negroes would remain to reduce Negro incomes. Becker conjectures that this type of discrimination (which depresses white incomes only negligibly) may reduce Negro incomes by something like 13 per cent. Whatever be the over-all reduction, it is much greater in the South, where the "taste for market discrimination" is about twice as high as in the North.[54] Becker's study does not disclose any recent tendency on the part of this type of discrimination to diminish appreciably, nor does it suggest that increase in the education of Negroes will reduce it appreciably. Improvement in the occupational position of Negroes has tended to parallel rather than to outstrip that of whites.[55]

IV. *Increasing Importance of Manufacturing*

Growth of manufacturing will probably do more than enlargement of any other single set of economic activities to enable the South to absorb its excess agricultural workers and large prospective increments in its labor force as well as to make better use of its ineffectively employed Negro and rural workers, the presence of whom remains a major depressant of per capita income in the South. Income per worker and per capita will rise in consequence of such growth, with the extent of the rise dependent in part upon the quality of the manufactures developed and of the employment provided therein. This growth will not be evenly distributed over the South, however, because, as is indicated below, it is only around foci of expansion that non-agricultural development is to be expected.

Several arguments may be advanced in support of this emphasis upon the importance of manufacturing, even though it occupied only about 25.5 per cent of the nation's labor force in 1950, at which time agriculture and other primary-resource extractors occupied 14.4 per cent, service industries occupied 52.5 per cent, and construction (which is dominated by population growth) engaged 6.1. First, manufacturing, though subject to its own locational determinants, is potentially more footloose than agriculture and mining, which are less correlated with population and which can therefore be highly developed only where the physical environment is suitable. This comparative footlooseness is more characteristic, of course, of forms of manufacturing that are not essentially transformers of resources and that are not highly correlated with population (as is also the supply of local services) or with industries that are correlated with population. Whether footlooseness manifests itself, however, turns in part on interregional differences in the cost of such potentially mobile inputs as labor. Second, the income elasticity of demand for manufactures as a group is in excess of unity, largely because their composition is continually modifiable and adaptable to changes in tastes and income. The income elasticity of demand for agricultural and most (if not all) mineral products, on the contrary, is low. Agriculture will continue to decline as a source of employment in the South and so will coal and probably some other types of mining. Mining engages only small fractions of the labor force outside of Kentucky, however; even in Texas, which has benefited far more than Louisiana from the development of oil and related mineral products, only about 3 per cent of the labor force is engaged in the extraction of these products.[56]

Third, although services (i.e., trade, government, etc.) engage over half the nation's labor force, they are largely oriented to local demand; they are also passive and adaptive rather than dynamic and employment-generating as manufacturing can be. The expansion of services is notably dependent, therefore, upon that of manufacturing and extractive industry. It will also be affected, of course, and especially in the South, by the development of recreation and tourism (of great importance in Florida and of considerable importance in Virginia, Georgia, Kentucky, Mississippi, Louisiana, and Texas),[57] by the distribution of federal governmental payrolls which (though much of the South has gotten a relatively small share of defense and related contracts) constitute two to three times as large a fraction of personal income in the South as in the rest of the nation (exclusive of the Mountain and Pacific Coast states),[58] and perhaps for a time by the South's catching up with the rest of the nation in "urbanization."[59]

1. *Trends.* The relative position of the South as a manufacturing region (with 21.4 per cent of its employed persons in manufacturing) has improved in recent decades, but it still lags behind the North and Northeast (with corresponding percentages of 30.2 and 33.4). Moreover, it is still largely though decreasingly engaged in manufactur-

Table 4. Manufacturing: Establishments, Employment, Trends, 1929–1958

State	Manufacturing Establish-ments	Manufacturing Em-ployees (000)	Relative no. (with 1954 = 100) 1929	1947	1958	Per 1000 population 1929	1954	% of U. S. total 1947	1958
United States	298,182	15,394	62	91	98	85	97	—	—
Virginia	4,414	252	55	90	105	55	68	1.51	1.64
North Carolina	7,289	455	53	89	106	73	102	2.67	2.96
South Carolina	2,888	225	52	86	102	66	97	1.32	1.46
Georgia	5,796	312	57	83	104	60	83	1.75	2.03
Florida	6,304	168	58	64	136	50	36	0.55	1.09
Kentucky	2,850	158	60	88	108	35	49	0.91	1.02
Tennessee	4,450	276	54	85	106	55	77	1.56	1.79
Alabama	3,927	225	60	95	104	50	71	1.44	1.46
Mississippi	2,414	108	62	85	119	29	43	0.54	0.74
Arkansas	2,571	88	62	84	112	27	43	0.46	0.57
Louisiana	3,125	136	67	92	94	47	50	0.93	0.89
Texas	10,338	464	38	72	114	28	48	2.08	3.03

SOURCE: Cols. 2–6, 9–10, *U. S. Census of Manufactures 1958*, III (1958), Table 6, 44 ff.; Cols. 7–8, V. R. Fuchs, *Changes in the Location of Manufacturing. . .* , *Since 1929* (New Haven: Yale University Press, 1962), p. 71.

ing marked by low wages and low national rates of growth, and insofar as this is true, it must pull industry from other regions instead of sharing in new or rapidly expanding industrial employment. Furthermore, as data in Table IV suggest, Southern states have participated unevenly in this improvement. By 1950 those engaged in manufacture in the South formed 17.5 per cent of its labor force and 21.8 per cent of its non-agricultural labor force; the corresponding percentages were 32.6 and 33.6 in the Northeast and 28.7 and 33 in the North Central regions.[60] The South's share of the nation's employment in manufactures, only 14.85 per cent in 1929, had risen to 15.67 by 1947 and to 18.65 by 1958. Even so (see Table IV), progress has been slow, with Texas alone accounting for three-eighths of this increase; and the annual rate of growth of manufacturing employment has been somewhat lower in 1947–1958 than in 1929–1947 in five Southern states (i.e., Virginia, the Carolinas, Alabama, and Louisiana) as well as in the United States. Furthermore, while manufacturing employment has expanded faster in every Southern state (except Louisiana) than in the nation, the ratio of manufacturing employment to the population in 1954 remained below the national level in all Southern states except North and South Carolina, and even in these states the ratio was below that in almost all states north of the Ohio River and east of the Mississippi River.

2. *Character of southern manufacture.* The character of Southern manufacture, as revealed in interstate and interregional comparisons, reflects the region's current comparative resource-structure, a structure that has enabled manufacturing employment to expand greatly in the South, albeit not so rapidly as on the Pacific Coast, whilst declining or barely holding its own north of the Ohio River and east of the Mississippi River. One or more Southern states experienced development in most of the major branches of manufacturing, in food, tobacco, textiles, apparel, lumber, furnitures, paper, printing, chemicals, petroleum and coal products, rubber, leather, stone, clay, and glass, primary metal products, machinery and electrical machinery, and transportation equipment; only fabricated metal products, instruments, and miscellaneous industries were almost unrepresented. Among the conditions which have helped to attract manufacturing to the South are low population density and the availability of space, important natural resources (including favorable climate), especially in Texas and Louisiana, and the relatively satisfactory terms on which less skilled labor was to be had (i.e., relatively low wages, low unionization). Market considerations (except in Florida), taxes, and power costs have exercised little influence. An abundance of relatively cheap unskilled labor made for the predominance of textile industries in Alabama and seaboard states other than Florida; and it fostered the development of other manufactures, among them apparel, furniture and fixtures, electrical machinery, and industries making use of produce or raw materials (e.g., canned and frozen foods, tobacco, pulp and paper mills, logging). Relatively cheap labor, together with abundance of water (a condition favorable also in the seaboard states) and centrality of location, favored the development of a number of manufactures in the East South Central states, among them textiles, apparel, chemicals, electrical machinery, pulp and paper mills, tires, tubes, and aircraft, furniture, and fixtures. In the West South Central states, natural resources (including climate) rather than relatively low wages have been of primary importance; they have facilitated the development of chemicals, aircraft, machinery and metal products, apparel, pulp and paper, and food products.

These developments have slightly improved the South's industrial structure; and they may also have slightly increased its "self-sufficiency," though one cannot be certain respecting any industry until one knows its consumption and product-mix patterns in detail. The South Atlantic states as of 1954 were apparently producing more than they consumed of pulp and paper, furniture, and (as were also the East South Central states) of tobacco, textiles, lumber, and chemicals. The East South Central states were also producing more than they consumed of rubber products, and the West South Central states, of chemicals and petroleum and coal products.[61] Inasmuch as Southern regions must trade with non-Southern regions, income in the South is affected by its terms of trade with these regions. These terms remain unfavorable to the South (though apparently somewhat less so than in the past), in that what it "exports" in raw or fabricated form is produced under somewhat more "competitive" conditions than what it "imports."[62]

The argument that expansion of manufacturing in the South constitutes a major key to the South's future economic development may be subject to one limitation, namely, that labor-saving technical progress in manufacturing may be at a substantially higher rate than labor-saving technical progress in the rest of the economy. In the future the growth of the nation's demand for manufactures will depend principally upon the income elasticity of demand for manufactures and the growth of the nation's income, and the growth of the latter will depend in turn upon the rates of increase characteristic of the labor force and of the output of goods and services per member of the labor force. How many persons will be employed in manufacturing, given the nation's income elasticity of demand for manufactures, will depend upon the rate of increase in output per member of the labor force engaged in manufacturing. If this latter rate is higher than the rate of increase in the output of goods and services per worker in the economy as a whole, the relative number of persons employed in manufacturing will decline unless the income elasticity of demand for manufactures remains sufficiently high to offset the margin of technical progress in manufacturing over that elsewhere in the economy. For example, suppose that the labor force is growing 1.5 per cent per year and that average output per member of the labor force is rising about 2 per cent per year; then aggregate output, or national income, is progressing about 3.5 per cent per year. Accordingly, if the income elasticity of demand for manufactures is around 1.0, demand for them will be increased about 3.5 per cent per year; then, if output per person engaged in manufacturing rises

3 per cent per year, the demand for labor in manufacturing will increase only about 0.5 per cent per year, or less rapidly than the rate (i.e., 1.5 per cent) at which the nation's labor force is growing. Indeed, under the assumptions made, the nation's income elasticity of demand for manufactures would have to remain close to 1.3, or be sufficiently re-enforced by price elasticity of demand, to permit the number of persons engaged in manufacturing to grow at the annual rate of 1.5 per cent supposedly characteristic of the nation's labor force. In view of the limitations suggested by this example, it follows, not that the South should place less emphasis upon manufacturing than has been suggested, but that it should concentrate increasingly upon manufactures, the income and/or price elasticity of demand for which is relatively high. The South should also favor manufactures which give rise to relatively many beneficial, income-increasing side-effects, or respecting which the South's climatic and related amenities constitute a differentially powerful source of attraction. If the South would follow the selective course indicated, it must equip its labor force with the requisite education and training.

In sum, the industrial composition of the South's economy has been unfavorable to economic and demographic growth, and it remains so in those parts of the South which have not adjusted sufficiently to changes in the structure of market demand, industrial and agricultural technology, and other conditions to which economies must adjust if they would grow. Its labor force has included a much larger fraction than has the nation's of workers engaged in slowly growing industries (i.e., agriculture, mining, transportation, and public utilities). Its agricultural labor force has included a larger fraction of workers engaged in relatively slowly growing branches of agriculture than has the nation's agricultural labor force; and its manufacturing labor force has included a larger fraction of workers engaged in relatively slowly growing branches of manufacture than has the nation's. This unfavorableness of composition has characterized the labor force of both the Deep South (i.e., South Carolina, Georgia, Alabama, Mississippi, and Arkansas) and the Appalachian South (North Carolina, Tennessee, Kentucky, and Virginia); it has not recently characterized the economy of Florida, or the part of Virginia's economy under the influence of Washington, D.C., or the whole of the non-agricultural portions of the economies of Texas and Louisiana. Because of the changes that have been taking place in the industrial structure of the economies of various Southern states, all are better situated than they were two decades ago; yet the prospects of these states differ appreciably, largely because of differences in the extent and character of their agricultural undertakings. For example, the competitive position of Louisiana, Virginia, Georgia, Alabama, Kentucky, Tennessee, and Arkansas seems likely to be superior to that of the Carolinas and Mississippi, and that of Florida and Texas will remain good.[63]

V. *Growth Loci*

Capacity for growth is very unevenly distributed in space. This was evident in the population trends summarized earlier. Growth within a region depends largely upon the number and strength of the foci of growth situated therein, since it is in the neighborhood of such foci that the tendency of employment to expand is greatest. It is in such neighborhoods also that capital and income per worker tend to increase most rapidly, in part because it is there that capital and skilled personnel of extra- as well as of intra-regional provenance tend to flow. It is there also that at least a portion of a region's rural-farm migrants move, with the result that both their incomes and those of persons remaining on farms tend to be higher than they otherwise would.

That the South (with roughly 4 of the nation's 13 economic regions, approximately 56 of its 119 economic subregions, and 189 of its 501 state economic areas) is not yet so well endowed with foci of growth becomes apparent when the progress of its geographical components is contrasted with that of the nation's.[64] In the 1940's and 1950's population grew more rapidly than in the United States only in Region IX, lying along the Atlantic and Gulf coasts and including Florida and much of Texas; it grew less rapidly in the other three regions (VII, VIII, and X). (Regions I, VI, and XI may be ignored since they include only very small portions of the South.) In the 1940's and the 1950's population grew faster in seventeen and fifteen, respectively, of the South's economic subregions than in the United States; the comparable figures for the nation are thirty-five and thirty-eight. However, only ten of the subregions lying in the South (rather than largely outside it) grew faster each decade.

Net immigration accounted largely for the high population growth rates encountered in Region IX and in expanding subregions; net

emigration accounted for much of the relatively slow growth encountered elsewhere in the South. Comparative money incomes in
turn accounted for a significant portion of this migration; for migrants tend to move into areas where money incomes are relatively
high, or where expanding economic opportunity is causing employers
to attract workers through recourse to relatively attractive rates of
remuneration. For example, in 1950 in growing Region IX, median
income, though still 19 per cent below the national median, was 10–32
per cent above that in the other three Southern regions. Moreover,
within three of four Southern regions, the 35–50 per cent of the
subregions ranking highest in per capita income included a dispro-
portionately large fraction of the subregions with the highest rates of
population growth within the region under consideration.[65] Rate
of population growth by subregion within a given region was not
significantly correlated with population growth for the whole of any
such region, however, because often factors other than income differences intruded.

While manufacturing has played a positive though not always a
dominant role in the development of the South's economic regions
and subregions, it has not accounted for regional differences, some
of which are associated with the unequal emergence of opportunities
other than in manufacturing and some of which reflect persisting inability to reduce agricultural employment compatibly with modern
technology. Thus in 1950 manufacturing provided only 15.1 per cent
of all employment in fast-growing Region IX, but 21.9 and 23.3 per
cent, respectively, of that in slower-growing Regions VII and VIII.
Region IX, however, with only 11.2 per cent of its employment in
agriculture, had carried adjustment in the agricultural sector further
than had Regions VII and VIII with 18.6 and 25.8 per cent of their
employment still in agriculture. In Region IX, furthermore, there
was no correlation by subregion between percentage of employment
in manufacturing and either median income or rate of population
growth. In Region X although subregional rank in population growth
was significantly correlated with subregional rank in median income,
neither rank in income nor rank in population growth was significantly associated with rank in manufacturing. When one turns to
Regions VII and VIII, however, one finds manufacturing playing a
decisive role. Of the eighteen subregions in Region VII the eight
ranking highest in manufacturing employment included six of the
eight ranking highest in median income and seven of the eight rank-

ing highest in population growth. Of the nineteen subregions in Region VIII the six ranking highest in manufacturing employment included the six ranking highest in median income and four of the six ranking highest in population growth.[66]

Some Southern states are relatively underequipped with actually or potentially expanding centers, such as metropolitan areas, in or near which manufacturing and often other types of economic opportunity tend to flourish. In 1950, of the 56 Standard Metropolitan Areas of 300,000 or more inhabitants, 16 were located in the South, but 12 of these were situated in 4 states (Texas, 4; Florida and Tennessee, 3 each; Virginia, 2) and only one each in 4 states (Alabama, Kentucky, Georgia, and Louisiana).[67] In 1960, of the nation's 212 SMSA, 65 were located in the South; but 19 of these were in Texas, 6 each in Alabama, Florida, Georgia, and North Carolina, 5 each in Louisiana and Virginia, and only 12 in the remaining 5 states. Manufacturing is relatively important in perhaps 54 of these areas, and in 36 employment in manufacturing increased 5 or more per cent in 1954–1958 while declining in the nation at large; but 22 of these 36 are located in 3 states (Texas, North Carolina, and Florida) and only one each in 6 states (Georgia, Kentucky, Louisiana, Mississippi, South Carolina, and Tennessee). Only 16 of the South's 122 non-metropolitan state economic areas as compared with 54 of its 67 metropolitan state economic areas experienced greater population growth in the 1940's and 1950's than did the nation; but 37 of the latter and 11 of the former are located in but 5 states (Florida, Georgia, Louisiana, Texas, and Virginia).

State-by-state comparison of population growth in metropolitan and non-metropolitan state economic areas corroborates the implication of data already presented that such growth is primarily an urban phenomenon. In the 1950's, of Arkansas's 12 areas only one (metropolitan Little Rock) experienced considerable· population growth while 10 of the 11 non-metropolitan areas lost population. In Mississippi only 2 areas (Jackson and the Gulf Coast area) grew appreciably and one (Hattiesburg) moderately, whereas 6 of the remaining 7 non-metropolitan areas lost population. In Kentucky 3 of 5 metropolitan areas and one out of 10 non-metropolitan areas grew appreciably; 4 non-metropolitan areas lost population, while 2 metropolitan and 5 non-metropolitan areas grew slightly to moderately. Two of Tennessee's 4 metropolitan areas grew appreciably and 2 increased moderately, whereas 5 of the state's 9 non-metropolitan areas lost population. Of Alabama's 6 metropolitan areas 3 grew appreciably and 3 moderately in 1940–1960 whereas 6 of the 9 non-metropolitan areas lost population and only one, situated on the Gulf Coast, grew appreciably. In Louisiana all 5 metropolitan areas and 2 non-metropolitan areas grew faster than the nation in 1940–1960, but 3 of the remaining 6 non-metropolitan areas declined while 3 grew only moderately. In Virginia in 1940–1960, 5 of its 6 metropolitan areas and one of its 10 non-metropolitan areas grew notably; 6 non-metropolitan areas grew slightly to moderately while 3 declined. In 1940–1960 five of North Carolina's 6 metropolitan areas and all 4 of South Carolina's grew notably, but only one non-metropolitan area in each state. Four of the remaining 11 non-metropolitan areas in North Carolina declined in the 1950's and 2 of the remaining 7 in South Carolina; other of these areas grew slightly to appreciably. In Georgia all 7 of its metropolitan areas and one non-metropolitan coastal area grew notably in 1940–1960, whereas 6 of the remaining 10 non-metropolitan areas lost population in the 1950's while 4 grew slightly to moderately. In 1940–1960 growth predominated in Florida, where all but one state economic area (a non-metropolitan one) grew remarkably, and in Texas, where all 15 metropolitan areas and 3 non-metropolitan areas grew notably; of the remaining 16 non-metropolitan areas in Texas 7 lost population in the 1950's while 9 gained slightly to moderately.[68]

Manufacturing contributed importantly to employment and development in some but not in all of the rapidly growing state economic areas. In 1950 in the United States manufacturing occupied 24–25 per cent of the labor force in rural non-farm territory and in places under 10,000 population; the corresponding percentage for places of 50–250 thousands and over one million was roughly 31–32 while that for places of 10–50 thousands and 250–1000 thousands was roughly 27–28 per cent.[69] In 1950 of the South's then 57 metropolitan state economic areas, in but 27 and 16, respectively, did manufacturing occupy over 20 and over 25 per cent of the labor force; in 19 the percentage was below 15. The corresponding percentages for the South's 118 non-metropolitan state economic areas were 37, 26, and 59. Manufacturing played an important role in Alabama, the Carolinas, Georgia, and Tennessee, and a relatively minor role in Florida, Texas, and Mississippi; its role was intermediate in the other Southern states, though more important in Virginia than in Louisiana, Kentucky, and Arkansas.[70]

VI. *Improving Prospects*

Improvement in incomes and in the employment structure of the South depends upon circumstances external as well as internal to the South. While the latter are far more important, illustrations of the former may be supplied. In general, when the nation's rate of growth is high, the South tends to benefit, for then the forces making for the convergence of incomes and the reduction of industrial and related differentials are especially powerful, with the result that laggard areas such as the South advance relatively rapidly. At present some rules governing taxation and the remuneration of workers favor other regions more than the South. For example, if the rate of corporate profits taxation declined as the rate of profits increased, and if regulations relating to the deductability of "business expense" accounts were tightened, corporations would become much more attentive to cost-saving than at present and industrial headquarters situated in very large and expensive urban centers (e.g., New York) would probably find it profitable to relocate at least part of their central offices. The South would stand to benefit, since its comparatively lower costs would have become additionally attractive. Similarly, the improvements being made in communication should favor the movement from very large metropolitan centers to smaller centers of both industrial headquarters (or portions thereof) and suppliers of non-local services or of products destined for final markets.[71] Again, suppose that employers were required to remunerate employees for at least a portion of the travel time lost in going to and from work. This requirement would appreciably increase the cost of carrying on production in those centers, especially large ones, in which much time is utilized in going to and from work. Many activities would therefore tend to move from these centers, in part to the South, where, though space per inhabitant remains high, travel time per job is quite low.[72]

It is, however, through change of circumstances in the South that improvement must be sought actively, principally by correcting the South's major current industrial and related shortcomings and by setting up institutions which will facilitate scientific planning and enable the South to capitalize on some of its major locational assets, among them abundance of water (a limitational factor in the West), a set of somewhat varied but generally favorable climates, plenty of well-situated but little-used space, and proximity to important external markets.

The general shortcomings of the Southern economy are fourfold. Most important is lag in education; for not only is the day past when an abundant supply of cheap, unskilled labor can draw industry to the South; the day is at hand when automation is beginning to convert the underskilled into the chronically idle and hence potential inner barbarians. Until the education of the South's population, together with provision for education, is on a par with that found (for example) in the urban Middle West or in California, the South will not be able to share as it might in the development of growing industries; for these are based upon modern technology and cannot flourish in areas where both scientific and technical education is underdeveloped at all levels. Second, so long as the Negro remains undereducated and, when educated, remains subject to adverse occupational discrimination, a large fraction of the South's labor force will be only (say) 40–50 per cent (if that) as productive as it might be. (As implied earlier, this statement is applicable, though in lesser measure, to every other region in the United States.) It is essential, of course, that the Negro make effective use of superior job opportunities as they become available and that he assume greater responsibility for fitting himself into modern industrial society.[73] Third, as W. H. Nicholls and E. L. Rauber have suggested, the South will have to give up what has been called "Southern Tradition," a tradition based upon agrarian values and rigidity of social structure which in turn have made for weakness of social responsibility, anti-intellectualism, and conformity of thought and behavior. It is essential that Huntsville (Alabama) become symbolic of the South. Unless its obsolete traditions are given up the South will fail in its efforts to accelerate its industrial-urban development, a must if low-income areas are to be eliminated.[74] Fourth, the inflow of capital into the South, together with increase in the rate of capital formation within the South, must be stimulated. For the South is lacking in capital, though it can overcome this in part if it affords, as it readily can, a higher rate of return to non-Southern capital than is to be had in parts of the United States where the rate of capital formation is high or the rates of return are depressed.[75] Employers and employees can facilitate this outcome by holding down minimum and union rates, excess in which is augmenting hard-core unemployment within and outside the South, and by putting greater emphasis upon training and retraining workers.

Two types of institutes need to be set up in one or several parts of the South (since it is a diverse region) whose function it would be to inventory the South's comparative advantages for various types of economic activity, to disclose how these advantages may be actualized, and perhaps to give publicity to them. (1) An Institute of Regional Science would play a major role in organizing relevant research, in discovering and inventorying comparative advantages, in suggesting developmental programs, and in conducting, on a custom basis, studies for communities and for business firms. An end might thus be made to the haphazardness of the search for "new industry" still characteristic of much of both Southern and non-Southern efforts to attract "industry" to particular states and areas. By now Regional Science has become a well-developed instrument and can supply many missing answers. (2) An Institute of Southern Metropolitan and Community Planning is equally necessary. As yet few of the South's cities have become so inflexible as the man-submerging agglomerations found in the North and East. The future of the urban South still remains relatively unshackled by bad planning in the past, though for the reason that the urban South has not had much of a past. If the urban South entrusts much of its "planning" to locally oriented and huckster-minded persons who disregard aesthetic and longer-run considerations, it will gradually dissipate that control over its future development which is perhaps the South's biggest single source of comparative advantage. An Institute concerned with the economic and governmental problems of metropolitan and community planning could undertake or sponsor the studies required and thereby provide guidelines based on scientific inquiry and longer-run considerations instead of upon short-run political advantage and trading profits which make for urban blight. It could also facilitate solution of Negro problems, most of which emerge with urbanization.

Inasmuch as the South's future economic development depends largely upon its foci of growth, together with their rates of expansion, proponents of such development must distinguish between *active* and *passive* sources of growth. Let us label the former A and the latter P, and let the indicator of growth be employment, with the aggregate amount designated E. If the sequence encountered in time is normally $A \rightarrow E \rightarrow P$ rather than $P \rightarrow E \rightarrow A$, we describe A as active since increase in it precedes increase in E and P instead of the other way around. In reality, of course, one does not encounter in the economy of a metropolis or other area the overwhelmingly unilateral and unidirectional flow of "causation" our formulation implies because the occupational sectors composing such an economy are interdependent.[76] Even so, we can have and probably do have stronger flows of "causation" from one source and in one direction than from another source and in another direction. We may therefore describe the usual temporal sequence as

$$A \rightleftarrows E \rightleftarrows P;$$

here A is predominantly active while P is predominantly passive. Should this relationship obtain, growth-fomenting policy would place major emphasis upon the expansion of A and count upon P to follow suit, particularly if (as is unlikely) there existed a "normal" ratio between A and P. In fact, some exponents of the so-called urban "economic base" thesis suggest that (say) a 10 per cent increase in the basic employment (usually defined as consisting in export-oriented activities) will be accompanied by roughly the same relative increase in other forms of employment; whence, if the amount of the latter is double that of the former, the increase in aggregate employment is three times that in basic employment and we have an employment multiplier of 3. The empirical conditions essential to the validity of this thesis are seldom realized, however.[77]

We have assigned to manufacturing a role analogous to that played by A in the preceding model. For if certain branches of manufacture can be established, then complementary branches (e.g., those supplying inputs or absorbing output) are likely to be established, and in time local services (which engage roughly as many workers as does manufacturing) and non-local services (which are of similar importance) will follow, at least in an amount sufficient to provide what is demanded in the form of local production. There may also be an increase in construction employment. There is no hard and fast sequence, however. If manufacturing employment increases 10 per cent, the net increase in income resulting to a community (after allowing for increase in imported inputs) may be spent there and elsewhere in various proportions, and the aggregate demand for local labor and other inputs will be affected accordingly.[78] There may be a marked increase in imports to the community, or there may be a partial substitution of home production for what had been imported. What happens will be much affected by the availability of labor in quantity and quality. If the increase in manufacturing absorbs all the unemployed labor, labor will have to be drawn from outside the community to supply local services, and there will be little immediate disposition to produce locally services that can be imported. In consequence the wage structure will be modified, and this in turn may even produce change in the structure of manufactures. Such labor shortage and such upward pressure against the wage level are likely to be less extreme in the South than in many other parts of the country, given that there exists a great deal of unemployment and underemployment, especially in surrounding rural areas; yet the utilizability of this labor may be and often is quite limited by its lack of education and training. In short, if manufacturing employment increases, a variety of sequels is possible, and their form will depend largely upon the policies pursued and upon the availability of competent labor.

In this discussion and earlier the role assigned services has been the essentially passive one of *P*, it being assumed that manufacturing shares the role of *A* only with extractive industry and that relative employment in construction depends principally upon the over-all rate of growth. It is true, nevertheless, that an increase in *P* (i.e., services) may necessitate some increase in *A* (i.e., manufactures), particularly if the relative amount of certain types of manufacturing is near the minimum for the type of urban community under analysis.[79] For local services are somewhat complementary to one another and to non-local services which can be exported much as goods are exported. Moreover, in Florida under the impact of tourism and attractive climate, in some coastal areas and in parts of Texas for several reasons, and in a number of larger urban centers, growth of *P* (services) has preceded and then stimulated that of *A* (manufactures) by generating demand and perhaps by attracting labor. It is not always clear, however, whether such an equilibrium-restoring process signifies that services have really played a highly active role. For, given some sort of equilibrium relationship between services and manufactures, *P* (services) could over-respond to an increase in *A* (manufactures), with the result that corrective action, under market influences, would become necessary on the part of *A*.

In sum, growth-fomenting policy cannot be carried out in the abstract. It must be adapted to the type of community and economic area under consideration. For even though it be assumed that the role of *A* in the South is most likely to be played by the expansion of manufactures, there will be many exceptions to this assumption, and policy must fit them as well as the more typical cases.

1. This paragraph, together with the one preceding, is based on returns in the 1950 and 1960 decennial censuses and upon *Statistical Bulletin* (Metropolitan Life Insurance Company), XXI (Nov., 1950), 9 ff.; XXIII (March, 1952), 7 ff.; (April, 1952), 1 ff.; (Aug., 1952), 6 ff.; XLII (March, 1961), 3 ff.; (April, 1961), 1 ff.; (July, 1961), 1 ff. On pre-1940 population and related problems in the South, see my series of papers, "Population Problems in the South," *Southern Economic Journal*, III–IV (April, July, Oct., 1937). On the emergence and peopling of Southern cities, see R. B. Vance and N. J. Demerath, *The Urban South* (Chapel Hill: University of North Carolina Press, 1954); and on the recent demographic history of the South's main problem area, see T. R. Ford, ed., *The Southern Appalachian Region: A Survey* (Lexington: University of Kentucky Press, 1962), chaps. iii–v. On pre-1950 urban, metropolitan, and regional trends, see Donald J. Bogue, *The Population of the United States* (Glencoe: Free Press, 1959), chaps. ii–iv. On regional differences, see H. S. Perloff *et al.*, *Regions, Resources, and Economic Growth* (Baltimore: The Johns Hopkins Press, 1960), chaps. ii, xv; and Edgar S. Dunn, Jr., *Recent Southern Economic Development As Revealed by the Changing Structure of Employment* (Gainesville: University of Florida Press, 1962), chap. i.

2. W. H. Graybill *et al.*, *The Fertility of American Women* (New York: Wiley, 1958), pp. 14, 64; Bureau of the Census, *Current Population Reports* (Series P-23, No. 4) (July 29, 1957); also Bogue, *op. cit.*, chap. xi, and Ford, ed., *op. cit.*, pp. 44–45.

3. In 1950 (as in 1940) the crude death rate was *below* the adjusted death rate in the South but *above* it in the nation at large (though slightly below it in 1940). See *Statistical Bulletin* (Metropolitan Life Insurance Company), XXXV (March, 1954), 9.

4. Based upon Graybill *et al.*, *op. cit.*, p. 70, and *U. S. Census of Population 1960, II: General Population Characteristics*, Table 13.

5. E.g., see C. V. Kiser, "Fertility Rates in the United States by Residence and Migration," *Proceedings, International Population Conference* (Vienna, 1959), pp. 273–286.

6. On differential fertility see Graybill *et al.*, *op. cit.*, chap. iv, esp. pp. 68–79; T. L. Smith, *Fundamentals of Population Study* (New York: Lippincott & Co., 1960), p. 326, also pp. 300–302, 313–316 on rural-urban differentials around 1950. In the United States between 1940 and 1959, white natality rose from 18.6 to 23.1 and non-white natality from 26.7 to 34; gross reproduction increased far more, from 1.082 to 1.730 in the white population and from 1.422 to 2.354 in the non-white population. See U. S. Bureau of the Census, *Vital Statistics of the United States 1959* (U. S. Department of Health, Education, and Welfare), Section 3, pp. 3–15, 3–25.

7. See Bogue, *op. cit.*, pp. 761, 767.

8. See Everett S. Lee *et al.*, *Population Redistribution and Economic Growth, United States, 1870–1950: Methodological Considerations and Reference Tables* (prepared under the direction of Simon Kuznets and Dorothy S. Thomas) (Philadelphia: American Philosophical Society, 1957), I, Table P-I; R. B. Vance and Nadia Danilevsky, *All These People* (Chapel Hill: University of North Carolina Press, 1945), chap. ix, esp. pp. 112, 117, 119. On cityward migration see Vance and Demerath, *op. cit.*; and on migration from the Southern Appalachian region, Ford, ed., *op. cit.*, chap. iv.

9. See Bureau of the Census, *Current Population Reports* (Series P-25, No. 247) (April 2, 1962), on which Table II is based.

10. Gladys K. Bowles, *Net Migration from the Farm Population, 1940–50* (Agricultural Marketing Service Statistical Bulletin No. 176) (Washington, 1956), p. 16.

11. Bureau of the Census, *Farm Population* (Series Census—ERS P-27, No. 31) (March 14, 1962). Under the new definition (which includes in the farm population only those living on farms and producing and selling at least a required minimum of produce), the farm population numbered 15,635,000 in 1960; under the old definition, 20,541,000.

12. E. L. Baum and E. O. Heady, "Some Effects of Selected Policy Programs on Agricultural Labor Mobility in the South," *Southern Economic Journal*, XXV (Jan., 1959), 328.

13. J. M. Brewster, "Long Run Prospects of Southern Agriculture," *Southern Economic Journal*, XXVI (Oct., 1959), 138–140. On the cotton prospect see Royall Brandis, "Cotton and the World Economy," *Southern Economic Journal*, XXIII (July, 1956), 28–38.

14. Baum and Heady, *op. cit.*, esp. pp. 322, 334–337.

15. E.g., see R. E. Wakely and M. E. Nasrat, "Sociological Analysis of Population Migration," *Rural Sociology*, XXVI (March, 1961), 15–23; R. D. Geschwind and V. W. Ruttan, "Job Mobility and Migration in a Low Income Rural Community," *Research Bulletin No. 730* (Agricultural Experiment Station, Purdue University, Sept., 1961); D. Gale Johnson, "Functioning of the Labor Market," *Journal of Farm Economics*, XXXIII (Feb., 1951), 75–87; Agricultural Policy Institute, *The Farmer and Migration in the United States* (School of Agriculture, North Carolina State College) (Raleigh, 1961).

16. On the stimulus of income differentials to migration and the capacity of migration to reduce income differentials, see Perloff *et al.*, *op. cit.*, chap. xxxiii; L. A. Sjaastad, "The Relationship Between Migration and Income in the United States," *Papers and Proceedings of the Regional Science Association*, VI (1960), 37–64, esp. 48–49, 51–54, 63–64; R. A. Easterlin, "Long Term Income Changes: Some Suggested Factors," *Papers and Proceedings of the Regional Science Association*, IV (1958), 312–325; F. T. Bachmura, "Man-Land Equalization through Migration," *American Economic Review*, XLIX (Dec., 1959), 1004–1017; G. H. Borts, "The Equalization of Returns and Regional Economic Growth," *American Economic Review*, L (June, 1960), 319–346. As to the mechanisms involved in the absorption of excess farm population, together with the role of "full employment," see F. T. Bachmura's case study, "Small Area Population Response to Full Employment," *Southern Economic Journal*, XXV (Oct., 1958), 159–173.

17. See Table III and R. E. Graham, Jr. and E. J. Coleman, "Consumer Incomes Up in All Regions in 1960," *Survey of Current Business*, XLI (Aug., 1961), 10. On earlier (1949) income differentials, see Perloff *et al.*, *op. cit.*, chap. xxvii, and on Negro-white differences in 1960, *U. S. Census of Population 1960*, II, Table 67.

18. R. J. Lampman, *The Low Income Population and Economic Growth*, Study Paper 12, prepared for consideration by the Joint Economic Committee (86th Congress of the United States, 1st session, Dec. 16, 1959) (Washington, D. C.), pp. 8–9.

19. T. R. Atkinson, "Money Income Distribution: South vs. Non-South," *Southern Economic Journal*, XXIII (July, 1956), 15–27.

20. The year-by-year changes are reported and graphed in Frank A. Hanna, *State Income Differentials, 1919–1954* (Durham: Duke University Press, 1959), pp. 38–41, 44, 48. See also C. F. Schwartz and R. E. Graham, Jr., "Personal Income by States, 1929–54," *Survey of Current Business*, XXXV (Sept., 1955), 12–22.

21. Inasmuch as cyclical and other non-persistent phenomena may affect personal income differently in Southern and in non-Southern states, the ratio of a particular state's per capita personal income to that of the nation may be affected temporarily by these phenomena even though the effect may not be great enough to modify the rank order of these incomes, by state. Incomes in all the states included in Table III (except Virginia, Florida, and the Carolinas) appear to be relatively sensitive to cyclical fluctuations, Hanna's careful analysis reveals. See Hanna, *op. cit.*, pp. 64–66. Accordingly, when there is a cyclical upturn, incomes in these states will tend to rise (fall) relatively more than the national average. *Ibid.*, pp. 73–74.

22. *Ibid.*, pp. 203–204. On interstate differences in the ratio of the labor force to the population, by state, see S. Kuznets *et al.*, *Population Redistribution and Economic Growth, United States, 1870–1950: Analyses of Economic Change* (Philadelphia: American Philosophical Society, 1957), II, 79–80. Regional changes in income and labor force are tabulated, pp. 221 ff., 228 ff.

23. See Simon Kuznets, "Industrial Distribution of Income and Labor Force by States, United States, 1919–1921 to 1955," *Economic Development and Cultural Change*, VI (July, 1958), 16–43; Perloff *et al.*, *op. cit.*, pp. 520–529.

24. Hanna, *op. cit.*, p. 192. "When the total explanatory values of the occupational and industrial compositions from the population census are compared, it is found that occupational composition accounts for about 46 per cent of the interstate variation left unexplained by industrial composition." *Ibid.*, p. 192.

25. Perloff *et al.*, *op. cit.*, pp. 532–534.

26. Hanna, *op. cit.*, p. 143. See also H. P. Miller, *Income of the American People* (New York: Wiley, 1955), chap. v.

27. F. A. Hanna, ed., *Regional Income* (Princeton: Princeton University Press, 1957), p. 186. E. F. Denison concluded that about 37 per cent of interstate variation in earnings

is due to differences in occupational composition and that most of the rest is due to differences in occupational earnings. *Ibid.*, pp. 170–171, 172–173.

28. The data for the late 1940's are given in C. A. R. Wardwell, "Regional Trends in the United States Economy," a Supplement to *Survey of Current Business* (Washington, 1951), pp. 75–76. The 1959 medians in the *U. S. Census of Population 1960: United States Summary, General Social and Economic Characteristics*, Tables 139–140, pp. 289–291.

29. Wardwell, *op. cit.*, pp. 12–13.

30. *Ibid.*, pp. 84, 86–89.

31. Many of these conditions and changes have been described in detail in C. B. Hoover and B. U. Ratchford, *Economic Resources and Policies of the South* (New York: Macmillan Company, 1951), esp. chaps. vi–vii.

32. Perloff *et al.*, *op. cit.*, pp. 547–548; see also Hoover and Ratchford, *op. cit.*, chap. xvi; also V. R. Fuchs, *Changes in the Location of Manufacturing in the United States Since 1929* (New Haven: Yale University Press, 1962), chap. vi and Table C:1; V. R. Fuchs and R. Periman, "Recent Trends in Southern Wage Differentials," *Review of Economics and Statistics*, XLII (Aug., 1960), 292–300.

33. U. S. Department of Labor, *Wages in Nonmetropolitan Areas, South and North Central States* (Oct., 1960) (B. L. S. Report No. 190) (Washington, 1961), 26, 31.

34. Wage data are given in U. S. Department of Labor, *Wages and Related Benefits; 82 Labor Markets 1960–61* (B. L. S. Bulletin No. 1285–83) (Washington, 1961), *passim*; J. H. Hawkes, "Job Pay Levels and Trends in 60 Labor Markets," *Monthly Labor Review*, LXXXIV (Feb., 1961), 163–169. See also Perloff *et al.*, *op. cit.*, p. 577.

35. See Hanna, *State Income Differentials*, pp. 204–214; Edwin Mansfield, "City Size and Income, 1949," in Hanna, ed., *Regional Income*, pp. 271–307 and comments by D. G. Johnson and Margaret R. Reid, *ibid.*, pp. 307–315, and by Mansfield, *ibid.*, pp. 315–317; also Miller, *op. cit.*, pp. 38–45; S. C. Sufrin *et al.*, "The North-South Differential—A Different View," *Southern Economic Journal*, XV (Oct., 1948), 184–190.

36. See Hanna, *State Income Differentials*, p. 36; Kuznets *et al.*, *Population Redistribution and Economic Growth, United States, 1870–1950: Analyses of Economic Change*, pp. 146–150, 163–165, 253–268, also p. 79 on labor force.

37. See data on property incomes in Kuznets *et al.*, *Population Redistribution and Economic Government, United States, 1870–1950: Analyses of Economic Change*, pp. 159–161; and Simon Kuznets' discussion of savings in his *Capital in the American Economy* (Princeton: Princeton University Press, 1961), pp. 110–116. He discusses the connection of income composition with saving but does not relate his discussion to regions. See Kuznets, *Capital in the American Economy*, pp. 97–110.

38. Kuznets, *Population Redistribution and Economic Growth, United States, 1870–1950: Analyses of Economic Change*, pp. 142–143, 147, 154–155, 190–191.

39. *Ibid.*, pp. 179–181.

40. R. J. Wolfson, "An Econometric Investigation of Regional Differentials in American Agricultural Wages," *Econometrica*, XXVI (April, 1958), 225–256.

41. Perloff *et al.*, *op. cit.*, pp. 559–560. For other evidence see my "Aspects of the Economics of Population Growth," *Southern Economic Journal*, XIV (Jan., 1948), 246–254.

42. Perloff *et al.*, *op. cit.*, pp. 556–567; see also Kuznets *et al.*, *Population Redistribution and Economic Growth, United States, 1870–1950: Analyses of Economic Change*, p. 251, on output and assets per worker; V. W. Ruttan and T. T. Stout, "Regional Differences in Factor Shares in American Agriculture 1925–1957," *Journal of Farm Economics*, XLII (Feb., 1960), 52–68.

43. Perloff *et al.*, *op. cit.*, pp. 572–585, 603–604; for data relating to other years and countries see my "Aspects of the Economics of Population Growth," pp. 254–256. For emphasis on the importance of industries with a low capital-labor ratio in the Southern economy and their past impact on the over-all ratio and Southern wages, see J. W. Markham, "Some Comments on the North-South Differential," *Southern Economic Journal*, XVI (Jan., 1950), 279–283.

44. These data are from *Current Population Reports, Labor Force*, (Series P-50, No.

78) (Nov., 1957), 11. See also *Current Population Reports, Labor Force* (Series P-20, No. 99) (Feb., 1960), on steady improvement in literacy and educational attainment; also "Educational Status, College Plans, and Occupational Status of Farm and Nonfarm Youths; October, 1959," *Farm Population* (Series Census-ERS P-27, No. 30) (Aug., 1961) and "Factors Related to College Attendance of Farm and Nonfarm High School Graduates," *Farm Population* (No. 32) (June, 1962).

45. C. A. Anderson, "Inequalities in Schooling in the South," *American Journal of Sociology*, LX (May, 1955), 547–561.

46. *Current Population Reports* (Series P-20, No. 110) (July, 1961), 14.

47. J. L. Fulmer, "State Per Capita Income Differentials: 1940 and 1950," *Southern Economic Journal*, XXII (July, 1955), 37, and "Factors Influencing State Per Capita Income Differentials," *Southern Economic Journal*, XVI (Jan., 1950), 262–266. Kuznets found that inclusion of states with large Negro populations increases the amount of interstate income inequality revealed by various indicators. See his "Industrial Distribution of Income and Labor Force by States, United States, 1919–1921 to 1955," pp. 95 ff.

48. See Fulmer, "Factors Influencing State Per Capita Income Differentials," pp. 266–269.

49. Lampman, *op. cit.*, pp. 9, 29; also *Current Population Reports* (Series P-50, No. 78) (Nov., 1957), 8.

50. This sentence and the one preceding are based upon a comparison of education data in Table D in *Current Population Reports* (Series P-50, No. 78) (Nov., 1957), 4, with income data in Table 25, *Current Population Reports* (Series P-60, No. 37) (Jan., 1962), 43. Data by state on the occupational composition of the male labor force in 1960 are reported in Table 57, *U. S. Census of Population 1960: II*.

51. See Gary Becker, "Underinvestment In College Education?," *American Economic Review*, L (May, 1960), 347–349, 352–354. See also "Factors Related to College Attendance . . ." (cited in note 44), pp. 4–5, where it is reported that of the 1959 high school graduates not in college "53 per cent were in the top half of the IQ distribution."

52. Gary Becker, *The Economics of Discrimination* (Chicago: University of Chicago Press, 1957), p. 107, also p. 104.

53. *Ibid.*, pp. 94–95; Wolfson, *op. cit.*, pp. 232–237; Perloff *et al.*, *op. cit.*, pp. 536–538, 549–551. For evidence that Negro aspiration levels are below those of whites, see J. V. Berreman, "The Educational and Occupational Aspirations and Plans of Negro and White Male Elementary Students," *Pacific Sociological Review*, II (Fall, 1959), 56–60; C. E. Silberman, "The City and the Negro," *Fortune*, LXV (March, 1962), 91 ff.

54. Becker, *The Economics of Discrimination*, pp. 21, 92–94, 101–102, 125; also his "Underinvestment in College Education?," p. 348, where it is indicated that "the rate of return to nonwhites seems to be about two percentage points lower" than that to urban male whites, that is, about 7 instead of 9 per cent, before taxes, on college costs.

55. Becker, *The Economics of Discrimination*, pp. 95, 106–107, also pp. 112–114, 124–125, on the stability of market discrimination against Negroes over time.

56. This paragraph is based on Otis Dudley Duncan *et al.*, *Metropolis and Region* (Baltimore: The Johns Hopkins Press, 1960), esp. chaps. iii, vii–ix; Fuchs, *op. cit.*, chap. v, on the mobility of manufacturing; and Perloff *et al.*, *op. cit.*, chap. xx, on mining and agricultural location, and pp. 303–305, 391, 409, 656–657, on employment trends by category and the slowness of growth of manufactures predominant in the South.

57. According to estimates reported in *Printer's Ink*, CCLXIV (July–Sept., 1958), 23, in 1957–1958 the annual dollar volume of tourism in the South ranged from $1,430,-000,000 in Florida to $128,000,000 in Tennessee; it amounted to $300,000,000 or more in the states named in the text.

58. Fuchs, *op. cit.*, pp. 150–151; Hoover and Ratchford, *op. cit.*, pp. 223–227; C. E. Mayberry, "Government Defense Industrial Activity in Relation to the South," *Southern Economic Journal*, XXIV (April, 1958), 458–470. See also Perloff *et al.*, *op. cit.*, pp. 463–466.

59. This paragraph is based largely on Perloff *et al.*, *op. cit.*, Part IV, and pp. 256–262, and on Duncan *et al.*, *op. cit.*, chaps. iii, vii–ix.

60. Kuznets *et al.*, *Population Redistribution and Economic Growth, United States*,

1870–1950: Analyses of Economic Change, pp. 70–71. On trends see also Fuchs, *op. cit.*, chap. iii.

61. Most of this paragraph and the one preceding is based on Fuchs, *op. cit.*, pp. 23–25, 51, 83, 94, 101, 124–127, 162–167, 174, 291–293, and chaps. iv–vii, ix. See also Perloff *et al.*, *op. cit.*, chaps. xxiii–xxv. On unionization see Leo Troy, "The Growth of Union Membership in the South, 1939–1953," *Southern Economic Journal*, XXIV (April, 1958), 407–420. On difficulties attending analysis of a region's trading relations, see Walter Isard, *Methods of Regional Analysis* (New York: Wiley, 1960), esp. chaps. v–vi.

62. E.g., Hoover and Ratchford, *op. cit.*, pp. 86–87, 405–406. Fuchs, *op. cit.*, employs one indicator of competitiveness, albeit an imperfect one, in his Table D.1 summarizing selected industry characteristics.

63. This paragraph is based upon Dunn, *Recent Southern Economic Development*.

64. D. J. Bogue and C. L. Beale, *Economic Areas of the United States* (New York: Free Press, Glencoe, Illinois, 1961), Table A.

65. Computed from data for regions VII–X, in *ibid*.

66. *Ibid*.

67. See Duncan *et al.*, *op. cit.*, chap. xi.

68. This paragraph and the preceding paragraphs are based on data for state economic areas in Bogue and Beale, *op. cit.*

69. See Duncan *et al.*, *op. cit.*, p. 60.

70. The data on state economic areas are based on Bogue and Beale, *op. cit.*

71. On the variation of occupational structures with size of community and of metropolitan area, see Duncan *et al.*, *op. cit.*, pp. 60, 210, 213 ff.

72. For data on density see U. S. Census of Population 1960, *United States Summary* (Final Report PC 1–1A), Tables E and 22; also Jean Gottmann, *Megalopolis* (New York: Twentieth Century Fund, 1961), chap. xii.

73. On the problems involved see Silberman, *op. cit.*, and Burt Schorr's survey of Negro recruitment, college standards, etc., in the *Wall Street Journal*, Aug. 6, 1962, pp. 1 ff.

74. See W. H. Nicholls, *Southern Traditions and Regional Progress* (Chapel Hill: University of North Carolina Press, 1960), *passim*; E. L. Rauber, "The South and Its Future," *Monthly Review of Federal Reserve Bank of Atlanta*, (June, 1962) p. 5.

75. E.g., see G. H. Borts and J. L. Stein, "Investment Return as a Measure of Comparative Regional Economic Advantage," in Werner Hochwald, ed., *Design of Regional Accounts* (Baltimore: The Johns Hopkins Press, 1961). See also J. L. Stein, "Interregional Comparisons and the Marginal Product of Capital," *Southern Economic Journal*, XXV (July, 1958), 24–32, and "The Predictive Accuracy of the Marginal Productivity Theory of Wages," *Review of Economic Studies*, XXV (1958), 182–189. We find in these studies support for the theory that rates of return and wage levels are highly associated with productivity, and hence support for the view that it is upon increase in productivity that increase in returns to capital and labor in the South depend.

76. For an illustration of the interdependence of certain variables underlying progress in urbanization and a critique of the unilateral causal assumption, made by those who premise urban growth upon the growth of an economic base, see C. E. Ferguson, "A Statistical Study of Urbanization," *Social Forces*, XXXVII (Oct., 1958), 19–26; also his "Statics, Dynamics, and the Economic Base," in R. W. Pfouts, ed., *The Techniques of Urban Economic Analysis* (West Trenton: Chandler-Davis, 1960) pp. 325–339. See also regarding difficulties besetting the isolation of factors responsible for metropolitan growth, Donald J. Bogue, *Population Growth in Standard Metropolitan Areas 1900–1950* (Housing and Home Finance Agency) (Washington, 1953), pp. 35–37.

77. For a discussion of the "economic-base" approach and the multiplier, see Isard, *op. cit.*, pp. 189–205, 222–227, 623–628; and for a critique, Ferguson, "Statics, Dynamics, and the Economic Base," in Pfouts, ed., *op. cit.*

78. See R. W. Pfouts and E. E. Curtis, "Limitations of the Economic Base Analysis," *Social Forces*, XXXVI (May, 1958), 303–310. On occupational structures, see Duncan

et al., op. cit., passim; and on interrelations of manufactures, see Perloff *et al., op. cit.*, pp. 394, 396–397.

79. E. L. Ullman and M. F. Dacey, "The Minimum Requirements Approach to the Urban Economic Base," *Papers and Proceedings of the Regional Science Association*, VI (1960), 175–194. See also C. M. Tiebout's comments on the controversy between B. Harris and R. W. Pfouts respecting economic base theory, *Journal of the American Institute of Planners*, XXIV (1958), 244–246.

John P. Frank

Legal Developments in Race Relations, 1945–1962

Introduction

The law, we have been told by the master, is a seamless web. The country and the society, we may add, are no less seamless and the law itself is only a completely intermingled part of country and society. Because this is so, the story of the development of law and its effects on the postwar South may begin instructively with a tale of the North and with a course of events which was only marginally affected by the law at all.

Our tale begins on a Middlewestern university campus with about a hundred Negroes among ten thousand students in the years 1946 and 1947. The campus was non-segregated but the community was not. The restaurants which fringed the campus and to which the students liked to go for cokes and snacks between classes, as well as for meals, were open to the white students only. The restaurant restriction was an aggravation. At fairly conventional hours, the Negro and white students could obtain snacks at a large, pleasant university restaurant. However, in this small town if a colored student missed a meal, as if for example he were on a job, he had no choice but to go hungry until the next one.

This pattern of race discrimination was deeply irksome to a substantial number of white students. The revolt against the restaurants began when, under the guidance of an exceptionally lively faculty member, a campus NAACP chapter was formed. More than six hundred students, almost all of them white, joined the chapter, making this proportionally probably the largest NAACP campus chapter among state universities. Within a few months the students were thoroughly conscious that some of their number were not having access to facilities which the overwhelming majority could enjoy.

The next step was action, with legal action included. The state had a thin civil rights law, one which was the subject of some long-gone compromise, and which was very nearly unenforceable by private action. Its enforcement was worth a try, but only as a part of an across-the-board attack on the problem because the legal recourse was simply not sturdy enough by itself to do the job. The NAACP chapter set out to raise funds to retain counsel, but it proved easier to do the former than the latter. A few hundred dollars was accumulated, but no local lawyer would take their case.

Help came from two quarters. The dean of the university law school, a figure of genuine distinction in legal education, together with a younger faculty member with some litigation experience, publicly announced that they would represent any students discriminated against by local restaurants. Moreover, an elderly and richly experienced lawyer in a neighboring community agreed to take the laboring oar on the representation and proceeded to draft injunction papers.

By now the community was thoroughly conscious of its problem and began to line up on one side or another. An excessively zealous faculty censor barred from the student newspaper the announcement by the law school dean. (The chapter got even wider coverage for its news by inserting the same story as an ad.) The across-the-board aspects of the program began to take effect. A national religious group interested in racial equality sent ministers into the community and local ministers began to line up on the same side. The chapter precipitated incidents, sending students into the restaurants to order something, be refused, and be carefully observed by student witnesses who would then be prepared to testify subsequently in court concerning the treatment given.

The members of the Restaurant Owners Association had no particular wish to discriminate. From their standpoint, one student's dime was as good as another's. But they believed that they had to rise and fall together. If one accepted colored business, he worried that his white trade might migrate elsewhere.

At this point, with lawsuits in the air but not yet tried, came crushing events. The NAACP chapter announced picketing of the restaurants. Then the many students of the men's dormitories met together and set about to resist discrimination against any of their fellow students. They knew their trade was essential to the merchants. They resolved to honor a picket line and to boycott any discriminating restaurant. The restaurant owners quickly capitulated. For the fifteen years last past, any student of this Middlewestern university who wants a bite to eat can get it on either side of a well-shaded university town street, for all will be treated alike.

The community wounds, though quickly buried, did not altogether disappear. The university dropped the instructor who had done so much for the NAACP when his contract renewal time came up, and there were those to wonder whether his concededly inadequate list of publications would have looked quite so serious to those passing upon his promotion if he had not been so conspicuously engaged in a community issue. Intrafaculty enmities over the entire incident had lasting effects.

Within its limited borders, this story portrays the relationship of the law and the South in the postwar years. Southern communities, in the manner of this Northern town, have gone through an apparently endless cycle of episodes of awareness, legal action, and community force and pressure to change practice. In each, to borrow a military analogy, the law is the landing force. It makes the beachhead. But the breakthrough, if it is to be significant, is broadened by forces from behind, which take advantage of the opening to go the rest of the way. Where these forces are present, significant alterations of social practices result. Where they do not exist, the law has been unable to hold its beachheads and the legal action becomes a kind of a military monument on which is only recorded, "We were here."

The supporting and capitalizing pressures in the wake of the legal attack are consumer pressures, religious pressures, voter pressures, and the public opinion pressure of moderate leaders. The dean of that university law school is like Ralph McGill and the Atlanta *Constitution*; when a person of such character moves into a controversy, the community tone changes and the public begins to give serious attention. The religious action in the restaurant case in the North is the parallel of the religious action in New Orleans and elsewhere. The restaurant reversal is a triumph primarily of consumer revolt against discrimination, and the owners of the buses in Birmingham would tell much the same story of their own disputes. The only basic element directly missing in the university case was the voter response, but this was very much present offstage. If the matter had lasted until an election the voters would have been heard from, and all the participants knew it. The sour side also has its parallels in the stories of bitterness and intragroup hostility wherever race relations come to issue.

Where the legal action has been sustained by one or more of these community pressures, there have been significant results. Where they have not been thus sustained, the condition is as it was. An example is Clarendon County, South Carolina, where the Supreme Court expressly but ineffectively directed non-segregation eight years ago.

This, then, has been the function of the law, the courts, and the Constitution in relation to the South in the postwar years. It has led the way in new directions. It has blazed a trail.

Developments

There have been five major areas of legal development in the postwar years: (1) voting; (2) housing; (3) administration of justice; (4) employment (public and private); (5) education and related problems of segregation. In addition there have been general problems of policy enforcement and a new method, passive resistance. The topics are scarcely new—the Civil Rights Acts of 1866 and 1875 also covered non-discrimination in the acquisition of property, in the administration of justice, in voting, and in at least some phases of segregation.[1] But each area has received new and more vigorous treatment since 1945.

While it is convenient to classify the subject for purposes of analysis, it would seriously obstruct understanding if we forget for even a moment how closely the divisions are interrelated, how common is their underpinning. What has happened in one area affects and often accounts for what has happened in the other areas, and all stand on a common foundation of moral awakening in the United States.

The last published symposium in which I appeared on the subject of race relations was ten years ago, and the intervening decade has lengthened the current which I there described:

The twenty-five years just past have seen an amazing re-establishment of moral opposition to racial discrimination in the United States. Indeed, though it would be impossible to prove, I suspect that in the past fifteen years the proportion of the whole population which has shared a sense of deep objection, on moral grounds, to mistreatment of Negroes is quantitatively greater than the proportion of the population which felt that objection in 1866. Once again, the courts have both gone along with and promoted this moral objection, and a series of judicial decisions has substantially broadened the modern meaning of equal protection of the laws.[2]

A. *Voting*

It has been apparent almost from the close of the Civil War that in the race relations field, the only lasting help must be self help, and that the only ultimate protection for a large minority is its voting power. It has been equally apparent that those who wish to limit the freedom of a minority must cut down that voting power. This was an old lesson long before the Civil War, having been fought out in terms of the incoming Irish in the 1840's and 1850's. The same lesson was rapidly applied to the freed Negroes, the next great difficult-to-digest minority. For example, Senator Charles Sumner of Massachusetts, the leading congressional abolitionist, had come to put his prime reliance on Negro voting by the time of his death in 1874.

The decision of *Smith v. Allwright*[3] overruled *Grovey v. Townsend*[4] and extended the protections of the Fifteenth Amendment to primary elections. The impact of this on one-party states is obvious, and an immense legal and practical development followed. There have been dozens of decided cases, numerous state statutes, and two important Acts of Congress. The 1957 Civil Rights Act[5] in Part IV deals with "means of further securing and protecting the right to vote," and the Civil Rights Act of 1960[6] provides further for direct court protection of voting rights on request of the Attorney-General.

Practical results have been outlined in a recent statement by Assistant Attorney-General Burke Marshall of the Civil Rights Division of the Department of Justice, who reported serious voting discriminations at the present time in about two hundred counties. Mr. Marshall described the operation of the recent statutes in Macon County, Alabama. This small county, the home of Tuskegee Institute, has an eligible white voting population of about three thousand and an eligible Negro voting population of about ten thousand. In 1958 substantially the entire white population was registered but only about one thousand, or 10 per cent, of the Negroes were.

Control of registrations had achieved this result. Whites could register almost automatically when they reached the age of twenty-one. Registration books were taken to the homes even of illiterate whites (despite the state restrictions against voting by illiterates) to make registration easy. On the other hand, Negro voters had virtually to jump through hoops of fire. Interminable literacy tests were run terribly slowly. Registration places were inconveniently located so that, as Mr. Marshall puts it, "Most Negroes did not get to apply for registration and those who did were rejected for trivial errors on tests on which the whites received aid and assistance."[7]

As a consequence of the procedures just described there were, in 1957 and 1958, only about fifty Negroes registered; in 1959 there were none; in 1960 eight were registered; and in 1961, up to the date of obtaining a federal court order, none. In the year 1961–62 after a court order was obtained, 1,300 Negroes had registered.

The voting right continues to be bitterly contested. Every device of gerrymander may be anticipated and the law will be slow to catch up. The most colorful example to date also arises in Macon County, Alabama. Prior to an act of the Alabama state legislature in 1957, the city of Tuskegee was approximately square in shape and had about four hundred Negroes within its borders. After the amendment, the town was revised into a structure with some twenty-eight sides which looked vaguely like a rooster with an arrow through its neck. The gerrymander, which was voided by the United States Supreme Court, put all but four or five of Tuskegee's Negro inhabitants outside its boundaries while not a single white citizen was lost to the community.[8]

Recent racial registration data on the Southern states are in Table I.

Table I. Recent White and Non-White Registrations, Ten Southern States

State	White percentage of adult population	White percentage of voters	Non-white percentage of adult population	Non-white percentage of voters
Alabama	73.8	92.9	26.2	7.1
Arkansas	81.5	87.7	18.5	12.3
Florida	84.8	90.9	15.2	9.1
Georgia	74.6	?	25.4	?
Louisiana	71.5	86.2	28.5	13.8
Mississippi	63.9	?	36.1	?
North Carolina	78.5	89.8	21.5	10.2
Tennessee	85.0	?	15.0	?
Texas	88.3	?	11.7	?
Virginia	81.1	?	18.9	?

These figures are taken from the analysis of registration statistics, U. S. Commission on Civil Rights, *Voting* (1961 Commission on Civil Rights Report) (Washington, 1961), pp. 104–111.

South Carolina is not included in the Civil Rights Commission statistics from which this table is composed, but other entries in the same report show that in 1958 the per cent of whites of voting age registered is 89.2, as against 10.8 in those counties which in fact have a majority of non-white residents.

Supplemental information from the same source shows that in two Alabama counties in which Negroes represent approximately 80 per cent of the total population, no Negroes were registered to vote. In Arkansas, from the statistics, there does not appear to be any large or greatly significant racial discrimination in voting. In two Florida counties in which Negroes represent 15.2 and 11.9 per cent respectively of the population, none are registered to vote. Georgia statistics are incomplete. In one block of thirteen counties, Negroes are registered in almost exact proportion to the population. On the other hand, in two counties in which Negroes are more than half the population, none are registered to vote, and in three counties in which they are about 25, 45 or 55 per cent of the total population, fewer than 10 per cent of the Negroes are registered. In Louisiana, in four parishes in which the percentage of Negroes ranges from 61–66, no Negroes are registered to vote. In Mississippi, figures on a racial basis are unavailable for some counties. In sixty-nine of eighty-two counties, where Negroes constitute 37.7 per cent of the voting-age population, 6.2 per cent of the voting-age Negroes are registered to vote. In thirteen counties, in which the Negro population ranges from a low of 9.9 to a high of 68 per cent, with a median of 33 per cent, no Negroes are registered. Figures from Tennessee are incomplete. In sixty-three of the ninety-five counties, whites account for 82.6 per cent of the voting-age population and 86 per cent of the number registered. Texas registration figures are incomplete. In 213 of the 254 counties, whites are 91.9 per cent of the population and 88.2 per cent of the voting population. Registration figures from Virginia are incomplete, but on the basis of very nearly complete figures, whites have 89.6 per cent of the registered voters.

Under the firm and steady pressure of the Civil Rights Division of the Department of Justice, the voting situation may be expected to continue to alter. The extent to which the change has already occurred is shown by the passage through the Congress of 1962 of the anti-poll tax amendment to the Constitution of the United States. Thirty years ago an anti-poll tax proposal was the trigger for the kind of filibuster now reserved for any real menace to the race relations status quo. In 1962 the anti-poll tax amendment passed both houses with no great difficulty, at a time when it had already been abandoned by all but five states.

The ease with which the poll tax measure is at long last moving demonstrates that today the important statistics on Negro voting are not those showing where the Negro does *not* vote, but those showing where he *does* vote. There are now clearly enough Northern Negro voters, whatever that number may be, to hold an important balance of power. As a political matter, their views must be conciliated and their wishes taken into account. In each of the two 1960 major nominating conventions, the greatest secondary interest after the choice of the candidates themselves was which party could outdo the other in soliciting Negro votes. As the Negroes become the most wooed political minority in the country, the pressure for civil rights legislation and civil rights enforcement will inexorably increase. As in so many other respects, Senator Sumner was a hundred years ahead of his time.

B. *Employment*

As America moves into the 1960's, the full and effective utilization of all of our resources, including our manpower resources, is the largest problem the nation faces. On a world scene in which powerful potential adversaries outnumber us to the extent of hundreds of millions of people, we cannot afford to waste. Where some phases of race relations involve primarily matters of moral value, the utilization of manpower presents as well a narrower and harder front of sheer national defense. We have troubles enough without leaving one in ten of our population on the economic sidelines.

The solution of this problem has presented legal questions in abundance in the postwar years, but they have not often been serious constitutional questions. Of the constitutional power of our various governments, there is not much room for doubt. The federal government through its own employment practices and its own purchasing practices has great leverage; and a general power which can control child labor practices can control discriminatory practices by labor unions.[9] Federal powers in the railway field have been equally upheld. There has been some lawmaking and—somewhat less—law enforcement concerning discrimination in employment in the last fifteen years, but there has not been much call for constitutional adjudication.

The underlying problem is that in the economic order Negroes are usually the last to be hired and the first to be discharged. Their employment is commonly restricted to unskilled and menial labor. They are frequently cut off from the opportunity of learning the better trades and if they do learn them, they may be severely inhibited in practicing them. During periods of pronounced unemployment, the Negro unemployment rate has been roughly double that of the white rate; a 1961 National Urban League survey of unemployment showed approximately 40 per cent or more of the Negroes unemployed in Detroit, Fort Wayne, Gary, and Louisville; 20 per cent unemployed in Cleveland; 25 per cent in Kansas City, Missouri; and 28 per cent in Philadelphia.

1. The armed services, which were altogether segregated at the beginning of World War II, have adopted the policy of fully eliminating segregation. In 1948 President Truman issued Executive Order 9981. Under the Order a distinguished American, Judge Charles Fahy, now of the United States Court of Appeals of the District of Columbia, headed a committee on Equality of Treatment and Opportunity in the Armed Services. Under the leadership of this committee, the task of integration went forward. Major problems continue to exist in the National Guard and in the Reserves.[10]

The first extensive military engagements testing the new policies came in the Korean War. Here, extended accounts demonstrated that Negro troops were consistently more serviceable in integrated than in segregated units. In a concise and immensely useful collection of materials, University of California anthropologist David Mandelbaum concludes that, "In combat, integration is militarily more efficient than segregation."[11]

The impact of the new policies on the South and on Southerners has been extensive. Southerners coming into the armed services have been compelled to accept associations which at home would be obnoxious. The frequent location of training camps at Southern points has created exceptionally severe problems of adjustment between integrated life on the post and non-integrated life off it.

2. With the national government as America's largest customer, the conditions under which it will buy can have extensive consequences on employment practices. The result has been a parade of Executive Orders aimed at eliminating discrimination in government purchasing.[12] In the Eisenhower Administration, the whole topic was kept at the highest level of government attention by the appointment of Vice President Nixon as chairman of the relevant committee, and President Kennedy has assigned similar matters to Vice President Johnson.

To date the end result of all these activities has been slight. The President's Commission on Civil Rights acknowledges that the Eisenhower program was not effective "in substantially increasing the overall employment of Negroes, or the numbers employed above unskilled or semi-skilled levels."[13] The structure of the Kennedy administrative program in this area is considerably better than its predecessors, but its actual hard accomplishments as of 1962 are not great.

3. The government as an employer of several million persons itself provides a market of great consequence. Here, too, the tendency has been strong for Negroes to have the custodial and menial jobs. In 1961, 76 per cent of all Negro government employees in Washington were at the bottom of the pay scale; 80–83 per cent were thus employed in Chicago, Detroit, and New York, and 97.4 per cent were thus employed in Atlanta.[14] The Civil Rights Commission concludes that, despite the efforts made to increase Negro opportunity in the federal service itself, "Patterns of Federal employment in the cities studied do not differ significantly from local employment patterns."[15]

4. On the problems of discrimination in completely private employment, World War II spurred an effort to insure full utilization of personnel which has languished since the end of the war. President Roosevelt established the Fair Employment Practices Committee in 1941 and enlarged its powers in 1943.[16] It dealt with government procurement and private employment with appreciable effect. This committee lapsed in 1946. At the present time the Commission on Civil Rights, by its hearings about the country, is doing a little to focus local attention on local problems, but this is not its primary assignment and any actual consequence in this regard is necessarily modest.

5. *Conclusion as to employment.* Minority employment is a legal problem and a social problem, but it is by no means peculiarly nor even particularly a Southern problem. I believe it to be the most important single part of the entire race relations problem in the United States. Every other phase is important, but this one transcends them all.

If there is ever to be an integrated American community, the Negroes must follow the pattern of the immigrant minority groups which have come into our society earlier in our country's history. The first representatives of each large such group have been predominantly poor. They have, at the time of their arrival, been an apparently totally indigestible mass, frequently bitterly resented by the established community here before them. The Irish, the Jews, the Poles, and the Italians are examples. Each has stood, at the moment of arrival, almost altogether on the bottom rung of the economic ladder. Then, scattered individuals have broken through to higher points. Finally, what was a completely lower-class minority becomes at least in part a middle-class minority with scattered upper-class members. At this point the process of acceptance is well under way. It may take at least three generations, but economic advance is at the heart of it.

As we come into the 1960's, the great need of this country is a substantial Negro middle class. This is a foremost national need, and it is certainly the foremost Negro need; the problems of crime, of inferior education, of absence of family stability will never be solved without it. When the American community is seriously ready to do something about the economic advance of the Negro, the law and the legal profession will not be short of resources.

C. *Housing*

As soon as the Civil War was over, the Congress turned to giving Negroes a right, without discrimination, to acquire land. The primary original object was not housing; it was agricultural land. The slaves, being owned themselves, had of course not owned the land on which they worked. Unless they were given the right to acquire some, they would have been a permanent tenant class. Hence, the Civil Rights Act of 1866 expressly provided that "all citizens" should have the same right as "white citizens" to buy, hold, or sell real property.

This simple mandate of the Civil Rights Act of 1866 has been far from enforced from then until now and its principle has caused one of the major constitutional decisions of the post-World War II years. In *Buchanan v. Warley*[17] the Supreme Court held that this principle of the Civil Rights Act of 1866 was included in the Fourteenth Amendment. Hence, it held that a Louisville ordinance which confined Negroes to one part of the town and whites to another was unconstitutional. But after *Buchanan v. Warley*, land owners sought the same result by private contract. Under these contracts, land was sold subject to racial restrictive covenants whereby land could not be sold to persons of undesired races. The practical consequence of this network of agreements, each of which the courts would enforce, was the same as the Louisville ordinance. The restrictive covenants were upheld in *Corrigan v. Buckley*.[18]

Corrigan v. Buckley, supported by restrictive mortgage practices and so-called "ethical standards" of real estate boards, led to the establishment of Black Ghettos in many cities. The entire system was under strong attack by the end of World War II. The leading opinion in the lower courts was a dissent of Judge Henry Edgerton of the

District of Columbia Circuit in *Mays v. Burgess*.[19] In 1948 the United States Supreme Court in *Shelley v. Kraemer*[20] junked *Corrigan v. Buckley* and held that no court could validly enforce a restrictive covenant based on race.

The decision of the Court in *Shelley v. Kraemer* has led to reconsideration of racial restrictions on housing. Prior to World War I, the federal government through its housing construction agencies was affirmatively encouraging segregation by the terms and manner in which it lent its money for private building, although it was promoting integration in units which were built altogether with federal funds.[21] Between 1947 and 1954 the FHA shifted from a policy requiring segregation to one encouraging non-segregation.

Nonetheless, so far as the federal government is concerned, the cure of the miseries of Negro slum housing is still more on order than on hand. In 1961 the President's Commission on Civil Rights reiterated its earlier conclusion that a considerable number of Americans, by reason of their color or race, are being denied equal opportunity in housing.[22] The resultant toll in terms of disease, crime, and misery is simply appalling. The national program for urban renewal, or elimination of slum conditions, has been substantial, but President Kennedy has acknowledged that the housing pledges of the past have by no means been realized. As of the early summer of 1962, it is widely reported that the President is on the verge of an extensive new Executive Order to insure that Federal support of housing is conditioned upon non-discrimination. But this is still in the offing; and there is so much unenforced law now on the books in this regard that one cannot be sanguine as to the results of new directives.

Once again, this is a race relations problem which is not particularly a Southern problem. Post-World War II housing for Negroes is only a segment of the total revolution in American cities which has occurred since 1945. The growth of the suburb and the regional shopping center has largely drained middle- and upper-class America out of the heart of the city and into suburbs into which the minorities could not follow economically even if there were no legal restrictions. Mortgage and real estate sales policies leave the minorities concentrated without regard to restrictive covenants. A prodigious withdrawal of city people from their own cities is abandoning much of downtown Washington, Philadelphia, Detroit, and Chicago to Negro and Puerto Rican populations.[23]

Pending possible serious control by the federal government through its insurance or financing activities, housing has been and remains primarily a state problem. Seventeen states have adopted legislation attempting to put at least some restrictions upon racial housing discrimination.[24] The validity of this legislation has been upheld in several instances, though not without exception.[25]

D. *Administration of Justice*

The classic major nineteenth- and early twentieth-century Negro legal problem was in the administration of justice. Our failures in this regard were the number-one world symbol of lawlessness in law enforcement; the Negro suspected of serious crime might be lynched. The number of lynchings, which peaked with more than 160 in 1892, receded to a 10 to 25 per year number in the early 1930's,[26] and has not quite disappeared in post-World War II America. According to Tuskegee Institute figures, Mack Charles Parker, a Negro charged with rape, who was taken out of a Poplarville, Mississippi, jail in April of 1959, shot twice and thrown into a nearby river, was the last person lynched in the United States and the 3,441st lynching victim since 1883.[27]

While lynching has virtually disappeared, the other forms of violence have not. The 1961 report of the United States Commission on Civil Rights dealing with justice elaborates the unhappy story in detail. In Birmingham a police commissioner elected on the slogan that he was "raising the Confederate flag" gave his police a holiday when disorders were expected. In May of 1961, great violence in Alabama included the burning of buses and an assault upon the President's personal representative, who was left unconscious in a Montgomery street after several white men kicked him. From 1956 to 1961 at least twenty violent acts were publicly reported in Birmingham alone, including allegations of racially motivated beatings, bombings, and one castration.[28] On August 27, 1960, a serious race riot occurred at Jacksonville, Florida. Once again this is not an exclusively Southern problem; the same report of the Civil Rights Commission narrates a series of ugly incidents in Chicago between 1954 and 1961.

We have been speaking of private violence, of lynching and mobs. But the greatest opportunity for outright brutality is police violence. The general run of the citizenry is not sufficiently provoked to take a hand in situations it regards as obnoxious except from time to time, and at great intervals. The police have the problem of administering justice every day, and in thousands of cases. Inevitably a certain number of the police, and particularly incompetents of the sort likely to be gathered together in a low-paid service, will be brutes by nature and racists by taste. The result may be serious disregard of constitutional rights.

One such incident was the death of James Brazier in Dawson, Georgia, in 1958. Imprisoned while objecting to the arrest of his father, Brazier was taken to a county jail in which he died with evidence of repeated beatings five days later. In 1958 the United States Attorney in Georgia sought indictments of the police officers responsible, but the grand jury refused to indict and the police officers most conspicuously involved were subsequently promoted.

In cases of this kind—and let it be clear that they occur in the North as well—it is the state of the laws as interpreted by the Supreme Court which has made federal prosecution of the police difficult. In *Screws v. United States*,[29] the Supreme Court construed the relevant Civil Rights Act as requiring a standard of "intent" which meant that the policeman beating up a prisoner must actually intend thereby to deprive him of a constitutional right. In the *Screws* case, a young Negro named Hall was beaten to death by Sheriff Claude Screws of Baker County, Georgia. While there was conflicting testimony, the most likely account is that Screws and his companions took Hall to the center of town, and there beat him to the ground and continued for some time to hit him with a two-pound metal blackjack at a time when their victim was handcuffed. Screws was never prosecuted locally and, under this interpretation, his federal prosecution was unsuccessful.

After *Screws* the Department of Justice continued to bring prosecutions, reaching a high of thirty-two in 1954. Since that time the number has declined and of late the Department has been particularly unsuccessful in this regard. The *Screws* and related cases show that the statutory law of the United States is inadequate. The right to be prosecuted for crime only in accordance with due process of law is absolutely and precisely what the draftsmen of the Civil Rights Act of 1866 and of the Fourteenth Amendment sought as the object of their work. A defendant who is given capital punishment before trial by the law-enforcement authorities is in the most obvious conceivable way deprived of his constitutional rights. The Civil Rights Commission has asked the Congress to consider appropriate criminal and civil remedies against law officers who thus grossly abuse their positions.[30]

E. *Education and Other Problems of Integration*

The progress of the law in respect to segregation between the end of World War II and 1962 can be seen in a few quotations:

1. In *Sipuel v. Board of Regents*,[31] plaintiff, a Negro woman, sought admission to the University of Oklahoma Law School. The defense was in substance that the University of Oklahoma did not then have a separate law school for Negroes, but that it would when there was enough demand. The NAACP, for the student, contended that Oklahoma must "admit petitioner to the only existing law school maintained by the state . . . the suggested substitutes of requiring her to elect either out of state aid, or demand that a new institution be erected for her, are inadequate to meet the requirements of equal protection of the law."[32] The Supreme Court reversed, saying that the state must provide for her legal education "and provide it as soon as it does for applicants of any other group."

2. The next law school case decided was *Sweatt v. Painter*.[33] In this case a Negro sought admission to the all-white University of Texas Law School, and the issue was whether he could, instead, be required to attend a state segregated law school. A committee of law teachers against segregation in legal education numbering something over 150 law professors from around the country filed a brief *amicus curiae*. The law professors asked that the decision of the United States Supreme Court in 1896, *Plessy v. Ferguson*,[34] which was the mother of the so-called "separate but equal" doctrine, should be overruled. Said the professors:

We grant, as *Plessy* implies, that the termination of segregation is a break with tradition. But we contend that there is nothing in the tradition of Negro slavery that is worth preserving. . . . This Court should return to the original purpose of the equal protection clause, to forbid distinctions because of race. State enforced segregation is unconstitutional because it makes such a distinction. As Senator Edmond puts it, it is "slave doctrine" to make color and race reasons for distinction among citizens. Segregation *is* discrimination.

The Supreme Court declined to re-examine *Plessy v. Ferguson*. Instead it found that the colored law school was inferior: equal "education is not available to him in a separate law school as offered by the state."

3. *Sweatt v. Painter* was nonetheless the turning point, because the grounds on which the Supreme Court found the University of Texas Law School (colored) unequal to the University of Texas Law School (white) were grounds inherent in segregation. These qualities, which the Court declared to be "incapable of objective measurement but which make for greatness in a law school," such as reputations of the faculty, experience of the administration, position and influence of alumni, and so on, could never be remedied. Hence it was but a short though immensely significant next step to *Brown v. Board of Education*,[35] the grade-school case, in which the Court held, "We conclude that in the field of public education the doctrine of 'separate but equal' has no place. Separate educational facilities are inherently unequal."

4. The history of *Plessy v. Ferguson* shows that constitutional questions may never be regarded as buried altogether, but on February 26, 1962, the Supreme Court buried the segregation issue as a constitutional dispute at least as deeply as it is ever possible to bury a constitutional question. In *Bailey v. Patterson*,[36] a group of Jackson, Mississippi, Negroes sought an injunction against segregated transportation services. In determining a jurisdictional issue relating to their case, the Supreme Court said, "We have settled beyond question that no state may require racial segregation of interstate or intrastate transportation facilities. The question is no longer open; it is foreclosed as a litigable issue." Citing both transportation and education cases as authority, the Court held that the unconstitutionality of segregation had been so absolutely and clearly established that it was "frivolous" to attempt to justify the constitutionality of any segregation state statute.

F. *Method and Enforcement*

1. The primary truly new development bearing on how law actually works has been the emergence of passive resistance as a major device in race relations. The attempt to turn the Christian ethic into a fighting tool of social relations is a direct importation of the use of similar methods by Ghandi. The transcending moral quality of the sit-ins and the Alabama bus devices are something a great deal more than our old legal acquaintances, the sit-down strike and the boycott. Passive resistance has proved a powerful method of resistance to dis-

crimination. While in no sense new, its transfer to this area was the most important development in method in the 1950's.

2. A chronicle of the history of the law of race relations from 1945 to 1962 necessarily must divide into two units. From 1945 to 1954, the issue was doctrine. From 1954 to 1962 the issue has been enforcement. This continental divide was in part recognized and in part created by the Supreme Court itself, which expressly asked for and had argument a year after the main decision of the school cases on the issue of how the decision should be enforced. The answer finally coming forth was "with all deliberate speed." Then, after the glorious days of dispute in the Marble Palace in Washington, the point of controversy changed to a schoolhouse in Louisville or Little Rock or Atlanta and the nation's attention was riveted on a bus station in Jackson, Mississippi.

The great and transcending jurisprudential question presented by the non-segregation program of the courts is, what can the courts do about it? When a court decides a dispute between two persons as to what happened at a stoplight, there is not much question about power; a judge can fairly well decide and dispose of the matter. But when the judicial determination is directed toward the folkways of a region or a country, then what are the limits of power?[37]

Experience gives some measure of that power. Where public opinion was substantially ready, desegregation proceeded almost without event. The District of Columbia, Louisville, Kentucky, and Missouri are in point. Where law enforcement was timid or uncertain, incidents occurred; and where law enforcement was downright hostile, there was great violence, as in Little Rock, Jackson, Birmingham, or Oxford, Mississippi. Some colorful political leaders have been brought to the fore by the new resistance, as for example in Arkansas and Alabama. Fundamentally, change has been dependent upon firm pressure by the courts coupled with a moderate response in the community. Where the moderates lose, as in Little Rock or New Orleans, there has been chaos until they regain control.[38] Where, as in Atlanta, such influential community leaders as Ralph McGill or Mayor William B. Hartsfield took the attitude that court orders must be obeyed in good faith, some movement toward desegregation began very slowly, but at least non-violently.[39]

The limitations of the judicial process in achieving desegregation have been both legal and practical, as for example, the pupil placement laws, the closing of public schools in Prince Edward County, and the drawing of school lines on geographic lines reflecting housing. While the Southern episodes have been most colorful, *de facto* segregation in education is by no means a purely Southern problem. Geographical segregation and the escape to the suburbs have created Northern segregation very nearly as rigid as that established by law in other places. Within the past two years, 14 per cent of the Philadelphia schools had more than 99 per cent Negro students; two Berkeley, California, schools have more than 90 per cent Negroes; and twenty-eight Detroit schools have almost exclusively Negro students.[40] These patterns are partially the product of segregated housing conditions, and partially the result of deliberate and systematic policy. Some significant counter-efforts have been taken, as for example in New York.

Institutions of the Law

And what of the institutions? In seventeen years since World War II, the law has cut new channels. The course may have been foreordained, patterned on an inevitable development since at least 1917. But since the war the legal trickle of equality has become a flood, and if its pathways are not altogether new, they are certainly different. New doctrine has had new reaction; old problems have caused new tensions. There has been blood in the streets, death in the land, and soldiers marching, not only in Caracas, or Leopoldville, or Berlin, but in American cities. How have the institutions of the law met the new demands put upon them?

The short answer is, magnificently. If the progress has been slow, the strain has been great. At no time in American peacetime history have such substantial social adjustments been attempted in so short a period of time. The westward movement in American history was proportionately more significant by far, but it took longer. The drift of foreign immigration for any seventeen-year period between 1890 and 1914 is perhaps comparable. Prohibition may have been a more dynamic experiment, but I suspect that in terms of the lives of millions it was more colorful than real. What else has attempted actually to change the lives of so many people in a significant way in so short a period as the progress of racial readjustment since 1945?

From the standpoint of judicial leadership, the only possible comparison in Supreme Court history is the nationalizing era of Marshall.

With the possible exception of the rise of due process between 1890 and 1905, the Court itself has never been so dynamic in a basic matter of social policy. The whole Court, with unerring consistency, and with the willingness of its members to sacrifice individual expression in almost every instance for the sake of a consolidated national position, has never hit the iron with more repeated or harder blows. Chief Justice Warren has a fair credit for pre-eminence, but this has not been a movement of either individuals or regions, so that Reed and Vinson of Kentucky, Black of Alabama, and Clark of Texas have risen above every local prejudice to join the national reform. The only reason that the character of Earl Warren does not altogether illumine our era like that of a Marshall is that Warren, unlike Marshall, is neither preceded nor flanked by ciphers such as most of Marshall's associates.

The lower federal judiciary has done an extraordinary job of meeting the challenge of the times. One analysis of the work of the Southern judges says that, "In the face of segregationist onslaught, judges back down."[41] I am simply not persuaded. Of course there have been the timorous and the fanatic, but a judge like J. Skelly Wright in New Orleans more than makes up for the weak ones. Wright, like all the judges of the Fourth and some of the Fifth Circuit Court of Appeals, is a Southerner from his mother's milk, but one who puts his judicial oath ahead of his habits or his traditions. Having accepted the duty of a federal district judge to enforce the law, Wright did it. His promotion to the Court of Appeals of the District of Columbia should give heart to every district judge who wonders whether he will be backed if he does his job. For courageous enforcement of the law, one could also take Judge Walter Hoffman of Virginia, Judge William E. Miller of Nashville, and Judge Robert L. Taylor in Knoxville. There are others—I would not pick and choose. The miracle is not that there have been weaklings but that there have been men of courage. The Supreme Court is the national quarterback—all it can do is throw the ball, and unless there are hands desirous of receiving it, it must ineffectively fall to the ground. There have been such hands.

Nor do I draw the same conclusions as Professor Peltason concerning the role of the bar. He observes that, "In the legal battles school-boards have the better talent. If one goes to a large southern city to interview the attorney for the board, one will be ushered into a posh law suite, past a battery of secretaries and young law school graduates,

and into the private office of one of the city's most successful and experienced lawyers. The carpet is thick, the furniture most chic." And
he recites the splendid fees available to the resistance movement.[42]

Of course, but it is always so. The way of the reformer is always
lonely, underfinanced, hard. The established order has never been
exactly renowned for a willingness to pay large sums of money to have
itself shaken. Again, the miracle is that so much has been done, that
the NAACP has been able to recruit talent, a good share of it for
nothing. It is doubtful that any legal movement for reform has ever
been as well financed or had as many volunteers; the original aboli-
tionists and the women's rights cause were even more at the mercy of
the tin cup than Thurgood Marshall for the NAACP. There must
have been at least a hundred volunteers to fetch wood and carry
water in the leading segregation cases. The role of the reformers may
have been on hard lines, but they have not been desperate.

This is the more so because of the role of government. The Civil
Rights Division of the Department of Justice, since its exceptionally
able early leaders, Henry Schweinhaut and Victor Rotnem, has been
doing a manful job. From the standpoint of sheer technical compe-
tence, as a lawyer who knows his trade, Burke Marshall, the head of
the Civil Rights Division, is one of the ablest lawyers in the country.
The three front-line lawyers on the program of this Administration
had, until a recent change of faces, been Harris Wofford in the White
House, Marshall at the Department of Justice, and Berl Bernhard,
staff director of the Civil Rights Commission. Each made great
sacrifice to accept this position, and each brought to his post ex-
ceptional experience and ability. Doubtless there will be shifts of
personnel—they may have already occurred before these words appear—but there is no reason to doubt that a high standard of ex-
cellence can be maintained. To say that the bar has not done as much
as it might to aid the orderly course of social readjustment is true,
but foolishness; of course the fur-lined rut and the status quo always
have their superior allure. What is remarkable rather is that so
much high quality is available.

Moreover, each national administration has done its best to do a
job. We have had three presidents since the end of the war. President
Truman, given the standards of the time, was perhaps the most aggressive civil rights president the country has had since Lincoln.
President Eisenhower has much in the affirmative on his record. His
bumbling comments on the segregation decision have been far too

much belabored. The fact is that he has a record of significant deeds, and that when the disturbances at Little Rock verged on revolution, he met the situation head-on.

It is too soon to measure the accomplishments of the present Administration. In its first year the Civil Rights Division and its parent, the Department of Justice, have been absolutely courageous in meeting the crises of the day, and the remarks of Attorney-General Robert Kennedy at the University of Georgia on May 6, 1961, set a new high for giving the same talk at the South that one would give at the North: "You may ask: Will we enforce the Civil Rights Statutes? The answer is: Yes, we will." Substantial work has been undertaken by the President's Committee on Equal Employment Opportunity. The Civil Rights Commission, an extraordinary aggregation of men of ability, integrity, and character, must be relied upon to give the country policy leadership in the Kennedy years.

In evaluating our legal institutions and their function between the close of World War II and this day, no honest man can claim special merit for either region or political affiliation. The judges and the public officials who have labored to carry out the program of equality in America have come from every region and from each of the major parties.

Problems Ahead

What of the future? What are tomorrow's problems for the law? Since the law is the mirror of the society, this is simply another way of anticipating the problems of the entire community. As its problems change, the law task will change.

It is by now almost the custom to say that general and widespread desegregation is coming. The observation may be made on an ascending or descending note—followed by either a jubilant "It's about time!" or a weary "And we might as well get used to it . . . ,"—but an end is, if not in sight, at least within reasonable forecast. And in some regions, it is upon us.

What then? The plain truth is that for the purpose of truly integrating the Negro into the American community, desegregation is not an end in itself; it is not enough. Three hundred years of slavery and oppression have consequences far deeper than can be cured by a rearrangement of seating on a bus or a commingling in classrooms.

Segregation is the badge of a condition, and an important one; but it is not the condition itself.

It does not matter where a person is to sit on a train if he is not going anywhere. It does not matter what high school a person is to attend if he is going to drop out anyway. It does not matter whether a person can buy a house in any part of the town if he cannot afford to get out of the slum.

There are at least three hard consequences of the three hundred years which desegregation, by itself, will not affect:

(a) Poverty, with all its consequences.

(b) A depressed and defensive outlook on life, with all this may mean in terms of meeting community responsibilities. That Negroes may gain the right to vote does not, for example, mean that they will necessarily exercise it for a long time to come. The child who turns a classroom, segregated or unsegregated, into a blackboard jungle is the child who entered from a street that was an armed camp, and desegregation may not affect his motivations at all.

(c) Learning limitations. These are the products today both of generations and of a personal lifetime of undernourishment and unintellectual environment. No amount of desegregation will make equal and educational opportunities for these two pupils: one born illegitimately to an eighteen-year-old mother, not knowing his father, having no home but a crowded room, no balanced and adequate nourishment, no touch of intellectual stimulus or even interest in the world beyond his street; the other born to a fairly routine middle-class background, adequately fed and housed, moderately traveled, his school progress an object of close attention by both parents. Meaningful educational opportunities for Number One requires considerably more than putting him into the same classroom as Number Two.

Our race relations thinking has not kept up with urban decentralization. For the long range, there may be more stimulus to serious thought on minority problems in Mumford on cities,[43] than in the excellent Blossom on Little Rock.[44] For all its immediacy, Blossom deals with a horrible and recent yesterday; Mumford carries us forward to tomorrow.

Compare two cities. In A, the Negroes are segregated by law and custom, in schools, restaurants, theaters, stores, transportation. They are poor, unhealthy, on the whole badly educated with a high dropout rate. The males do heavy manual labor or custodial work, the females do housework for whites.

In city B, there is no segregation. Restaurants are open to those who can afford them; theaters are frequented by all; the midtown stores are patronized by whoever wishes. The schools may be segregated by geography because of living locations, but not by law. And the Negroes are poor, unhealthy, on the whole badly educated with a high dropout rate. The males do heavy manual labor or custodial work, the females do housework for whites.

City B has no very strong race prejudice. Insofar as its ruling group thinks about it, its members are proud of their unsegregated condition, and almost all of them believe that all is well in their community. True, about 98 per cent or so of the minority population lives south of X Street. The only mass contact between the two societies occurs each morning when northside buses pass each other, the bus going south with a solid white load to offices, stores, or factories, while the northbound bus carries a solid colored load of women moving north to clean the houses and mind the children of the people in the other lane. In the evening the pattern is reversed, the relationship equally distant.

In Community B, the three I's—ignorance, isolation, and indifference—on the part of the white community take the place of conscious, deliberate, and aggressive segregation—and the effect is very much the same.

This leads to the view, as *Fortune* in an exceptionally significant analysis has put it, "The United States must learn to look upon the Negro community as if it were an undeveloped country."[45] For the Negroes of Ghana who are attempting to catch up with the twentieth century, or for those of Nigeria, we have aid from peace corps to dams. How about those in New York, Detroit, or Birmingham?

What can be done for our own citizens raises truly difficult constitutional problems for tomorrow; and that tomorrow is very, very close. The premise of desegregation is that all classes must be treated alike—equal protection in the racial context means that there shall be no discrimination based on race. Applying this principle, take three problems:

First, slum clearance and improved housing. Can there be discrimination in favor of Negroes by expenditure of public funds to get them into decent housing?

Second, education. Can there be special schools for Negroes to help them close the gap as they move from poorer to better schools? This, of course, is pure segregation. Can there be "good" segregation?

Third, employment. If the vital problem is the creation of a Negro middle class, can there be employment policies, governmental and private, in which Negroes are deliberately chosen for employment? If Mr. A, colored, and Mr. B, white, both apply for a job, and the two appear to be equal, can there be any justification for giving A the job—and thus discriminating against B—for the sake of redressing the inequities of three centuries? Suppose the Negro is a little short of qualification. Should he be put on the job anyway?

The best discussion so far of the legal problems involved in pro-Negro discrimination is that of Professor Bittker.[46] He puts the problem of a community which wishes to encourage integration, and so *requires* that half of its homeowners be Negroes. The social purpose of enforced integration is quite opposite from enforced separation; but insofar as each governs human relationships in terms of race, Bittker suggests that legally they may be just the same.

In housing, at the simplest level, the problem of unabashed discrimination in favor of Negroes need not arise. A solution is suggested by the First Amendment cases on religion. The Amendment puts two restrictions on government as to religion: government can neither discriminate against nor establish religion; it shall neither hurt nor help. Yet general legislation which happens to aid a religion, though this is not its primary purpose, is perfectly valid so long as it has a legitimate, independent, other objective.

Thus organized religion would be prodigiously handicapped if the fire department could not put out a fire in a church or if policemen could not be detailed to guide traffic at a church corner on a Sunday morning. The goals of fire protection and public safety are primary; the religious benefit incidental. Sharper questions are presented when free textbooks are distributed or free transportation furnished. Yet it has been held that, the primary object being public welfare legislation, the fact that the books are used or the students carried to private or parochial schools is immaterial. Books may be so expensive or transportation so burdensome that without the public assistance the parochial schools would lose much of their drawing power, but under the doctrine of dominant legitimate purpose, this is immaterial.

So also with problems of slum clearance or urban renewal. At any given point in American history, the worst-housed segment of the population will usually be a definable minority and has frequently been the most recent immigrant group. Nonetheless no one seriously challenges the constitutionality of these projects on the grounds that Negroes may be primary beneficiaries.

The critical problem is just one notch beyond these public projects. Suppose the administrators of such projects seek to require integration by providing that not more than a certain percentage of a given project be occupied by any one group, white or colored. At this point what is euphemistically called "balanced occupancy" instead of "open occupancy" becomes the objective. The resultant discrimination may work against either group, depending upon whether a white or a colored apartment happens to be the one next turning up.

The same problem of benevolent discrimination arises in education. At its simplest, a university admissions committee has certain standards for admission. It receives an application from a Negro youngster who, by objective standards, is almost but not quite qualified. On the ground that the Negro community needs trained persons, will it make a little allowance in favor of the Negro applicant to bring him in? In the Northeastern states it is a rare admissions committee that has not been confronted with this problem, and almost as rare a committee that has not on occasion blinked the standard to take the admission. Yet if the school has only a fixed number of admittees, the practical effect is to discriminate against someone else, presumably better qualified, and solely because of his color, because he happens not to be a Negro.

For the private universities this is essentially a moral rather than a legal problem. We may leave them to struggle with it as they will, though we note that there certainly have been instances in which the Massachusetts legal requirement that there be no indication of race on student application papers has operated to keep Negroes out who otherwise, by virtue of "benign discrimination," would have been in. But the problem of whether ability or background grouping may have the practical effect of segregation in the public schools has not yet been clearly faced, and will need to be.

The problem, which may be avoided under the guise of general welfare legislation in housing and which may be ducked or ignored in education, is completely inescapable in employment. At the present time the Negro occupies the bottom level of the employment ladder. If he is to be moved up, it can only be by purposeful action aimed at achieving that result, or so at least if the result is to be achieved within a generation. As an Assistant Secretary of Labor has

bluntly put it, "You cannot bring into balance a Negro unemployment rate double that of whites without a step-up rate of hiring
Negroes. You cannot give a Negro a long overdue promotion without
denying some other persons that same promotion."[47] I can recall
from personal experience some of the consequences, both wholesome
and tragic, when an Attorney-General of the United States directed
that some Negro lawyers be hired in the divisions, for all the years
of discrimination had made qualified applicants hard to come by.
The present policy of the federal government of generally increasing
Negro employment at the above-custodial ranks necessarily means
that personnel directors must to some extent discriminate against
other applicants. The whole process of stopping or lessening discrimination at plants producing for the government has plant managers suddenly scurrying about for some Negroes to hire.

For the law to look more kindly on benign discrimination than on
hostile discrimination requires a total reversal of legal doctrine. Such
reversals have occurred so frequently in the past that one is not incon-
ceivable here. To the extent that doctrine is a means rather than an
end, means may sometimes out and out reverse themselves without a
shifting of the objective. The archconservative of John Marshall's
time was the great nationalist and the great conservative of today
may be an extreme states' rights man. Herbert Hoover still has more
fundamentally in common with Marshall than with Thomas Jefferson, even though the great Republican and the great Chief Justice
appear to be altogether at odds on doctrine. By similar reversal, it is
possible the racial liberals who from 1920 to 1960 were against any
thought of discrimination may from 1970 to 1990 find themselves its
exponents.

As one whose roots are deep in the decades past, may I say that this
would be all wrong. The movement for desegregation is in part a
matter of humanity, and part a matter of pure morality. This morality has its own legitimate force, and from the standpoint of this
morality, discrimination is not made the more palatable by substituting one for another.

The consequences of three hundred years cannot be erased overnight. Cessation of segregation will not inaugurate the millennium.
There is a grave educational duty to make this clear, for otherwise
the reformers, seeing how little is accomplished by their reform, may
sink back into despair. The greatest enemy of progress is not iniquity,
it is frustration, and the greatest cause of frustration is expecting too

much.[48] Impatience will in turn give rise to a new intolerance. To those who are frustrated by the slowness of the pace with which the Negro is both freed and able to assume his rightful place in the community, the answer was given by Mr. Lincoln in his Second Inaugural, "Yet, if God wills that it continue, until all the wealth of the bondsman's two hundred fifty years of unrequited toil shall be sunk, and until every drop of blood drawn with the lash shall be paid by another drawn with the sword, as was said three thousand years ago, so still it must be said, 'The judgments of the Lord are true and righteous altogether.' "

The great social change in America between 1945 and 1962 is that by the end of this period the segregated and unequal society is inexorably on the way out. These have been the years of a world-wide colored revolution. On most of the earth's surface and for most of the earth's population that dominance which for about a century and a half has been in white hands has finally shifted to the other races of the world. Two continents, containing most of the world's population, have passed almost altogether out of white control. Unlike the colonialism of the English or the French, our own has been vertical, not horizontal, and has predominantly reached down into the society instead of across national lines.

We, too, in our own way, might have had our Algeria, our Kenya, our India. The primary function of the law since World War II has been to change our course without these dislocations by firm adherence to the simple mandate of the Constitution of the United States, "Nor shall any state deny to any person within its jurisdiction the equal protection of the laws." The years from 1945 to 1962 have not been the years of the mission accomplished; but they have been years of the crossing of the stream.

1. 14 Stat. 27, 18 Stat. 336.
2. J. P. Frank, "Can Courts Erase the Color Line?," *Journal of Negro Education*, XXI (Summer, 1952), 305–306, and in *Buffalo Law Review*, II (Winter, 1952), 28.
3. 321 U.S. 649, 64 Sup.Ct. 757, 88 L.Ed. 987 (1944).
4. 295 U.S. 45, 55 Sup.Ct. 622, 79 L.Ed. 1292 (1935).
5. 71 Stat. 634.
6. 74 Stat. 86.
7. Burke Marshall, *Special Issue of the ADL Bulletin* (Anti-Defamation League of B'nai B'rith) (March, 1962), pp. 9–10.
8. *Gomillion v. Lightfoot*, 364 U.S. 339, 81 Sup.Ct. 125, 5 L.Ed. 110 (1960). For the conclusion, in the light of the Supreme Court opinion, that the action was void, see *Gomillion v. Lightfoot*, Civ. No. 462E, M.D.Ala., Feb. 17, 1961.
9. *Railway Mail Association v. Corsi*, 326 U.S. 88, 65 Sup.Ct. 1483, 89 L.Ed. 2072 (1945).

10. U.S. Commission on Civil Rights, *Employment* (1961 Commission on Civil Rights Report) (Washington, 1961), pp. 45–53.

11. David Mandelbaum, *Soldier Groups and Negro Soldiers* (Berkeley: University of California Press, 1952), p. 120. Major Mandelbaum had extensive military experience in the Far East in World War II.

12. In 1951 President Truman established, by Executive Order 10308, a Committee on Non-discrimination in Government Contracts. President Eisenhower pushed the matter a step further in 1953 with his Executive Order 10479 and in 1961, President Kennedy issued his Order 10925 establishing a Committee on Equal Employment Opportunity.

13. U.S. Commission on Civil Rights, *Employment* (1961), p. 66.

14. Statistics for these and other cities are set forth in *ibid.*, Table 4, p. 34.

15. *Ibid.*, p. 38.

16. Executive Order 8802, June 25, 1941; Executive Order 9346, May 27, 1943.

17. 245 U.S. 60, 38 Sup.Ct. 16, 62 L.Ed. 149 (1917).

18. 271 U.S. 323, 46 Sup.Ct. 521, 70 L.Ed. 969 (1926).

19. 147 F.2d 869, 873 (D.C.Cir. 1945).

20. 334 U.S. 1, 68 Sup.Ct. 836, 92 L.Ed. 1161 (1948).

21. U. S. Commission on Civil Rights, *Housing* (1961 Commission on Civil Rights Report) (Washington, 1961), pp. 11–17.

22. *Ibid.*, p. 144.

23. The most rewarding discussion of this entire urban development, viewed from the standpoint of the growth of cities rather than of race relations, is Lewis Mumford, *The City in History* (New York: Harcourt, Brace and World, 1961), chaps. xvi and xvii. For more direct attention to the Negro problem in cities, see Charles E. Silberman, "The City and the Negro," *Fortune,* LXV (March, 1962), 2–10. The comparison of the Negro immigrant of the twentieth century to the European immigrant of the nineteenth is discussed with particular acuteness at pages 4–5.

24. For a tabular listing, see U. S. Commission on Civil Rights, *Housing* (1961), p. 198.

25. For discussion of cases, see *ibid.*, pp. 126–131. The important adverse holding is *O'Meara v. Washington State Board*, reported in *Race Relations Law Reporter*, IV (Fall, 1959), 664.

26. E. Franklin Frazier, *The Negro in the United States* (New York: Macmillan, 1949), p. 160.

27. The figures are taken from U. S. Commission on Civil Rights, *Justice* (1961 Commission on Civil Rights Report) (Washington, 1961), p. 42.

28. *Ibid.*, p. 34.

29. 325 U.S. 91, 65 Sup.Ct. 1031, 89 L.Ed. 1495 (1945).

30. U. S. Commission on Civil Rights, *Justice* (1961), pp. 112–113. For a statistical review of this problem, see Henry Putzel, Jr., "Federal Civil Rights Enforcement: A Current Appraisal," *University of Pennsylvania Law Review*, XCIX (Jan., 1951), 439–454, and see the table attached to the opinion of Mr. Justice Douglas in *Irvine v. California*, 347 U.S. 128,153, 74 Sup.Ct. 381, 98 L.Ed. 561 (1954).

31. 332 U.S. 631, 68 Sup.Ct. 299, 92 L.Ed. 247 (1948).

32. From the summary of the brief as set forth in 92 L.Ed. 247.

33. 339 U.S. 629, 70 Sup.Ct. 848, 94 L.Ed. 1114 (1950).

34. 163 U.S. 537, 16 Sup.Ct. 1138, 41 L.Ed. 256 (1896).

35. 347 U.S. 483, 74 Sup.Ct. 686, 98 L.Ed. 873 (1954).

36. 368 U.S. 346, 82 Sup.Ct. 549, 7 L.Ed.2d 332 (1962).

37. J. P. Frank, *op. cit.*, 304, and in *Buffalo Law Review, op. cit.* 28, considers these problems of power.

38. Perhaps the best account of the conflict between moderates and extremists is the volume by Virgil Blossom, Little Rock Superintendent, a volume fairly described on its dust jacket as revealing "how a law abiding American city, striving to solve a harsh and complex problem by democratic means, was demoralized and dominated by certain power-hungry men coldly exploiting the passions of their neighbors." Virgil T. Blossom, *It Has Happened Here* (New York: Harper, 1959).

39. For a state by state report in useful detail see U. S. Commission on Civil Rights, *Education* (1961 Commission on Civil Rights Report) (Washington, 1961); and for a breakdown of the developing rules of law in terms of the various problems presented, see "Education, Survey of Developments 1957–1961," *Race Relations Law Reporter*, VI (Fall, 1961), 905–922.

40. U. S. Commission on Civil Rights, *Education* (1961), p. 100.

41. J. W. Peltason, *58 Lonely Men* (New York: Harcourt, Brace and World, 1961), p. 244.

42. *Ibid.*, p. 94.

43. Lewis Mumford, *op. cit.*

44. Virgil T. Blossom, *op. cit.*

45. Charles E. Silberman, *op. cit.*, p. 151.

46. Boris Bittker, "The Case of the Checkerboard Ordinance: An Experiment in Race Relations,"*Yale Law Journal*, LXXI (July, 1962), 1387–1423.

47. *New York Times*, Oct. 30, 1961.

48. The article by John Fischer, "What the Negro Needs Most," *Harper's*, CCXXIV (July, 1962), 12 ff., and the correspondence attendant, is an important reflection of the impatience of liberals.

Edgar T. Thompson

The South and the Second Emancipation

I

The South is a history in search of a country. In the middle of the nineteenth century various interests and values incubated in this history sought to structure themselves into a separate country, but the effort failed and left the South, as the 1949 edition of the *Encyclopaedia Britannica* tersely defined it, "a large area of the United States which presents certain distinctive characteristics." Within the frame of the United States the people of each region intuitively have defined the boundaries and characteristics of their own and of every other region. The South, then, is that part of the nation regarded as the South by non-Southerners and Southerners alike, and that popular assignment refers not merely to geographic location but to broad cultural distinctiveness as well. In the moral geography of the United States the South has been the most sensitive area. Today, in a shrinking world with nations in a position to look over into the backyards of each other and ever ready to pass judgment, this area, like South Africa, Germany, and others, has become one of the most morally sensitive areas of the world, an exasperated subject of prolonged criticism from the outside. The setting in which there is a public that appears to hiss the actors in the Southern scene is changing from the nation to that of the world, but white Southerners, like white South Africans, continue to deny the right of the rest of the world to reprimand and to pass judgment. Nevertheless, in the struggle to accommodate itself to changes and to judgments from without, the South has changed and will continue to change from within. In a special sense the South is a product of change and of reaction to change throughout its history. Its basic constitution has been determined by the way it has dealt with the problem of change in the past, and the changes it faces now and in the future may involve nothing less than a revolution in its fundamental institutional structure.

II

Perhaps the central problem of every society is that of preserving enough consistency to maintain a relatively stable organization on the one hand while coping with inevitable changes on the other. How much change can a society admit and yet remain the same society? This is the ancient and universal problem of preserving a balance between order and change, and it has occupied the thought of many generations of philosophers. The ideal solution, of course, is orderly change, and this is what modern constitutional government aims to achieve. But when the members of a society cannot agree on what the goals of change are, or even upon the desirability of change at all, and this usually is the case, the ideal of orderly change can only be approximated. Almost always and everywhere the social process is punctuated by disorderly episodes of one kind or another, but, orderly or disorderly, change is inevitable in all social life. It is, as John Dewey has somewhere put it, "the primary social fact as surely as motion is the primary physical fact."

Things lying inert and seemingly changeless tend to escape notice. Change induces attention, observation, concern, reflection, and study; it is at least one source of social awareness of diversity leading to conflict, particularly when individuals and groups change at different tempos. Hence something is learned about the nature of things and about ourselves in the course of efforts to effect, prevent, or minimize change. Often efforts to block change unwittingly help bring about subsequent changes more drastic than otherwise might have been the case. In this sense the true radicals may, in the perspective of the history of a society, be the conservatives.

Social change is, of course, not the same thing as the mere passage of time. Nor is it just the accumulation of culture and of the artifacts of culture. It is something more than social circulation as in the elimination and replacement of group personnel, and it is something more than social succession as represented in the procession of the generations. In social change just what is it that changes? The central fact in social change appears to be alteration in the individual or group positions of the members of a society, that is, status change. An established social order is one in which there is an established status system; in the absence of such a system there is only a frontier.

Status is a broad term for the position of a person or group in a hierarchy of persons or groups. Like the struggle for existence, which operates in a biological and economic context, the struggle for higher status, which operates in a social and moral context, is, apparently, universal and eternal. "From this struggle," said Robert E. Park, "no philosophy of life has yet discovered a refuge."

It is important to distinguish status from the "condition" of an individual or group. "Condition" is more or less an environmental accident; the term describes the material and moral circumstances and standards under which individuals live, changes in which may occur without a corresponding change in social station. A status, on the other hand, is a position in a system of statuses, a position in a society. We speak of improving a condition but we speak of advancing a status. A status is organically bound up with every other status in the system. There could be no one to experience that "sickening sense of inferiority" if there were no others around to display the satisfactions and advantages of higher position. The items of a given condition become important for status when they are defined, not so much in terms of physical misery or comfort, but mainly in terms of personal or social degradation or prestige. This happens when events and an enlarging community bring about opportunities for sensitive inner comparisons and contrasts which in turn generate self and group consciousness. It happens when one becomes aware of what one's grievances or special privileges are in a world of those people whose estimate of one's self and of one's group seems important.

This is why the revision of the status system of a society will have repercussions throughout the entire social order. Any such revision *is* social change even though the causes of such change need not be social in their origins.

III

What, now, is the source of the popular commitment to race in social relations? If we abandon all the many good reasons that have been advanced and face the real reason, white Southerners and a great many white Americans generally would have to acknowledge that it stems from uncompromising status considerations, such as those having to do with interdining and intermarriage. It is important for the Best People of any society to know where to draw the line, and "racism," says Ruth Benedict, "is essentially a pretentious way of saying that 'I' belong to the Best People." Where the status of Best People entails some mark of obvious, permanent, and transmissible distinction, such as skin color, a distinction open to all born with the right complexion, it is possible to assert the claim of aristocratic status without benefit of education, wealth, family, or even good manners.

Southern society knows the discriminating force of education, family, fortune, office, religion, and other usual features of class in its status system, but cutting across all these features and distinguishing this society from most others is the long-time presence in it of an inherited status principle based upon race. The South, in a very special sense, is that part of the nation which is race-bound: race is the chief axis around which Southern life and thought has revolved for at least a hundred and fifty years. This region, as Jonathan Daniels put it, is two races, a racial moiety, with one race automatically assigned a superior status and the other just as automatically assigned an inferior one. This is true in spite of the fact, or perhaps because of it, that the two races have interdigitated, like the lacing of the fingers of the two hands, so that the lives of whites and of Negroes have played into the lives of each other. It is because the two groups have been so thoroughly intermixed in the same territory, because physical distance between them has been so insignificant a factor, that the ideology of race has been generated to effect a wide social distance. The believed-in differences between them pertain to little or nothing that is biologically or psychologically in one race that is not in the other, but rather to the social and historical situation in which both exist; only the intervention of the Other establishes the identity of individuals of different complexion as white or as Negro. Race functions as a contrast conception.

We have to understand the establishment of this kind of a status system in the South as a reaction to the problem of social change as this problem was presented in its early history. The changes presently going on amount to a veritable status revolution which is shaking the South to its very foundations, that is, in its social structure.

IV

At this point it may be useful to distinguish between change *in* race relations and change *and* race relations. A number of anthropologists and sociologists since W. H. R. Rivers have made us aware of the difference between those more formal and material aspects of a culture which change more or less easily and readily and those aspects which persist or offer considerable resistance to change. These institutional and persisting relationships constitute the social structure. In the social structure of most if not all societies, sex, age, and blood attributes and relationships get codified and legitimated. Insofar as such attributes and relationships are transmitted by educational institutions and sanctioned by religious institutions these, too, must be regarded as part of the structure. The more or less superficial changes which occur in the superstructure may have relatively little effect on the structural foundations of the society itself. All this is analogous to the different types of changes which physiologists observe in a developing organism. The point may be illustrated by the acculturation which, in the course of American history, fairly quickly erased the external signs of costume, mannerisms, and dialect that originally distinguished the members of one immigrant group from another, as well as from old-line Americans. But the resulting apparent homogeneity often obscured deeper differences of outlook and attitude which existed and probably continue to exist between them.

It is apparent that many changes have occurred in both our white and Negro populations, and in the relationships between them, during the past hundred years or more. But how deeply into the structure of Southern society do such changes go? Basic in the structure of a society are its institutions and its family and kinship relationships. Individuals in Southern society are born into a world of new artifacts and circumstances, but they continue to identify their membership in this society with a structure that they have been reared to believe is everlasting. They continue to regard themselves and to be regarded by others as Southerners. The institutional and kinship system of the South today may be described in almost precisely the same terms employed a century ago. Institutions then and now are divided along racial lines. Kinship as a network of communication and personal bonds divides itself now—as it did then—at the color line, notwithstanding an extensive amount of miscegenation which has occurred outside marriage. These elements of the social structure are regarded as of much more than temporary significance—factors of constancy and continuity are involved in them. One reading the journal of a Southern planter or matron of an earlier period often is impressed with the sense of certainty, the assurance, that the order of society in which they enjoyed high prestige would last forever. To-day this sense of assurance is being deeply shaken, but it is likely that many, if not most, white Southerners feel that when the tumult of mass race demonstrations have passed, as similar threats have passed before, the basic tenets of their way of life will remain the same.

An integral part of the social structure of the South is and has been its status system, one predicated upon the complete acceptance of the idea of race. No idea has ever yet separated the strata of a society more completely, nor with a greater assumption of finality, than has that of race. In its most extreme expression the idea leads people who face each other across a status line to see the others as members of a different species. The idea contains the notion that race is something primary, something that goes back into a far past and will continue into a far future. How did the idea arise and establish itself in the structure of Southern society? The answer requires an examination of the connection between change *and* race relations.

V

The evidence indicates that blacks in Virginia and in the South were not originally identified as racially different from the Euro-pean settlers, but as religiously different. They were "Moors" or at least non-Christians. However, this conception, inherited from the religious wars of Europe and used to justify the slave trade, broke down with the problem of maintaining Negroes in a state of slavery on the plantations. The religious rationalization implied emancipa-tion upon conversion until colonial legislatures, following the ex-ample of the Maryland assembly in 1664, "altered the religious sanc-tion for slavery and based its validity frankly upon race."[1] To be sure, the alteration had been building up in custom before it was formalized in the law. It was, nevertheless, a drastic alteration since it shifted social stratification from the English contractual and class arrangement to a biological heredity principle, a principle at once, in the case of the black man, highly visible, durable, predictable, and economically and socially meaningful. The asserted correspondence between color and slave status served to shunt the black man back into his racial place as he tried to imitate whites and climb higher in the social scale.

The racial principle was to take deepest root in what possibly was the most democratic part of the American frontier, the Southern frontier, an area productive of the leadership and doctrines of Jefferson and Jackson.[2] All along its course westward from North to South the American frontier developed practical working arrangements in which every man regarded himself and was regarded by others as being as good as any other man, that is, until the man of strange feature came along. The frontier had its own peculiar prejudices in that it demanded some kind of uniformity of outlook and appearance. Within such wide limits the stranger on the frontier easily fraternized with others and learned to compete and to co-operate with them. But the man of strange feature and color could not, in the nature of the case, conform to such requirements. The democratic code broke at the color line. Men who ardently believed in liberty became the masters of slaves.

In a feudal and military order assumptions of superiority and inferiority appear not to require elaborate ideological justifications. Concerning the virtual enslavement of native "kanaka" labor on the plantations of New Guinea by the Germans prior to World War I, Stephen W. Reed notes the absence among the Germans of assertions about high moral purpose on the one hand and justifications of exploitation on the other. Apparently the Germans felt no need to rationalize the subordination of native labor in racial terms. In the South it became an article of faith to be proclaimed at every opportunity that the Negro was a racial inferior, but in German New Guinea such a profession about the natives would have sounded like an assent to the alphabet. Reed goes on to say that the white and democratic Australians who took over the plantations from the Germans in World War I, and who recruited and controlled labor in much the same manner, could not be indifferent to the contradictions in their own culture and behavior. They came to rationalize their relations with the natives in terms of race.[3]

A parallel with developments in the American South would seem to be obvious. The suggestion is strong that the Negro was established here as a separate race, not in spite of our democracy, but actually because of it. If democratic values for whites were to be retained it seemed necessary to introduce another component, that of race. If the white Southerner was to subordinate the Negro in slavery and at the same time maintain his democratic and Christian dogmas, it was necessary to deny the Negro the attributes of a human being. The idea of race thus permitted whites to affirm their belief in the freedom and equality of all men, even as they excluded Negroes from the scope of that belief, by persuading whites that Negroes were not really men. At the same time the idea of race induced in many Negroes an acceptance of his own and his race's inferiority. It is perhaps because Negroes in America have been excluded from the circle of conventional white Christian values and democratic rights that they have become among the most uncompromising supporters of these values and rights. They cannot demand these values and rights for themselves without demanding them for all. In a larger sense it appears to be true that the struggle of the lower classes generally to rise is the source of the theory of democracy. The men who are struggling to rise are the men who define and maintain it.

VI

It has been suggested that the intense democracy of the Southern frontier broke at the color line. We need now to examine some further aspects of the role of color and other physical markings in connection with social change and with the processes of acculturation which resulted in the making of Americans and the distinctions which they created among themselves. It seems reasonable to argue that it was the black man from Africa who became the original American. Certainly the tribal Indian who met the white settlers at the boat was not an American either in his own eyes or in the eyes of the newcomers. He was not even an Indian in his own view of himself. He was a tribesman bearing the name of a tribe, the only name for himself and for his fellows he knew. Only much later did he accept the white man's view of himself as an Indian, and this was when he identified with other tribesmen in a common opposition to the whites who were taking over the country. Much more time was to pass before he left the reservation, became detribalized, and came to regard himself as an American citizen. But for the most part he and his fellows continued to be regarded as native aliens.

The cultures of the white colonists from Europe, and especially England, underwent change as they adapted to a new environment and to a new social order, but the language they spoke, the religion they professed, the spirit of the laws and constitutions they adopted, the marriage, family, and kinship system they took for granted—all these features of their cultures they transplanted with little significant change from their European homelands. They infused a new spirit into their culture and institutions, to be sure, but the newness was largely a matter of degree.

The man almost totally transformed in the American environment, the man to whom the transplanted European culture and institutions were completely new, was the black man brought to these shores from Africa. Some authorities say he came almost culturally naked, but whether this is true or not it is certain that, as compared with those who came from Europe, the African cultural heritage was relatively small. In America he became a new man to a far greater extent than the white man.[4] He was a tribesman in Africa, but he did not remain for long a tribesman in America. Many if not most of the Negroes originally brought to the West Indies and to America were tribally designated and sold as such, but practically all tribal distinctions were lost in the second generation. As a slave on the plantations of the South he rapidly, even if imperfectly, took over a European language as a *lingua franca* not merely to understand the commands of his master, but even more importantly to understand his fellow blacks who came from linguistic backgrounds in Africa different from his own. In later generations this European language became a *lingua madre* as children were born into such slave family life as existed. Uprooted from an old way of life and thrown into the company of other detribalized strangers, he became a member of a new and greater tribe as represented by the Christian church.

The Negro was introduced into Virginia in 1619 before any white settlers had arrived in New England, before the Dutch came to New Amsterdam, the Germans to Pennsylvania, the Scotch-Irish to the back country of the Carolinas, the Swedes to New Jersey, or the French Huguenots to Charleston. From 1619 until the very eve of the Civil War he was brought to this country by the thousands, antedating most of the Irish and the Scotch, and all the Italians, the Norwegians, and the Poles. Today the Negro is an Old American, and many of his race could qualify for membership in the Colonial Dames or the Sons and Daughters of the American Revolution if only the records had been kept and the rules of these organizations allowed it.

In Africa he was never a Negro and he is not there a Negro today. Modern American newspapers and magazines now reporting the activities of the "Negroes" of Africa use this word in order to make the news intelligible in terms of our vocabulary, but the word as it pertains to Africans is entirely misleading. In Africa the black man still is a tribesman, albeit a tribesman in the process of becoming a Ghanian, a Nigerian, or some other kind of nationalist. Only in America is the black man a Negro, and he became so by reason of peculiarly American conditions and experiences. In America vis-à-vis the whites practically all persons with a black ancestor came to think of themselves as Negroes and were in turn regarded by whites as Negroes. But the American culture, which he so thoroughly acquired and which he has expanded perhaps more than any other single ethnic in our population, is the most distinctive thing about him. The statement by George Burton Adams is not overly exaggerated: "With most marvelous certainty, when we consider the conditions, the negro in the South could be trusted to perpetuate our political ideas and institutions, if our republic fell, as surely as the Gaul did his adopted institutions."[5] Kelly Miller, one of the most perceptive of Negro spokesmen of an earlier generation, said that one of the greatest injustices suffered by the black man in America was that he was not permitted to be patriotic, not permitted to feel at home in the only country and culture he knew. Up to now nothing has perhaps been more difficult than to interest him in tribal Africa.

VII

As cultural differences between Europeans and Negroes in the colonies receded, alleged racial differences advanced. Both race and counter-race would appear to be incidents of acculturation and assimilation. There is no marked emphasis upon race when ethnics are culturally recognizably different; the idea seems to come to the fore when members of the lower-status community begin to acquire the manners, the tastes, the costume, the speech, and the religion of the upper-status community. In his study of relations between the Spanish-speaking Ladinos and the Indian language-speaking groups of Guatemala, John Gillin has called attention to a separating status line almost as great as anything we know in the South between whites and Negroes.[6] In this situation, however, there has been no need to resort to racial ideas since individuals are readily identified as Ladino or Indian on the basis of speech, dress, and other cultural criteria.

The situation in the South developed very differently. As acculturation progressively stripped away cultural differences there was practically nothing of distinctiveness left to the Negroes but a black skin, a flat nose, large lips, and woolly hair. There was danger of Negro absorption into the European community and consequently of a breakdown of the exclusiveness of this community. It was expedient to seize upon those differences which acculturation could not erase, differences fixed in an inherited physical form, and to make the most of them. Making the most of them led to the assertion of race. Skin color, in particular, was to become a significant symbol of status difference. It was easy to impute to individuals of different color moral and social characteristics such as laziness, improvidence, immorality, stupidity, doglike fidelity, and criminal tendency. These alleged behavioral characteristics also were believed to be biologically inherited, and what is in the biological nature of a people is there to stay, the business of God alone since He put it there. Such ideas in the past have given us "the eternal feminine" and "the Jewish character," as well as "the black soul." Many of us may regret these ideas, and we may have enormous sympathy for such people because of the handicaps with which they must live. There appears to be nothing, however, that anyone can do about it. From such ideas come the themes of human tragedy, of the struggle of man, not against other men but against fate, and, of course, fate is bound to win.

It is most comforting for the man of high station to feel that his lot in life is in accord with the will of God. It is agreeable to believe that some immutable principle sustains the status quo unless, of course, one happens to be near the bottom of the order. Ordinarily, the man of high station will agree with Aristotle, who, considering the matter from the point of view of an Athenian aristocrat, laid it down that changes in an established order should be as few and as slight as possible. Conservatives in general tend to deprecate change since it impugns the security of that to which they have given their allegiance and which guards their status. Liberals in general are at least more charitable toward change, especially when they are members of a class that is dissatisfied and motivated to remove barriers that obstruct their interests. In various situations the issues may be differently defined and the opposed parties may be differently labeled, but it may well be true that the basic cleavage in every society is the one between conservatives and liberals in their varying degrees. The racial situation is no different in kind; with reference to certain issues it tends to divide conservatives and liberals at the color line. Race prejudice, Robert Park remarked, "is merely an elementary expression of conservatism."

It is not true, of course, that all men instinctively fear and oppose change. Most men are always ready to enter into such new relationships as appear to them to involve a rise in their relative status or to be necessary to maintain existing status. They expect thereby to gain by change and they welcome it, especially when they are acutely conscious of the gap between their own status and that of those immediately above them. The narrower the status gap becomes the more sensitive are men to the differences that remain. The gains American Negroes have recently made can be expected to promote more, not less, dissatisfaction on their part.

Other men are just as quick to reject new relationships that appear to involve a loss of status. When circumstances force them lower on the scale in any way they are deeply hurt in the most sensitive aspect of their lives, their conception of themselves. They try desperately to hang on to the self-image they enjoyed at the highest point of the history of their class. They will respond, as white Southerners for some time have been doing, by an overemphasis upon the past, an orientation that tends to close the channels of interracial communication at just the times and points where communication is most needed. Incidentally, it would appear that in our more systematic investigations we have paid considerably more attention to the status-advancing aspirations of groups suffering from an oppression psychosis than to the consequences for personality and social organization of individuals and groups declining in status. (The opposite assertion might be made of themes popular among Southern novelists and playwrights.) Yet it may be just this fact that in our day is converting the race problem in the South from a Negro into a white problem. One is, to be sure, born a "white" man, but one has to wage continuous battle to remain a white man. When the Southern white loses some part of the social estate which his white skin has in the past automatically given him, he at the same time loses some part of his identity. He ceases by so much to know exactly who he is, and it is not at all surprising that he does not willingly surrender himself in the partial loss of his sense of self. Most of us today, white and black alike, might well consider that no effort in behalf of the black man that is not matched by a real sympathy for, and understanding of, the white man can really be socially constructive.

VIII

There is no true interracial society until and unless the idea of race enters the social structure and becomes a part of the society's "way of life," or "civilization," or "*pietas.*" The idea may be of only local or provincial application but its adherents regard it as a universal. Always it appears to be the disposition of those who oppose change to appeal to something beyond experience, since experience is ever in a state of flux, in order to find stability and peace. The concept of God, "the rock of ages," has often been adopted as the solution to this problem, but lesser principles also have been found useful. It was not by accident that it was the aristocratic philosopher Plato who discovered the perfect and unchanging concept of the concept and who rooted concepts in the original nature of man. The principle of the divine right of kings supported the view of absolute and eternal monarchy until the execution of Charles I showed that circumstances could both make and unmake kings. God made the climate what it is, and climate requires the labor of people especially qualified for work on tropical plantations while other men not so qualified can repose on their verandas. We recognize, as firm and fixed, the ground beneath our feet—until there is an earthquake.

The very human need for some principle of certainty in a world of flux has led to an unending search for some sort of spiritual or cultural anchor without which we cannot hold on to what we have and to what we are or think we are. We have to understand our deep emotional investment in race in this context. It is one of the ideas thrown up in the more recent history of mankind and passed along from generation to generation because it has worked, and worked more or less satisfactorily until now, to stabilize the social hierarchies of whole social orders. When we look under the heading "race" in the *Oxford Dictionary*, we notice quite a large number of meanings historically associated with this word. Should we reflect upon these various meanings and uses of the word with the hope of uncovering some common denominator, we would in all likelihood conclude that each in its own way and with respect to its own reference implies the idea of something built in or entrenched, something permanent and immutable. The English language, and perhaps other languages as well, is rich in the variety of words expressing this idea, words such as inherent, constitutional, ingrained, inborn, intrinsic, incarnate, and many others. The idea of race is like a condition that was written into the lease at the time of creation governing relations among the men who are allowed to inhabit the earth. It came into the South, as in certain other interracial societies, to do duty as an absolute, as a symbol more effective and lasting than language or religion to insure the continued economic, political, and social security of the classes of highest status. To be sure, it had to be shared with landless and impecunious whites, but this was not a complete disadvantage since these whites functioned as a buffer class to absorb the shocks of race conflict. The poor whites of the South, because they were white men, served the cause of the Confederacy in behalf of economic interests they did not share. Statements documenting the proposition that the idea of race in the South has functioned in the manner indicated might be quoted almost without end. Let this quotation from the speech of a contemporary Southern Senator suffice: "By this bill [FEPC] there is an attempt to change something that God made. We did not make it. God made my face white and some other face yellow and some other face black. I did not do it. Congress cannot change that state of affairs."[7]

IX

A comparison between the roles and experiences of the Negro and the immigrant in American life may shed more light upon the difference between change *in* race relations and change *and* race relations. In 1930 Negroes and foreign-born in the United States were approximately equal in numbers, but, of course, Negroes now far outnumber the foreign-born as these two groups are identified and counted in the census. Technically, we all are descendants of immigrants, unless we are Indians, but we have come to use the word "immigrant" in a special way since the American Revolution and particularly since the coming of the Irish during and after the 1840's. Until about 1890 the influx from northern and western Europe predominated; after that date the tide turned increasingly toward newcomers from southern and eastern Europe. It was then that America began to be conscious of an "immigrant problem" and of the difficulties of assimilating alien peoples to what were deemed to be the values and standards of American life. There are a large number of autobiographies by immigrants, and even at this late date when the problem of the immigrant, if the Puerto Rican be excepted, no longer agitates us, these books constitute an instructive body of literature that vividly describes the personal and subjective aspects of "Americanization."

These are not, however, the aspects that concern us here. Nor can we detail the many and important differences between the experiences of various immigrant groups. Rather, we want to see if there is some pattern in the process of change in each immigrant group that may throw some light upon the prospective course of the Negro in American civilization.

Perhaps the first thing to be noticed is that in no case from first to last did the national elites of Europe break home ties and depart for America. On the contrary, to take the case of Sweden, the aristocracy considered the country to which their laborers were migrating to be a "paradise of scoundrels, cheats, and rascals."[8] The recurrent waves of mass immigration consisted, in the main, of the poor and the depressed strata of Europe. It began when such strata had to be "planted" in early Virginia by men of capital who remained in England, and it continued with the white indentured servant class for a century or more later. Then came Welsh, French Huguenots, Scotch-Irish, Austrians, Croats, Czechs, Hungarians, Greeks, Italians, and Jews to fill the territorial and economic vacancies at the bottom of American society, and thereby to facilitate the rise of the immigrant groups which preceded them.[9] Lord Bryce in *The American Commonwealth* explained the relatively high status of the skilled worker in America by the fact that "all unskilled labourers are comparatively recent immigrants."

On the whole, the members of each migrating group were desperately poor, but perhaps no migrations were ever more strongly motivated. Nothing else could account for the willingness to pull up stakes in a loved homeland, travel across a large and dangerous ocean in steerage accommodations, and then endeavor to take root again in a strange land among people of even stranger customs. Reporting what he had heard on a ship bringing a number of elderly Italians to America, a journalist wrote:

And the word that turned up most frequently in their conversation was "America." In colloquial Italian, "America" has come to mean something more than a geographical place. It is, by extension, any deposit of hopes, any tabernacle where all things too big, too difficult, too far beyond one's grasp take shape and become true—so true that all one needs in order to touch them is a ship that will take one there. "America" is, again, something one finds or makes, a stepping stone, a rung in the ladder that allows one to climb a little higher—not, of course, in the country called America but back home. "America" also means the treasure one finds when "America" (the rung in the ladder) is steadily under one's feet. Inevitably, the question that the old people asked one another, over and over, was "Is America America?"[10]

That America was to people such as these Italians a land of opportunity is no mere literary expression. In truth it was a land of hope and promise, and the immigrants of each wave and each group set out to make the promise come true. They identified with the country —their children even more so—and they came to say "we Americans" along with other Americans here long before them. But in their case it was a "we" of aspiration used in the same sense that the first white "Americans" had used the expression, as if they were saying "we are the people who are helping to build a better land for ourselves and for our children." The reference was to the future.

But as members of each group moved up the status ladder and acquired land, skill, or a place of residence outside the city ghettos in which they first had settled, as each group differentiated middle and upper classes within itself and produced successful men, they began to say "we Americans" in a somewhat different sense. Looking back at the past and considering the distance thay had traveled and the degree of success and recognition they had won, they were more disposed to say, in effect, "We are the people who have made America what it is."[11] They now were concerned to establish societies called the Sons and Daughters of Something or Other intended to preserve and to glorify the record of their achievements and perhaps to object to the admission of any more lower-class immigrants.

Wave after wave of immigrants were destined to start at the very bottom with their eyes upon the hills. Very often they became the servants or the employees of the preceding group, but they were confident that hard work would win for themselves and their children an honorable place in the new land. To them this ideal conception of a country with a future was America.

The story of hopeful immigrants and successful self-made men of foreign birth or descent leap-frogging over each other was to be repeated many times as American history moved on. Both the relatively successful who had some status advantage to defend and the lowly beginners who hoped to rise had a kind of vested interest in preserving the essential social and institutional structure of the nation, since outside of it the positions they occupied or hoped to occupy would have been meaningless. Thus the changes sought by the immigrants posed, in general, no great threat to that structure. On the contrary, they supported it. To be sure, there did develop among old-line Americans, particularly in the North, a cult of Anglo-Saxonism provoked by the coming of large numbers of Catholics, Jews, and Latins from eastern and southern Europe, a cult which found some common ground with the racism of the South, but the chief effect of this concern was the final restriction of all immigration after World War I.

From the story of the immigrant we learn something of the true meaning of America and of Americanism. We began learning it in the social settlements that were established in the slums of our great cities of the North and that were intended to help solve the immigrant problem by teaching the newcomers the ideals of Americanism. These ideals were presumed by the teachers to have been derived from our history, and so the emphasis in this teaching was upon American achievement. But the immigrants did not agree with the assumption that almost everything valuable in American life had been handed down from the Teutons in the German forests, from the English, or from the pioneers on the American frontier. They insisted on the recognition of their own cultural contributions. The settlement-house experiments wound up with the immigrant students teaching the teachers that America meant aspiration, especially to the immigrants who still lived in slums. These new Americans were not interested in looking back over American history, although over their shoulders they might hear the men of the past saying, "We were concerned to build a great cathedral but we had to leave it unfinished. It is for you to build on." It was an unfinished cathedral to which each new group of different culture might add a stone.

From the immigrants we learned this: the real America is something more than the America of the Daughters of the American Revolution. America is a nation of many histories and peoples, with relatively little by way of a common past. For this reason in times of national emergency this country cannot effectively appeal, as can England or France, to a common past in order to mobilize its people of many origins. It becomes necessary to appeal to a common hope, to a common aspiration, to a common future. Our literary historians have come to call this "the American Dream"—the conception that the future is ours to create.

In our very mobile population the differences between peoples upon which economic and symbiotic relations originally were based have been continually disappearing as peoples of low estate have been encouraged and even driven to struggle upward and to bring about occupational successions. While, on the one hand, this process has been accelerated by our "100 per cent American" policy and ideal, the same process on the other hand has supplied motives for the development of doctrines to prevent upward occupational movement from happening. As has been shown, such doctrines have been most effective in the case of the black man, but they also have operated against the Puerto Rican, the Mexican, and certain other minorities. The black man had not wanted to come to America, and after he came here he had no reason for wanting to remain here. He came because he was compelled to come, and he remained here without motive or purpose of his own. His life here, and the lives of his children, served the purpose of someone else. His conception of America was neither that of aspiration nor that of achievement. One neither looks back upon slavery in terms of achievement nor looks forward to sharecropping in terms of aspiration. There were exceptions, of course. Even before the Civil War free Negroes, many of whom were mulattoes, were establishing themselves as a class apart both in the South and in the North. But the black masses remained on the plantations of the South where their fathers before had lived and worked out their lives. They were American Negroes but not Negro Americans.

During the Civil War Negro slaves were freed by presidential proclamation. Their descendants have since learned from bitter experience that real emancipation is never achieved by proclamation. In the long run people have to emancipate themselves. And white people, too, at least some of them, have learned or are learning that freedom is never really handed over to another people by the simple device of issuing a proclamation. Real freedom is never within the prerogative of one people to give another. Members of the master race have at the same time morally to emancipate themselves, and it may be that Negroes cannot effectively gain their freedom until whites have freed themselves from race-bound self-conceptions. It is just now, one hundred years after Lincoln's proclamation, that both Negroes and whites in the South, and throughout the nation generally, are at last beginning to free themselves in some large and significant way from both the slavery and the mastership of the past. This does not involve just one more form of racial adjustment; it involves nothing less than the threatened penetration of the social structure itself.

Behavioristically described, freedom is freedom to move and to get about. After 1865 the Negro freedmen of the South manifested their freedom by moving from one plantation to another, and from the plantations to the villages, towns, and cities of the South and then later to the cities of the North. This greater liberty to move about is doubtless what the freedmen meant when they spoke of the "looseness" of freedom. But many of them moved through the gates of isolated rural plantations only to enter the gates of the segregated ghettos of the cities of both the South and the North.

If emancipation involves freedom to move it also involves freedom to appear. As slaves Negroes were hidden away on the private estates of the planters and as migrants to the cities they were concealed behind the walls of ghetto slums. Slavery consists not only in being deprived of freedom to move but also in being denied a public and visible existence. The changes we now are witnessing describe a process of Negroes rising into public sight from their previous obscurity in city ghettoes. They are putting in an appearance in the theaters, on the streets, on the highways, on the trains and buses, in the voting booths, and in the schools and colleges. They are everywhere, in places where before they rarely ventured. They are conspicuous, they are out in the public, they are being noticed. They are, in short, being emancipated a second time.

We are living in an age of worldwide emancipations. All sorts and conditions of people—women, children, teen-agers, sectarians, workers, natives, colonials, peasants—are being emancipated from real or fancied states of oppression all over the world. Again we hear much talk of the "natural" rights of man, a kind of talk which tells more about situations of change than it does about what natural rights are, but all these people seeking more freedom agree on at least one natural and inalienable right in common and that is, the right to complain about their lack of rights. They are complaining so effectively that the holders of traditional status powers are recognizing rights of some sort on the part of those surging up from below and demanding them.

The second emancipation of the Negro, the American phase of this world-wide status struggle, is more fundamental and, for the future, far more important than the first one. Its present manifestations —such as freedom rides, restaurant picketing, school and university desegregation, and other events which command the headlines—may be mere surface manifestations of a more profound change taking place in the *ethos* of the Negro and an earnest of changes taking place or about to take place in the basic structure of Southern society. The first emancipation gave Negroes freedom to move around and to choose their own employers, but it widened racial distances and made Southern institutions much more racially exclusive. Legal slavery disappeared with the first emancipation, but the idea of race, which in part originated as a rationalization of slavery, became an end-value in itself and went even deeper into the structure of Southern society than before.

A social order based upon slavery or race will, of course, be especially sensitive to behavior and language which touches these nerves and which consequently will be deemed subversive. The Japanese have a term, *kiken shiso*, which is translated as "dangerous thought." In old Japan a man might be thrown into prison if suspected of dangerous thought or if he merely had read an outlawed book or had a knowing smile on his face.[12] Dangerous thoughts are thoughts regarded as dangerous to entertain even for a moment. They threaten, not just political authority or economic interests, but the fundamental social order itself. Since the Civil War dangerous thought in the South has turned, more than upon anything else, upon the issue of race. In 1903 Professor John A. Bassett, Professor of History at Trinity College, now Duke University, gave it as his opinion that Robert E. Lee and Booker T. Washington were the two greatest men produced in the South in a hundred years. To outsiders it seemed a harmless enough remark but to Southerners the linking of the name of Lee with the name of a Negro was an expression of dangerous thought, a sacrilege, and there were widespread demands for Bassett's expulsion from the state. Against this background it is easily understandable why the Supreme Court school desegregation decision opened to public view ideas long defined in the South as dangerous and subversive. It is understandable why Americans and especially Southerners who entertain dangerous thought about such things as racial equality should so often be regarded by other Southerners as Communists.[13] One step short of this is the disposition of Southern newspapers to label such people as "sociologists" and to refer to the 1954 decision of the Supreme Court as a "sociological" decision. Since the social sciences raise for objective consideration questions which people ordinarily feel are already settled in the mores, much of the thought of social science in all its branches presents itself to the people as at least near-dangerous thought.

XI

Yet no matter how deep into the social structure the idea of race might penetrate, the South was not permitted to become a separate nation completely free to control its domestic affairs and keep out all dangerous thought. The presence of the North made it impossible for relations between the races to avoid critical evaluation from some source, even from within the South itself. Impersonal forces of change, in addition, brought such pressures upon Southern society as to force something to give. Reaction to change brought the idea of race into existence as part of the Southern "way of life" in the first place; reaction to change is dramatically altering that way of life and the idea of race implicit in it today. These modern changes include the collapse of an obsolete cotton culture, geographic shifts in agriculture, the mechanization of agriculture, the movement away from share-cropping and the trend toward wage labor in agricultural enterprises, the development of competing areas in other parts of the world, over-population, urbanization, industrialization, the migration of both whites and Negroes northward and westward, the foreign policy requirements of the State Department, the cold war with the Soviet Union, and many other developments. All these cannot be discussed in detail, but attention may be directed to a few of the more significant domestic changes now in process.

There now are more Negroes living outside the South than in it. The South, however, remains that part of the United States where rural Negroes are distributed; Northern and Western Negroes are concentrated in the large cities. The old adage that "city air makes free" continues to operate in behalf of Negroes in Northern and Southern urban areas as it has done historically in behalf of other disadvantaged groups. In the cities, especially in the North and West, Negroes have taken their place alongside the foreign-born whites and their children as a sort of belated immigrant group. The descendants of old-line black Americans have taken up where the white immigrants left off in 1924. In the manner of the newly arrived European immigrants, the contemporary Negro is saying "we Americans" in the same spirit of aspiration and with the same orientation toward the future. Largely because of the Negro, America continues to be what the steerage immigrants first taught us it was, an unfinished cathedral. The Negroes of our time intend to add more than one stone to the building.

There may, however, be an important difference between the aspiring white immigrant American and the aspiring Negro immigrant American. The former was drawn from a traditional European peasantry which declined to continue as such in America and which produced a pride of achievement when it developed middle and upper classes. Among Negroes, on the other hand, the "we" of aspiration appears first in the middle and upper classes and especially in the lower middle class, the class just one notch ahead of the ambitionless lower class. These Negroes are the ones who feel most acutely the need to affirm a distinction and some sense of equality with whites. They are the yeast of Negro society determined to move into a preferred position. Race makes the difference, and in America advance in class status does not erase it. So long as there is a color line there is still much that Negroes have to aspire to, satisfactions that the children of white immigrants have long since achieved.

Until the relatively recent past there was little by way of a Negro middle class in America. Some semblance of such a class made its appearance before the Civil War and the first emancipation added a few small landowners in the rural areas and a few small merchants and artisans in the villages and towns of the South. It was the ghettos of the large cities of the South and even more those of the North that made possible a rapid and extensive enlargement of this class, especially after about 1890. The statement that there is a large and growing Negro middle class in America will hardly be challenged by any competent student, but perhaps many whites, especially in the South, would be astonished to learn that all Negroes are not lower class by nature. A black middle class appears to be rising in parts of Africa; there are blacks in Brazil, but perhaps no middle class as such, since race and class are practically identical ideas there; and over most of the West Indies what would be a Negro middle class in America has become a separate "colored" group no longer locally identified as Negro. Certainly the development of a substantial Negro middle class differentiates the black population of America from Negroid populations in other parts of the world, and constitutes a critical factor in changes in race relations here. A Negro middle class has been taking form, almost entirely outside the awareness of whites, in segregated urban ghettoes. Indeed, it might be said that middle-class Negroes generally are those who have least contact with whites and who, consequently, are the most segregated. No matter how much modern Negro leaders may inveigh against these segregated areas, it is reasonable to suppose that in them were incubated and protected the occupations and institutions that trained large number of Negroes in middle-class skills and values.

The Negro middle class formed in urban black belts is now in the process of trying to break out of these areas by bidding for the respect and deference of the surrounding white world. With each success the Negro middle class becomes stronger. Every middle class anywhere seems to arise, where there was not one before, when a segment of the depressed population begins to refuse to play the role assigned to it by the traditional status system. When, inevitably, they meet resistance from sources in the traditional order, they are led to define the barriers as "discrimination." In the course of such encounters between those who would maintain or expand traditional status barriers and those who would set them aside and substitute other status standards, a middle class is born. The process is similar in the evolution of middle classes generally. In England, for example, as R. H. Grotton describes it, merchants and professionals pushing their way upward constituted themselves into a class between the aristocratic stratum on the one hand and the stratum of menial workers on the other. They encountered resistance from below as well as from above.[14]

In America the process of Negro middle-class formation has resulted in some degree of change in the conception, in both Negro and white society, of who a Negro is. Increasing awareness of the existence of a Negro middle class seems to have confused the lines of traditional racial identification just as the appearance of the mixed-blood, the mulatto, did in colonial America. The traditional dominant white race tries to strengthen the laws and customs against the upstarts but the latter counter by disciplining themselves in new rules of behavior appropriate to their new conception of themselves. A consequence of such discipline is the development of traits and attitudes that are thought to characterize people of middle-class standing anywhere, that is, an emphasis on virtue, respectability, and individual worth, and an intense effort to instill such values into the ambitions of their children. Observers have often noted a kind of puritanism among middle-class Negroes and a concern for precision in speech. It appears as overprecision to white observers; Will Rogers once remarked of Negroes at Tuskegee Institute that they spoke such good English he could hardly understand them.

Incidental to urbanization and the emergence of an aspiring Negro middle class have come formal organizations designed to clarify objectives, to mobilize effort among Negroes and their white sympathizers, and to develop plans for action, e.g., the National Association for the Advancement of Colored People. They are countered by organizations like the White Citizens Councils. The first emancipation in the last century was the result of efforts on behalf of an enslaved people by organizations formed and led by whites in the North. The second emancipation in this century is the goal of organizations spearheaded by Negroes themselves. They have launched into the general complex society of America a series of organizations that interact with other organizations—industrial, labor, religious, political, regional, and social—in ways that have produced interlockings, conflicts, compromises, and accommodations that have measurably transformed the racial struggle into a more impersonal and indirect affair. The shift away from the study of race relations in direct and personal terms to their study in terms of mass organizational interaction is registered in the writings of such students as Herbert Blumer, Joseph Lohman, and Dietrich Reitzes. The course of future study of change and race relations in the United States is likely to proceed further in this direction, and from it we may expect to get a more realistic understanding of the racial shape of things to come.

XII

But despite the obvious impact of these powerful new forces on race relations, there remains the question of how deeply into the fundamental structure of Southern society they can and will go. Few white Southerners of intelligence, good will, and moderation will deny that the problems presented the South by the status advance of the Negro count as practically nothing compared with the problems that would be presented by his failure to advance both in status and in material culture. They are inclined to put their faith in education and in gradual economic advance. These programs can shift the color line somewhat nearer the democratic ideal without, however, erasing that line. The structural foundations of the color line may undergo comparatively little change. When we consider the question of structural change in other societies in the long perspective of history it would appear that gradual educational and cultural changes have had relatively little to do with it. The major transformations of historical societies have had their setting in periods of intense collective excitement, such as war, revolution, and migration. It may be that societies are more often and more fundamentally changed by mass action than by individual action. We may now be involved in a sort of slow-burning racial revolution in America, but unless the movement reaches a stage of more violent upheaval than we anticipate, it is likely that the idea of race and the deeper social structure that supports it will be with us for a very long time to come. Few white Americans are prepared to act, and to train their children to act, as if no such structure existed.

The Negro will continue to be, as he has always been, a symbol of change. We can expect him consciously to become more and more a protagonist of change. We will do well to support the conviction he inherited from the steerage immigrants that America stands for the future, and all of us can join him in helping the South take a more positive hand in the making of its own future as a part of America, a future of democracy and good will as well as of material progress.

There is in the conduct of race relations in the South much to repent, but there is no point in a people repenting its virtues as well as its sins. And certainly there is no point in repenting that which was brought about by the impersonal forces of the past. Whites can and should repent when they use their position of racial ascendency for unworthy purposes, or fail to use it for worthy ones. Insofar as they can, by taking thought, they should deliberately enter into and help to guide toward worthy ends the changes that the future will have in store for us.

1. Marcus W. Jernegan, "Slavery and Conversion in the American Colonies," *American Historical Review*, XXI (April, 1916), 506.

2. For documentation of this proposition, see Charles Grier Sellers, "The Travail of Slavery," in Sellers, ed., *The Southerner as American* (Chapel Hill: University of North Carolina Press, 1960).

3. Stephen W. Reed, *The Making of Modern New Guinea* (Philadelphia: American Philosophical Society, 1942), pp. 245–246.

4. Crèvecoeur does not consider the case of the Negro in his famous essay, "What, Then, Is the American, This New Man?" See Arthur M. Schlesinger, *Paths to the Present* (New York: Macmillan Co., 1949), chap. i.

5. George Burton Adams, *Civilization during the Middle Ages* (Rev. ed.; New York: Charles Scribner's Sons, 1914), p. 30.

6. John Gillin, " 'Race' Relations without Conflict: A Guatemalan Town," *American Journal of Sociology*, LIII (March, 1948), 337–343.

7. *United States Congressional Record*, Seventy-ninth Congress, Second Session, XCII, Part 1 (Jan. 30, 1946), 563.

8. Hans Mattson, *Reminiscences: The Story of an Immigrant* (St. Paul: D. D. Merrill Co., 1891), p. 111.

9. See, for example, Maldwyn Jones, *American Immigration* (Chicago: University of

Chicago Press, 1960); Marcus L. Hansen, *The Immigrant in American History* (Cambridge, Mass.: Harvard University Press, 1940); and Oscar Handlin, *The Uprooted* (Boston: Little Brown and Co., 1951).

10. Niccole Tucci, "The Underground Letters," *New Yorker*, XXVII (Aug. 4, 1951), 24.

11. Everett and Helen M. Hughes, *Where Peoples Meet* (Glencoe: Free Press, 1952), p. 140.

12. John Paul Reed, *Kokutai* (Chicago: University of Chicago Libraries, 1940), chap. iii, "Dangerous Thoughts."

13. The South African Nationalist government has gone so far as legislatively to define such people as Communists. See Leo Kuper, *Passive Resistance in South Africa* (New Haven: Yale University Press, 1957), chap. ii, "Communism by Statute."

14. R. H. Grotton, *The British Middle Class* (London: G. Bell and Sons, Ltd., 1917).

Donald R. Matthews and James W. Prothro

Negro Voter Registration in the South*

On August 18, 1961, John W. Hardy, a twenty-one-year-old Negro student from Nashville, Tennessee, opened a voter registration school for Negroes at the Mount Moriah Baptist Church in Walthall County, Mississippi. Mr. Hardy, a political science student at Tennessee Agricultural and Industrial University and an active member of the Student Non-Violent Coordinating Committee, spent several weeks training twenty to fifty local Negroes in Mississippi's literacy test and registration requirements. Up to that time, these requirements (and their administration) had proven sufficiently intricate that not one of the 2,500 Negroes of voting age in Walthall County had been able to satisfy them. On August 30, four Negro graduates of the training school—including one college student and a former school teacher—presented themselves to the registrar of voters, Circuit Court Clerk John Q. Wood, in the county courthouse in Tylertown. The next day Wood announced that they had failed to meet the legal qualifications necessary to register. On September 7, two more graduates of the school, this time accompanied by Mr. Hardy, attempted to register. Mr. Wood said that he could not administer the test pending the outcome of a Justice Department suit against him claiming discriminatory treatment of potential Negro voters. An argument between Wood and Hardy ensued, at the conclusion of which Wood reached into his

* This study has been supported by a grant from the Rockefeller Foundation to the Institute for Research in Social Science of the University of North Carolina. It has been aided by grants from the Social Science Research Council of a Senior Award for Research on Governmental Affairs and an Award for Research on American Governmental and Legal Processes to the authors, respectively. We wish to express our gratitude to these organizations for providing the resources needed to engage in this analysis. Professors V. O. Key, Jr., Warren E. Miller, and Allan P. Sindler have commented generously upon an earlier version of this paper. While we have learned much from their criticism, neither they nor the organizations named above should be held responsible for the contents of this paper.

Most of this paper, together with additional materials, was published in the form of two articles, one in the March, 1963 and the other in the June, 1963 issue of the *American Political Science Review*. We appreciate the reprint permission granted to us by the holders of the copyright, the American Political Science Association.

desk, pulled out a gun and ordered the three Negroes to leave. After the Negroes turned toward the door, Wood struck Hardy on the head with his pistol. As Hardy staggered from the Clerk's office assisted by his Negro companions, County Sheriff Ed Craft arrived on the scene, arrested the student for disturbing the peace, and threatened to "beat him within an inch of his life."[1]

*   *   *

Six days later, municipal elections were held in Atlanta, Georgia. More than 28 per cent of the Atlantans qualified to vote in the contest were Negroes. Two of the five candidates for Mayor—Ivan Allen, Jr., and M. M. (Muggsy) Smith—openly pledged themselves to continue the enlightened racial policies of retiring Mayor William B. Hartsfield; two were silent on racial matters but were believed to be in general sympathy with Hartsfield's handling of the city's racial problems. A fifth candidate, Lester Maddox, was an avowed segregationist. A spirited contest between Allen and Smith for the endorsement of the powerful Atlanta Negro Voters League dominated the early stages of the campaign. Allen won the endorsement of the League and went on to lead in the first election, polling 39,000 of the 102,000 votes cast. Mr. Maddox, who polled 20,000 votes, was second. Between the first election and the run-off contest held on September 22, Maddox campaigned almost exclusively on the racial issue. He charged that the Negro voters "were out to get him" and that if Allen were elected "Auburn Avenue [predominantly Negro] will run your city." The voters chose Allen by a two-to-one margin. Post-election analysis showed that the votes in predominantly white precincts were evenly divided, with Maddox enjoying a small plurality of 2,000 or 3,000 votes. In the predominantly Negro portions of Atlanta, Allen received 31,224 votes—about half his total—while Maddox received 179.[2]

*   *   *

Neither the assault on John Hardy in Tylertown nor the victory of Ivan Allen in Atlanta is "typical" of the South today. But they do indicate the wide range of situations found in the region, so far as Negro voting is concerned. At one end of the continuum, no Negroes vote, politics is the white man's preserve, and he is willing to resort to violence and intimidation in order to preserve this monopoly; at the other end, Negroes virtually have achieved parity at the ballot box and have very substantial political power. In this paper we shall describe this range of Negro voting situations in some detail and attempt to explain why the variation exists.

This is more than an academic exercise. The vote may be the key which unlocks the door to full citizenship and social and economic equality for Southern Negroes. A John Q. Wood would not last very long as an elective official in Atlanta—unless, as the shrewd politician that he is, he treated Negro citizens very differently from the way in which he treats them in southwestern Mississippi. Once Negroes vote as heavily all over the South as they do in Atlanta, white politicians should prove more responsive to the desires of the Negro community. "Political rights pave the way to all others."[3]

Such, at least, seems to have been the reasoning behind the Civil Rights Acts of 1957 and 1960, both of which deal primarily with the right to vote. The mere passage of these statutes indicates that the white South—and Southerners in Congress—are less resistant to federal action on voting rights than to action involving schools, jobs, or housing. Attorney-General Robert F. Kennedy and Herbert Brownell, first attorney-general in the Eisenhower Administration, are both reported to believe that the vote provides the Southern Negro with his most effective means of advancing toward equality, and recent actions of the Justice Department seem to reflect this view.[4]

Negro leaders apparently share this belief in the overriding importance of the vote. Hundreds of Negro registration drives have been held in Southern cities and counties since 1957. Martin Luther King, usually considered an advocate of non-violent direct action, recently remarked that the most significant step Negroes can take is in the "direction of the voting booths."[5] The National Association for the Advancement of Colored People, historically identified with courtroom attacks on segregation, is now enthusiastically committed to a "battle of the ballots."[6] In March, 1962, the Southern Regional Council announced receipt of foundation grants of $325,000 to initiate a major program to increase Negro voter registration in the South.[7] The Congress on Racial Equality, the National Association for the Advancement of Colored People, the National Urban League, the Southern Christian Leadership Conference, and the Student Non-Violent Coordinating Committee are among the organizations now participating in the actual registration drives.

While the advocates of the unique importance of the vote to Negroes in the South are numerous and persuasive, there is an alternative point of view. Most Southern Negroes are characterized by low social status, relatively small incomes, and limited education received in inferior schools. These attributes are associated with low voter turnout among *all* populations. The low voting rates of Negroes in the South are, to perhaps a large extent, a result of these factors rather than a consequence of direct political or legal discrimination by the white community. Moreover, the low status, income, and education of Southern whites foster racial prejudice. Thus poverty and ignorance may have a double-barreled effect on Negro political participation by decreasing the Negroes' desire and ability to participate effectively while increasing white resistance to their doing so. Negro voting in the South is not, according to this line of argument, easily increased by political or legal means. A large, active, and effective Negro electorate in the South may have to await substantial social and economic change.

These sharply differing evaluations of the significance of Negro voting in the South hinge upon an empirical question which political scientists ought to be able to answer—the relative importance of socio-economic versus political factors in determining Negro voter turnout in the South. Can registration drives, legal pressures on the region's voter registrars, abolition of poll taxes, revision of literacy tests, and similar political and legal reforms have a significant impact on the amount of Negro voting in the former Confederate states? Or do the social and economic realities of the region make the goal of Negro parity at the ballot box difficult if not impossible to achieve for generations?

A short paper cannot hope to "answer" such large questions. However, an analysis of the relationships between county social, economic, and political characteristics and Negro voter registration rates may provide important clues to the unsolved mystery.

Registration rather than voting statistics are employed in this paper because registration figures are available by race whereas the number of Negroes actually voting is not known.[8] The use of registration rather than voting figures tends to exaggerate the size of the active Negro electorate since, for a number of reasons, some registered Negroes seldom if ever exercise their franchise. Moreover, voting lists in rural areas are often out of date, containing the names of many bona fide residents of New York, Detroit, and Los Angeles, to say nothing of local graveyards. In some states the payment of a poll tax is the nearest equivalent of voter registration and numerous exemptions from the tax make lists of poll-tax payers not strictly comparable to the enfranchised population. Finally, statewide statistics on voter registration (or poll-tax payment) by race are collected only in Arkansas, Florida, Georgia, Louisiana, South Carolina, and Virginia. In the remaining states the number of registered Negro voters must be obtained from estimates made by county registrars, newsmen, politicians, and the like. Nonetheless, when analyzed with caution, the sometimes crude data on Negro voter registration can throw considerable light on Negro voting in the South.

First, we shall consider the development and the distribution of Negro registration in detail. Then we shall examine the correlations between a battery of social and economic variables and Negro voter registration in order to determine the extent to which the former are predictive of the latter for the South as a whole. Then we shall examine the relationships between some political variables and Negro voter registration, controlling for the effects of social and economic structure. Finally, we shall estimate the relative importance of social and economic versus political variables and Negro voter registration and draw a few conclusions and implications from the analysis.

Negro Voter Registration: An Overview

Immediately after *Smith v. Allwright* declared the white primary unconstitutional in 1944, the number and proportion of Negro adults registered to vote in the Southern states increased with startling speed (Table 1). Before this historic decision, about 250,000 Negroes (5 per cent of the adult non-white population) were thought to be registered voters. Three years after the white-primary case, both the number and proportion of Negro registered voters had doubled. By 1952 about 20 per cent of the Negro adults were registered to vote. Since then, however, the rate of increase has been less impressive. In 1956 the Southern Regional Council estimated that about 25 per cent of the Negro adults were registered. Four years, two Civil Rights Acts, and innumerable local registration drives later, the proportion of Negro adults who were registered had risen to only 28 per cent, as compared with about 60 per cent for the adult whites in the region. Of course, the fact that Negroes held their own during this period is a significant accomplishment when one considers such factors as heavy out-migration by Negroes, increased racial tensions stemming from the school desegregation crisis, the adoption of new voter restrictions

Table 1.   Estimated Number and Percentage of Voting-Age Negroes Registered to Vote in Eleven Southern States, 1940–1960

Year	Estimated number of Negro registered voters	% of voting-age Negroes registered as voters
1940	250,000	5
1947	595,000	12
1952	1,008,614	20
1956	1,238,038	25
1958	1,266,488	25
1960	1,414,052	28

SOURCES: Derived from U. S. Census data on non-white population and Negro registration estimates in G. Myrdal, *An American Dilemma* (New York: Harper, 1944), p. 488; M. Price, *The Negro Voter in the South* (Atlanta: Southern Regional Council, 1957), p. 5; Southern Regional Council, "The Negro Voter in the South—1958," *Special Report* (mimeo.), p. 3; U. S. Commission on Civil Rights, *1959 Report* (1959 Commission on Civil Rights Report) (Washington, 1959), and U. S. Commission on Civil Rights, *Voting* (1961 Commission on Civil Rights Report) (Washington, 1961).

in some states, and the stricter application of old requirements in other areas.

The 250,000 Negroes estimated to be registered before *Smith v. Allwright* were unevenly distributed among the Southern states (Table 2). In Mississippi, Alabama, South Carolina, and Louisiana, less than 0.5 per cent of the adult Negroes were thought to be registered to vote in general elections and non-partisan contests in 1940. At the other end of the continuum, in Tennessee, 16 per cent were registered. Negro registration increased rapidly after the death of the white primary, but with conspicuous differences from state to state. The slowest increases occurred in the Deep South states of Mississippi and Alabama and in the three states—Texas, North Carolina, and Tennessee—which had the largest amount of Negro voting prior to *Smith v. Allwright.* In Arkansas and Florida, on the other hand, the proportion of Negroes registered has increased more than tenfold, from 3 per cent in 1940 to almost 40 per cent in 1960. The uneven response to *Smith v. Allwright* is evident. The "Solid South" is a fiction, then, but the source of these variations is not so obvious.

Table 3 shows the different registration rates, by county, *within* the eleven Southern states and for the region as a whole. Two general

Table 2. Estimated Percentage of Voting-Age Negroes Registered to Vote, 1940–1960, by States

State	Year					
	1940	*1947*	*1952*	*1956*	*1958*	*1960*
Mississippi	*	1	4	5	5	6
Alabama	*	1	5	11	15	14
South Carolina	*	13	20	27	15	***
Louisiana	*	2	25	31	26	31
Georgia	2	20	23	27	26	***
Arkansas	3	21	27	36	33	38
Florida	3	13	33	32	31	39
Virginia	5	11	16	19	21	23
Texas	9	17	31	37	39	30**
North Carolina	10	14	18	24	32	38
Tennessee	16	25	27	29	***	48**

* Less than 0.5%.
** Incomplete data; the data for Tennessee are especially unreliable.
*** No data.
Sources: Same as for Table 1.

conclusions can be drawn from this table. First, the range of Negro registration rates in the region is sizable. In most counties, the rate of Negro voter registration is very low—indeed the most common (modal) situation is for less than 5 per cent of the voting-age Negroes to be registered. In a significant minority of cases, however, the level of Negro registration compares favorably with that of white Southerners. Second, the Southern states differ markedly not only when compared with one another on a statewide basis, but also when compared in terms of their internal distributions of Negro registration.

The greatest diversity in Negro registration rates is found in Louisiana (standard deviation, 26.9), North Carolina (26.5), Georgia (25.6), and Tennessee (25.1). In Louisiana, for example, the bottom third of the parishes have less than 10 per cent of their voting-age Negro population registered, while the top third have over 50 per cent registered. The diversity in Negro participation rates is almost as great in Georgia. In North Carolina, over 50 per cent of the counties have from 10 to 30 per cent of their adult Negroes on their voting lists, but there is a wide spread in both directions from this norm. Tennessee has an equally broad range of Negro registration situations, although here there is a higher norm than in its neighbor to the east.

Table 3.   Rates of Negro Voter Registration in the Southern States, 1958

% of voting-age Negroes registered to vote	States (% of counties)											South-wide (% of cos.)
	Miss.	S.C.	Ala.	Va.	Ark.	Ga.	La.	N.C.	Tex.	Fla.	Tenn.	
0–9	89	30	38	10	3	25	32	5	2	9	4	21
10–19	6	50	26	31	24	16	11	30	7	7	0	18
20–29	4	20	11	31	28	19	12	23	24	18	4	19
30–39	1	0	6	15	33	10	5	7	28	18	2	13
40–49	0	0	3	8	7	11	9	5	21	19	11	10
50–59	0	0	9	1	3	5	16	9	12	15	4	7
60–69	0	0	3	2	2	3	5	6	2	5	18	4
70–79	0	0	2	0	0	3	5	5	1	5	11	2
80–89	0	0	2	0	0	5	3	3	1	3	17	3
90+	0	0	0	2	0	3	2	7	2	1	29	3
Total	100	100	100	100	100	100	100	100	100	100	100	100
No. of counties on which figures based	82	46	66	124	58	153	64	96	190	67	54	997
Unweighted mean of county percentages	3.4	12.5	20.5	24.1	27.6	30.4	31.2	36.0	36.8	39.1	72.3	30.4
Standard Deviation	6.6	7.8	20.3	15.6	11.2	25.6	26.9	26.5	15.6	21.0	25.1	24.3

SOURCES: U. S. Commission on Civil Rights, *1959 Report* (1959 Commission on Civil Rights Report) (Washington, 1959) and U. S. Commission on Civil Rights, *Voting* (1961 Commission on Civil Rights Report) (Washington, 1961).

Nothing like this diversity in Negro registration rates exists within Mississippi (standard deviation, 6.6), South Carolina (7.8), Arkansas (11.2), Virginia (15.6), or Texas (15.6). Whether this lack of variation results from social and economic homogeneity, the characteristics of the state political system, or some mixture of both is not now clear. It is evident, however, that striking differences are found from state to state in the patterns of Negro registration.

Social and Economic Correlates of Negro Registration

What accounts for the wide variation in Negro voter registration rates both between and within the Southern states? While no comprehensive explanation has been offered, previous studies of Southern politics and political participation suggest a number of possible influences. Drawing upon this literature, we collected data from the U.S. Census and other sources on thirty-one social, economic, and political characteristics of all Southern counties with populations containing more than 1 per cent Negroes.[9] We then computed simple correlations between each of these variables and the per cent of voting-age Negroes registered to vote in the same counties.[10] The coefficient of correlation (*r*) varies from 0 (no association between the independent and dependent variables) to 1.0 (one variable perfectly predicts the other). A positive correlation indicates that as one variable increases the other also increases; a negative correlation indicates an inverse relationship—as one variable increases, the other decreases. In order to control for the effects of one variable upon another, we also computed partial correlations, which tell us the association between each social, economic, and political variable and Negro registration controlling for every other variable, one at a time.

Omitting the details of this analysis, which of necessity are often complex and technical, we concentrate on the main conclusions drawn from this mass of data.

Twenty of our variables concern the social and economic characteristics of Southern counties. The simple correlations between each of these and the per cent of the voting-age Negroes registered to vote are presented in Table 4. What do they tell us about the relationships between social and economic structure and Negro registration?*

The size of the Negro middle class. The higher the educational level, occupation, or income of a person, the more likely he is actively to participate in politics: these are among the more strongly supported generalizations in contemporary research on political participation. Moreover, these three factors are probably a pretty good index of the size of the county's Negro middle class. It is widely believed by students of Negro politics that the low rate of voter registration by Southern Negroes is partly the result of a lack of leadership.[11] Only when there is a pool of educated and skilful leaders whose means of livelihood are not controlled by whites can sufficient leader-

---

* The correlation coefficients between these same variables and the registration rates of *whites* is radically different than for Negroes. For fifteen of the twenty social and economic factors considered, the direction of the association is *reversed* for the two races. Not one of the variables is substantially and consistently related to both Negro and white rates of registration. Thus the registration rates of the races are differently related to county social and economic structure as measured by our indexes.

Table 4. Correlations Between County Social and
Economic Characteristics and Percentage of Voting-
Age Negroes Registered to Vote, By County, in
Eleven Southern States

County characteristics	Simple correlations (r)	Partial correlations, controlling for percentage Negro, 1950
Percentage of non-white labor force in white-collar occupations	+.23	+.15
Non-white median school years completed	+.22	+.01
Non-white median income	+.19	+.02
Percentage of total church membership Roman Catholic	+.15	+.10
Percentage increase in population, 1940–1950	+.08	.00
Percentage of labor force in manufacturing	+.08	+.09
White median income	+.08	−.03
Percentage of population urban	+.07	−.02
Percentage point difference in percentage population Negro, 1900–1950	+.04	−.02
Percentage of total church membership Jewish	+.004	+.01
Difference in white–non-white median school years completed	−.02	−.02
Difference in white–non-white median income	−.02	−.05
Number of Negro colleges in county	−.05	+.01
Percentage of total church membership Baptist	−.10	−.07
Percentage of population belonging to a church	−.17	+.01
Percentage of labor force in agriculture	−.20	−.07
White median school years completed	−.26	−.15
Percentage of farms operated by tenants	−.32	−.13
Percentage of population Negro in 1900	−.41	−.01
Percentage of population Negro in 1950	−.46	—

NOTES: No tests of significance are reported in this paper since the correlations are based upon a complete enumeration rather than a sample.

The inaccuracy of some of the registration figures tends to reduce the magnitude of all correlations obtained by this analysis. The assumption of linearity underlying the computation of *r* also reduces the size of the correlations where the relationship between dependent and independent variables is, in fact, a curvilinear one. It is therefore safe to assume that the *r*'s reported in this article err in the conservative direction.

ship and political organization develop to ensure a relatively high rate of Negro registration in the South.

Our data support both lines of argument. The three largest positive correlations with Negro voter registration are per cent of the non-white labor force in white-collar occupations (+.23), the median number of school years completed by non-whites (+.22), and the median income of non-whites (+.19). While these are not very large correlations, these factors are more closely associated with high rates of Negro registration than any other social or economic variable tested. Furthermore, the correlations between per cent in white-collar jobs and Negro registration is not reduced very much when controls for other variables are introduced. (The partial correlation is +.15 when per cent Negro in 1950 is held constant, one of the highest partials obtained while controlling for the important factor of Negro concentration. See Table 4.)

Small increases in the size of the Negro middle class are associated with large increases in Negro voter registration, and these higher rates cannot be attributed simply to the registration of white-collar workers themselves. The average Southern county with 1 per cent of its non-white labor force in white-collar jobs has only 4 per cent of its voting-age Negroes registered to vote; at 5 per cent white-collar, 15 per cent of the Negroes are registered, and so on, each percentage point increase in white-collar occupations being associated with a 3 to 4 percentage point increase in voter registration. This trend continues until 12 per cent of the non-whites are in white-collar jobs and 42 per cent of the potential Negro electorate is registered. After this point, additional increases in the proportion of Negroes in white-collar jobs is no longer associated with increases in voter registration; indeed, voter registration actually declines somewhat as the size of the middle class grows beyond 12 per cent. Perhaps when the Negro middle class becomes this large, it tends to become more isolated from other Negroes, more preoccupied with the middle-class round of life, less identified with the black masses. A sharpening of class cleavages within the Negro community may lead to some loss of political effectiveness. Even so, this decline in effectiveness is not enough to wipe out the added increment from jobs to registered voters; it merely declines from three or four voters for every white-collar job to about two.

Despite this finding, it should be pointed out that the correlations between Negro registration and Negro education, income, and occupation are far smaller than many of the correlations between Negro registration and the characteristics of the white-dominated community. The level of Negro voter registration in Southern counties is far less a matter of the attributes of its Negro population than of the characteristics of its white population and of the total community.

The rest of our analysis, therefore, deals with community and white characteristics rather than with Negro attributes.

Negro concentration. In virtually every study of Negro politics in the South, the proportion of Negroes in the population emerges as the primary explanation of variations in rates of participation.[12] It is not surprising, therefore, that the per cent of Negroes in the county population has the largest simple correlation (−.46) with the county's rate of Negro registration. Moreover, when partial correlations are computed between these two variables, controlling for a large array of other social and economic factors, the association between Negro concentration and registration is not sizably affected. As the proportion of Negroes in the population goes up, the Negro registration rate goes down no matter what statistical controls are introduced.

The decline in Negro registration associated with increasing Negro concentration does not occur at a constant rate. Increases in the proportion Negro from 1 per cent to about 30 per cent are *not* accompanied by general and substantial declines in Negro registration rates. As the proportion Negro increases beyond 30 per cent, however, Negro registration begins to decline very sharply until it approaches zero at about 60 per cent Negro and over.

Given the fact that the proportion of Negroes in the South is now less than 30 per cent and is steadily declining, proponents of enlarged Negro electoral participation would appear to have reason for optimism. But Negro concentration *in 1900* is almost as highly (and negatively) correlated with Negro registration (−.41) as is Negro concentration a half-century later. This strong negative correlation is impressive evidence of the stability of Southern racial practices.

It would be a mistake, however, to conclude that decreases in Negro concentration in the South are not associated with increasing Negro voter registration. When one looks at the relationship between registration and decreases in Negro concentration, holding constant the proportion of the population Negro in 1900, several otherwise hidden relationships emerge. (1) In counties with heavy (over 70 per cent) Negro concentrations in 1900, decreases in the proportion Negro seem to make little difference—their Negro concentration was still relatively high in 1950 and the proportion of Negroes registered is negligible. (2) In counties with relatively few (less than 30 per cent) Negroes in 1900, rates of Negro registration tend to be high whether a decline in the proportion Negro was experienced or not. A decline in Negro concentration in these counties, however, is associated with a somewhat higher rate of Negro registration than in those counties where the division of the two races remained approximately the same between 1900 and 1950. (3) In counties with moderate (30 to 70 per cent) Negro concentrations in 1900, a decline in Negro concentration is clearly related to higher Negro voter registration. Moreover, the larger the decrease in the Negro population percentage, the higher the registration. The average county in this moderate group with a 30 percentage point decrease in Negro proportions has a voter registration rate double or triple that of the average county which did not experience significant change in the numerical balance between colored and white inhabitants.

The agrarian economy. It is widely believed that the South's relatively poor agricultural economy contributes to the low levels of Negro political participation in the region.[13] People living in poverty are unlikely candidates for active citizenship anywhere. The Negroes' economic dependence upon local whites in the rural South serves as a potent inhibition to those few who are not otherwise discouraged from voting. Rural whites are both more hostile to Negro voting and in a better position to do something about it than are their urban kin.

Our correlations tend to support this line of reasoning. The per cent of the county's labor force in agricultural employment and the per cent of the farms operated by tenants are negatively correlated with Negro voter registration to the extent of −.20 and −.32. But the region's Negro population is still primarily rural: the simple correlation between per cent in agriculture and per cent Negro is +.30; between farm tenancy and Negro concentration, +.49. Are these two characteristics of the counties still associated with low Negro voter registration when Negro concentration is controlled? The partial correlation between farm tenancy and Negro registration is −.13 when Negro concentration is controlled; between per cent in agriculture and registration it is reduced even further to −.07. There is, therefore, some tendency for Negro voter registration to decline as farm tenancy increases, a tendency that holds true even when differences in Negro concentration from one county to the next are taken into account. Nonetheless, it is a far less important factor than Negro concentration and probably is less important than the size of the Negro middle class as a factor explaining Negro participation and non-participation.

Urbanization and industrialization. If the South's agrarian economy tends to discourage Negro registration and voting, then industrialization and urbanization should facilitate them. The urban-industrial life is more rational, impersonal, and less tradition-bound; both Negroes and whites enjoy more wealth and education; the Negroes benefit from a concentration of potential leaders and politically relevant organizations in the cities. The urban ghetto may provide social reinforcement to individual motivations for political action. Many other equally plausible reasons might be suggested why urbanization and industrialization should foster Negro registration.[14] Our Southwide correlations, however, cast serious doubt upon the entire line of reasoning.

The simple correlations between the per cent of the county population living in urban areas and Negro registration is a mere +.07; between per cent of the labor force in manufacturing and Negro registration the correlation is +.08. When partial correlations are figured, controlling for Negro concentration, the association between urbanization and Negro registration completely disappears (the partial correlation is −.02), a fact which suggests that the initial +.07 simple correlation is largely the result of the low proportion of the urban population that is Negro. The partial correlation between per cent in manufacturing and Negro registration goes up slightly to +.09 when controls for Negro concentration are added. Partial correlations figured while controlling for many other social and economic variables do not significantly increase either correlation.

It seems plausible to assume that if urbanization does facilitate Negro voter registration, the effect should be particularly clear in the region's largest urban complexes. If the Negro registration rates of the seventy counties contained in the South's Standard Metropolitan Areas are compared with the distribution of registration rates for non-metropolitan counties, we note that the "metropolitan" counties are far more likely to have from 20 to 40 per cent of their voting-age Negroes registered than the other counties. Moreover, there is a tendency for counties in larger metropolitan areas to have slightly higher registration rates than counties in less populous SMSA's. However, the metropolitan counties have smaller concentrations of Negroes than the rural and small-town counties. Do these relationships hold true when comparisons are made between metropolitan and non-metropolitan counties with approximately the same proportion of Negroes within their boundaries? The answer is no; there is no meaningful difference in the rate of Negro registration between metropolitan and non-metropolitan counties when Negro concentration is controlled. Thus, neither "urbanism" nor "metropolitanism," as crudely defined by the census categories, appears to be independently related to high Negro voter registration.

The very low correlation between per cent of the labor force in manufacturing employment and Negro voter registration appears to be the result of other considerations. The word "manufacturing" conjures up images of the "New South"—with belching smokestacks, booming cities, and bulging payrolls. For the South as a whole this is a quite misleading picture. While manufacturing in 1950 was associated with somewhat higher income for both Negroes and whites (the correlation between per cent in manufacturing and median income was +.19 for both races), it was not primarily an urban phenomenon (the correlation between per cent in manufacturing and per cent urban was +.08), nor was it associated with rapid population growth (the correlation with population increase between 1940 and 1950 is +.05). Manufacturing was negatively correlated with school years completed by both whites and Negroes (−.14 and −.05, respectively). This kind of low-wage manufacturing centered in relatively stable small towns is not strongly associated with growing Negro voter registration.

While our analysis should not be taken as the last word on the subject, it does strongly suggest that urbanization and industrialization are vastly overrated as facilitators of Negro voter registration. Urbanization and industrialization may provide necessary conditions for high levels of Negro political participation but, by themselves, they are not sufficient to ensure them.

White educational levels. If, as we have argued, Negro registration rates in the South respond far more to the characteristics of the white community than to the attributes of the Negroes themselves, then it seems reasonable to expect Negro voter registration to be positively correlated with white educational levels. Numerous studies have shown that racial prejudice and discrimination tend to be related to low levels of formal education. Where the whites are relatively well educated, there should be less resistance to Negro political participation and, therefore, more Negro voter registration.

Just the opposite is the case for the South as a whole. The correlation between median school years completed by whites and Negro voter registration is −.26, one of the largest negative correlations obtained in this study. When white education increases, Negro voter registration decreases.

How can we account for this surprising finding? Since it is so unexpected, we might suppose that the relationship is merely a reflection of some third variable that happens to be related both to Negro registration and to white education. If so, it should disappear when other factors are held constant. But the correlation holds up surprisingly well when other variables are controlled. The most powerful third variable is, once again, Negro concentration in the population. With Negro concentration controlled, the partial correlation between white educational level and Negro registration is reduced to −.15. While this is a substantial reduction, the partial correlation remains one of the largest obtained after controlling for the extraordinarily important factor of Negro concentration. The strong correlation (+.30) between Negro concentration and median school years completed by whites is almost as unexpected as the correlation between Negro registration and white education. The whites in the black belt counties tend to be better educated—at least quantitatively—than other white Southerners. And, regardless of the percentage of Negroes in the population, proportionately fewer Negroes are registered in counties where whites have more education.

A second explanation for the negative relationship between white education and Negro registration might be that their relationship is curvilinear: at the lower educational levels, increases in white median school years might be associated with declining rates of Negro registration but, at higher educational levels, the relationship might be reversed. If this were the case, then the over-all negative relationship would be a result of the generally low educational levels of the South, concealing the fact that the few counties with high white educational levels had the highest rates of Negro registration. Close analysis suggests only a moderate tendency in this direction. As the number of school years completed by whites goes up through the primary and secondary grades, the proportion of voting-age Negroes registered declines. Eleven of the twenty-eight counties in which the average white adult has completed less than seven years of schooling are

French-Catholic parishes in Louisiana. Even when those parishes are eliminated, the trend remains the same. (The partial correlations between white school years and Negro registration, controlling for per cent Roman Catholic, is —.25.)

In the very few counties in which the average white adult has completed high school or received some higher education, the trend reverses and Negro registration rates begin to increase. But the reversal is not sharp enough for the counties with the highest white education to reach as great a Negro registration rate as the counties with the lowest white education. Southern counties with extremely high white educational levels have only about average rates of Negro registration.

Being unable to "explain away" our finding entirely, either by testing for hidden third variables or by examining the regularity of the association, we must conclude that white education is independently and negatively associated with Negro registration. Up to the highest levels, the more educated the whites the more actively and effectively they seem to enforce the traditional mores of the region against Negro participation in elections. The usual effect of an increase in average schooling for whites in the South as a whole appears to be to give the white people more of the skills that are needed effectively to express their anti-Negro sentiment. For example, the correlation between median school years completed by whites and the presence or absence of a White Citizens Council or similar organization is +.32. It seems to take considerably more formal education than the average Southern white receives to *alter* his attitude toward the Negro's place in Southern politics.

White religious affiliation. A variety of studies suggest that religion plays some role—either as an independent or intervening variable—in the racial politics of the South. Churchgoers have been found to be less tolerant than non-attenders,[15] and the South is a churchgoing region. Studies in Louisiana politics have found substantial political differences between the Catholic and Protestant sections of the state.[16] It seemed worthwhile, therefore, to examine the correlation between white religious affiliation and Negro registration rates for the South as a whole.

We find that Negro registration rates are depressed as church membership among whites increases (—.17), despite the fact that white membership in different churches has different functions—

Baptist membership is negatively related to Negro registration (−.10), while Catholic membership is positively related (+.15). On a South-wide basis, the percentage of Jews in the county's total church membership is not significantly associated with Negro registration (−.01).

Granted that Catholicism is positively related to Negro registration, we can partial out the influence of Catholicism in order to determine the correlation between non-Catholic white church membership and Negro registration. This partial correlation is, as expected, slightly greater (−.23) than the simple correlation. But the negative correlation between white church membership and Negro registration disappears when Negro concentration is held constant. (The partial correlation is +.01.) Apparently, then, white church membership per se is unimportant for Negro registration. White people in the kinds of counties with more Negroes and in predominantly Catholic counties are more often members of churches. In the former kinds of counties, fewer Negroes will vote regardless of non-Catholic church membership. Most non-Catholic churches presumably take on the racial attitudes of their localities; or, if they do not, they have little effect on those attitudes insofar as the attitudes are reflected in rates of Negro registration.

Per cent of Roman Catholics in the white church population is by far the most important of our religious attributes of Southern counties. And the relationship between Catholicism and Negro voter registration does not disappear when Negro concentration is controlled. (The partial correlation is +.10.) The presence of Roman Catholics, then, does seem to facilitate Negro voter registration on a Southwide basis. Roman Catholic churches presumably respond less directly to other county attributes than most Protestant churches; in any case, Catholicism is independently and positively related to Negro voter registration.

Multiple correlation of social and economic factors and Negro voter registration. So far, we have examined the association between selected social and economic factors and Negro registration one at a time. While controls for the impact of one social and economic factor on another have been introduced, we have not yet attempted to estimate the extent of the association between all the social and economic factors taken together and Negro registration.

In order to do this, we have figured the multiple correlation coeffi-

Table 5. Multiple Correlation of Twenty-One So-
cial and Economic Variables and Percentage of
Voting-Age Negroes Registered to Vote, By County,
Within Eleven Southern States

State	R	R²
Alabama	.79	.62
Arkansas	.65	.42
Florida	.76	.58
Georgia	.66	.44
Louisiana	.89	.79
Mississippi	.82	.67
North Carolina	.74	.55
South Carolina	.85	.72
Tennessee	.79	.62
Texas	.59	.35
Virginia	.55	.30
Southwide R	.53	.28
Mean, State R	.73	.53
Median, State R	.75	.56

cient between all twenty social and economic factors (plus the size of
the Standard Metropolitan Area, if any, within which the county is
contained—a qualitative variable for which simple correlations could
not be obtained) and Negro voter registration. The results of this
undertaking are presented in Table 5.

The Southwide correlation between these twenty-one social and
economic variables and county registration rates of Negroes is .53,
which explains about 28 per cent (R^2) of the variation in Negro
registration. When the same variables are used to compute the multiple correlation coefficient with Negro registration within each
Southern state, the R's go up considerably. Our twenty-one social
and economic variables are most successful in predicting Negro
registration rates in Louisiana ($R = .89$) and least successful in
Virginia ($R = .55$). For the states, then, our twenty-one social and
economic variables explain between 30 and 80 per cent of the vari-
ance in Negro registration.

Political Factors and Negro Registration

Having accounted for this much of the variation in Negro voter
registration rates, we might simply stop with the conclusion that

social and economic forces have a great deal to do with the problem. But our underlying hypothesis is to the contrary and must be directly tested. Do political and legal factors not only shape Negro registration rates but also exert an influence on Negro voter registration *independent* of social and economic structure?

The multiple regression equation obtained in the process of computing the multiple correlation reported in the preceding section can be used to predict the level of Negro registration every county in the South "ought" to have on the basis of its social and economic attributes. Some counties behave politically just as would be expected from these demographic features, but others have registration rates which are above or below the predicted level. By examining the pattern of these deviations above and below predicted registration—the deviations are called "residuals" in statistical parlance—we are able to control the effects of social structure on Negro registration, and thereby to ascertain whether political and legal factors have any independent association with Negro registration.

When the average (mean) percentage of voting-age Negroes registered to vote, by county, is compared to the average predicted rate of county registration for each state in the South, the variation and range are found to be quite high (Table 6). The average county in Mississippi should have, in terms of its social and economic characteristics, about 18 per cent of its Negroes registered to vote; a little

Table 6. Mean Percentage of Voting-Age Negroes Registered to Vote, By County, Compared to Mean Percentage Predicted By Twenty-One Demographic Variables, By County, Within Eleven Southern States, 1958

State	Actual mean percentage	Predicted mean percentage	Actual mean as percentage of predicted mean
Mississippi	3.4	17.7	19.2
South Carolina	12.5	19.4	64.4
Alabama	20.5	26.8	76.5
Virginia	24.1	34.3	70.3
Arkansas	27.6	32.3	85.4
Georgia	30.4	24.9	122.1
Louisiana	31.2	31.2	100.0
North Carolina	36.0	32.8	109.7
Texas	36.8	36.7	100.3
Florida	39.1	32.6	119.9
Tennessee	72.3	39.7	182.1

less than 4 per cent were actually registered in the average Mississippi county in 1958. The predicted registration for South Carolina is 19.4 per cent while the actual per cent registered is 12.5. The actual per cent registered is 70 per cent of the social and economic prediction for Virginia, 76.5 per cent for Alabama, and 85 per cent for Arkansas. Louisiana and Texas have just about the proportion of Negroes registered that one would expect on the basis of their social and economic characteristics; North Carolina and Florida, somewhat more than one would expect, and Georgia and Tennessee a great deal more. When it is understood that *these contrasts among the states exist when the states are viewed as if each had identical social and economic characteristics,* one can easily see that the state political systems must be an additional independent influence. Two socially and economically identical counties—one in Mississippi and the other in North Carolina—will have very different rates of registration. To say that this is the result of different state political systems is not to say very much. What aspects of state politics account for these differences? We have been able to isolate a few of the relevant factors.

Voting requirements. The Southern states have different requirements for registration and voting. Alabama, Arkansas, Mississippi, Texas, and Virginia have poll taxes. These vary in size from Mississippi's $2.00 to Arkansas' $1.00, and in Alabama, Mississippi, and Virginia they are cumulative. Alabama, Georgia, Louisiana, Mississippi, North Carolina, South Carolina, and Virginia require potential voters to pass a literacy test. Locally administered, these tests are highly responsive to local racial prejudices and vary greatly in form and difficulty within each state. Tennessee and Florida have neither a poll tax nor a literacy test.

To what extent are these differences in formal voting requirements related to differences in registration rates, controlling for social and economic structure? The answer is given in Table 7. The three states with both literacy tests and poll taxes have, on the average, actual registration rates which are 10.3 percentage points below the predicted value. The six states with either poll taxes or literacy tests have Negro registration rates which, on the average, are about what one would expect. The two states with neither poll taxes nor literacy tests have, on the average, about 19.2 percentage points more Negroes registered than one would expect on the basis

Table 7. State Voter Requirements and Negro
Voter Registration Residuals*

State voter requirements	Mean residual	Range of residuals
Poll Tax and Literacy Test	−10.3	−14.3 to − 6.3
Either Poll Tax or Literacy Test	− 0.5	− 6.9 to + 5.5
Neither	+19.2	+ 6.5 to +32.4

* The county residual is the percentage point difference between the actual per
cent of voting-age Negroes registered to vote in 1958 and the registration rate predicted
by twenty-one social and economic variables. The state residual is the mean of county
residuals. A positive residual indicates that the actual rate is larger than predicted;
a negative residual that the actual rate is less than predicted.

of their social and economic characteristics. If we were able to take
into account the way these requirements are variously administered
by different officials within each state, this factor would undoubtedly
prove to be more important than Table 7 indicates. Voter requirements, then, do seem to have an important effect on Negro registration over and above the admittedly large impact of social and economic structure.

The structure of competition. Another political reason why Negro
registration tends to be low in the South may be that state politics
often present no meaningful alternatives to the Negro voter.

Confronted with a choice between Senator Eastland and a chal-
lenger attempting to outdo that Mississippian at his own game, scores
of potential Negro voters may decide to go fishing rather than attempt to register. Given a choice between Frank Porter Graham and
Willis Smith, they will turn out in droves. The Southern Negro vote
is an "issue-oriented" vote and race is the only important issue. But
in some states in the South, all the candidates for public office are
unsatisfactory from the Negro's point of view. In other states, it is
usually possible for the Negro to distinguish one or more candidates
as favorably disposed to Negro interests—despite the candidate's best
efforts to avoid being labeled by whites as the "Negro candidate"—
and these candidates have some chance of winning.

Southern state political systems also vary in another way which
affects the nature of the choice confronting potential or actual Negro
votes. While the South is no longer solidly Democratic in presidential
elections, state and local politics are still largely confined to contests

between Democrats. The factional alignments within the Democratic party are rather different from state to state. In some states, two fairly clear-cut factions battle it out on even terms and these factions tend to persist from one year to the next. In others, Democratic factionalism is more fluid and unstructured. The number of candidates tends to be larger, and there is little relationship between one electoral contest and the next. Finally, there are states in which one Democratic faction clearly dominates the others—Virginia is the classic example.

The factional structure of a one-party system has an effect upon the turnout rate of *all* citizens, but perhaps particularly those of low social and economic status and limited intellectual skills. Obviously there is less reason to vote where one dominant faction runs the show; there is no realistic choice to be made. It is a good deal easier for a voter of limited political interest and skill to determine where his self-interest lies in a bifactional state than in a fluid multifactional one; there are fewer candidates to choose from and they tend to be identified with long-standing political cleavages. Candidates can be identified as belonging to the Long faction, or Talmadge faction, or Kerr Scott faction, and these labels have some policy meaning.

We expect, therefore, that both the type of Democratic factionalism and the extent to which candidates are identified with different racial views would be associated with different rates of voter registration among Negroes. When the eleven Southern states are classified according to these two criteria[17] and the mean state residuals of each type of state examined, we see that this is the case (Table 8). Two states, Virginia and South Carolina, have been dominated by one faction since 1948. In neither state are there discernible racial differences between factions. The mean residual for the two states is −8.5. Alabama and Mississippi have multifactional systems combined with white racial consensus: their mean residual is −10.3. Arkansas and Georgia have had bifactional Democratic politics, but it has been difficult for Negroes to ascertain significant differences on racial policy between them: their mean residual is +0.4. Louisiana, Florida, and Texas have had multifactional politics in recent years, but there have been discernible differences between the candidates from the Negro point of view. Taken together, they have a residual of +2.2. Finally, North Carolina and Tennessee have had both bifactional politics and significant differences on racial matters between the factions. The mean residual of these two states is +17.8.

Table 8.   The Structure of Competition in Southern States, 1948–1960, and Negro Voter Registration Residuals*

	Generally no major candidate favorable to Negroes	Generally one or more major candidates favorable to Negroes	Total $\bar{X}s$
One dominant faction	Virginia (−10.2) South Carolina (−6.9) $\bar{X} = -8.5$		−8.5
Two competitive factions	Arkansas (−4.7) Georgia (+5.5) $\bar{X} = +0.4$	Tennessee (+32.4) North Carolina (+3.2) $\bar{X} = +17.8$	+9.1
Multifactionalism	Alabama (−6.3) Mississippi (−14.3) $\bar{X} = -10.3$	Louisiana (0) Florida (+6.5) Texas (+0.1) $\bar{X} = +2.2$	−2.8
Total $\bar{X}s$	−6.5	+8.4	

* See note to Table 7 for explanation of the term "residual." The numbers in parentheses immediately after the names of the states are state residuals. All other numbers are means of state residuals.

Table 9.   Extent of Race Organization and Negro Voter Registration Residuals*

		Extent of white race organization		
		HIGH (46%+ of counties organized)	LOW (Less than 17% of counties organized)	
Extent of Negro race organization	HIGH (43%+ of counties organized)	South Carolina (−6.9) $\bar{X} = -6.9$	Virginia (−10.2) Florida (+6.5) North Carolina (+3.2) $\bar{X} = -.01$	$\bar{X} = -6.9$
	LOW (Less than 28% of counties organized)	Mississippi (−14.3) Louisiana (0) Alabama (−6.3) $\bar{X} = -7.0$	Arkansas (−4.7) Tennessee (+32.4) Texas (+0.1) Georgia (+5.5) $\bar{X} = +8.3$	$\bar{X} = +4.7$
		$\bar{X} = -1.8$	$\bar{X} = +1.8$	

* See note to Table 8.

Thus the structure of competition does seem to make a difference, and these differences are in the expected direction. The presence of observable differences in the racial views of candidates seems somewhat more important than the character of Democratic factionalism, but both factors are independently related to Negro registration rates.

The same tendency can be observed in elections for president. The states which the Republicans are most likely to carry are Tennessee, Florida, and Virginia. The first two states have large plus residuals, while Virginia has a negative residual.

Race organization. The South has seen a plethora of new racial organizations created in the wake of *Smith v. Allwright* and *Brown v. Board of Education.* The Southern Christian Leadership Conference (SCLC), the Student Non-Violent Coordinating Committee (SNCC), and the Congress on Racial Equality (CORE) have entered the lists along with the NAACP and the National Urban League as champions of the Negro cause. The White Citizens Councils, sometimes called by other names in different states and communities, have sprung to the defense of white supremacy. Are these politico-racial organizations associated with higher or lower rates of Negro voter registration when the effects of social and economic characteristics are controlled?

We have made strenuous efforts to ascertain, through correspondence and a search of newspaper files, the location of all chapters of all Negro and white race organizations in the South. While our list is no doubt incomplete, we believe that it is probably accurate enough to classify the states according to the degree to which they contain Negro and white race organizations. The four Deep South states with the largest Negro concentrations have been far more heavily organized by the White Citizens Councils than the others. North Carolina, Virginia, South Carolina, and Florida have been better organized by the Negroes. When we examine Table 9, we see that the Negro registration residuals are definitely lower in states with numerous white race organizations than elsewhere. The opposite, however, apparently is not the case: the states with a large proportion of their counties organized by Negro racial groups actually have a lower mean residual (−6.9) than those in which they are not so strong (+4.7). But this is largely because Negro organization is weak in four states where White Citizens Councils are also weak; the largest Negro

Table 10. Southern Cities With Known Negro Voters' Leagues and Negro Voter Registration Residuals*

City, State	Residual for central county (A)	Mean state residual (B)	Adjusted residual (A − B)
Houston, Texas	+19.6	+ 0.1	+19.5
New Orleans, La.	−16.0	0	−16.0
Atlanta, Ga.	+ 1.4	+ 5.5	− 4.1
Dallas, Texas	+ 5.7	+ 0.1	+ 5.6
Birmingham, Ala.	−12.4	− 6.3	− 6.1
Memphis, Tenn.	+43.0	+32.4	+10.6
Tampa, Fla.	+ 0.4	+ 6.5	− 6.1
Richmond, Va.	− 4.8	−10.2	+ 5.4
Jacksonville, Fla.	+13.0	+ 6.5	+ 6.5
Chattanooga, Tenn.	+43.7	+32.4	+11.3
Mobile, Ala.	− 8.3	− 6.3	− 2.0
Charlotte, N. C.	+ 5.0	+ 3.2	+ 2.8
Greensboro, N. C.	− 1.3	+ 3.2	− 4.5
Winston-Salem, N. C.	+23.3	+ 3.2	+20.1
Columbia, S. C.	+ 1.2	− 6.9	+ 8.1
Jackson, Miss.	+ 2.8	−14.3	+17.1
Montgomery, Ala.	− 3.8	− 6.3	+ 2.5
Durham, N. C.	+25.5	+ 3.2	+22.3

MEAN = + 5.2

* See note to Table 7 for explanation of term "residual."

voter registration residuals are found in the four states (Arkansas, Georgia, Tennessee, and Texas) where neither kind of racial organization is very prevalent.

We should not jump to the conclusion that Negro racial organizations do more harm than good, so far as voter registration is concerned. Our data are proximate at best, no evidence is available as to how actively these Negro organizations have pursued registration drives, and we are dealing with statewide tendencies while Negro political organizations are generally far more potent at the local level.

Therefore, we shall examine the Negro registration residuals for Southern cities where we know that local Negro voters' leagues are relatively active. Table 10 presents the Negro registration residuals for the counties containing these cities. If the mean state residual is subtracted from this figure, it can be seen that the existence of a Negro voters' league does tend to be associated with relatively high Negro registration rates—on the average about 5 percentage points above the statewide norm, even after one controls for social and economic factors.

Political versus Socio-economic Variables and Negro Registration

We have seen that both social and economic factors *and* political and legal factors are associated with Negro voter registration in the eleven Southern states. Which type of factor is more important in shaping Negro registration rates?

Earlier we reported that the multiple correlation between all twenty-one social and economic variables and Negro registration was .53, which means that they explain about 28 per cent of the variation in Negro registration. If we add ten political variables* to the equation and calculate the multiple correlation between all thirty-one variables—socio-economic *plus* political—we obtain a multiple correlation of .70, which explains about 50 per cent (R^2) of the variation in Negro registration figures. The addition of the political variables to the Southwide equation almost doubles the explanatory power of the analysis. Insofar as statistical analysis can answer such a broad and complex question, it would appear that political variables are of about equal importance to socio-economic ones.

Implications

One must approach the drawing of policy implications from our analysis with extreme caution. Our data are crude, our units of analysis (counties and states) are large. The dividing line between what is "social" or "economic" and what is "political" is arbitrary (at worst) or merely conventional (at best). Correlations are not "causes" but merely associations; attributing causal relationships to variables which are correlated with one another is to engage in the drawing of inferences, which sometimes are spectacularly wrong. Nonetheless, we believe that tentative implications can be drawn from our analysis.

* These ten political variables are states; per cent of presidential vote States' Rights, 1948; per cent of presidential vote Republican in 1928, 1948, and 1956; per cent of vote Republican in race for statewide office in year of highest Republican vote, 1950–1959; presence or absence of Negro race organization in county; presence or absence of white race organization in county; presence or absence of desegregated school in county; number of incidents of racial violence in county.

First of all, the low rate of Negro voter registration in the South is heavily conditioned by the social and economic realities of the region. Most Negroes in the South are poor, undereducated, and not strongly motivated toward political activity. Political "apathy" is the *normal* reaction to such conditions, regardless of one's skin color. Add to this the hostility of most of the white South to effective Negro political participation, the frequent lack of adequate Negro leadership, Negro economic dependence on whites, and so on, and it is rather surprising that 28 per cent of the adult Negroes are already registered voters.

Moreover, one cannot help being impressed by the massive indications of stability in the situation—the extremely high negative correlation between per cent Negro *in 1900* and Negro registration in 1958, the apparent failure of urbanization and, to a lesser extent, industrialization to provide favorable conditions for Negro political participation, the *negative* correlation between white educational levels and Negro registration, and so forth. Clearly, political and legal reformers should not expect miracles. Talk of Southern Negroes being "able to elect at least five Negroes to Congress in the next few years"[18] seems wildly to underestimate the social and economic barriers to Negro political participation.

At the same time, Negro registration has increased rapidly since 1944 and changes in the Southern society and economy suggest that this trend will continue. Every one of the social and economic variables that we have found to be positively associated with Negro registration is on the increase—some have doubled in twenty years and all but one have increased by at least 50 per cent. Only one of the variables associated with low Negro registration—white educational levels—is also increasing and there is reason to believe that a good many Southern counties will soon reach the stage where this factor may tend to facilitate rather than hinder Negro political participation. If white school years completed continues to increase at the 1950–1960 rate, the average Southern white will have completed 11.4 years of schooling by 1970 and many Southern counties will have average white school years completed of 12 years or more. Assuming that the present relationship between years of formal education received by whites and Negro registration continues to hold true, the effect of white education on Negro registration may gradually reverse. All the other factors negatively correlated with Negro registration (except, of course, per cent Negro in 1900) are declining rapidly. Thus the South's social and economic structure may be, at one and the same time, the reformer's major short-run obstacle and his long-run cause for hope.

Moreover, our analysis suggests that substantial changes in the level of Negro voter registration can be attained by political and legal means. It is not necessary to await the arrival of basic social and economic changes before attempting, *with reasonable expectations of moderate success,* to enfranchise more Southern Negroes. The abolition of the poll tax and modification of literacy requirements to assure fair treatment of Negroes might enhance the Southwide rate of Negro registration by 10 or more percentage points. Encouraging the candidacy of politicians—both Negro and white—who are favorable to the Negro cause should bring out many more Negro votes, even when they have little chance of success. Finally, heightened organizational efforts by Negroes would increase Negro registration levels over what they would otherwise be. All of these reforms would have a positive effect on Negro registration rates without waiting for massive social and economic change.

Whether the Southern Negroes, more effectively armed with the vote than ever before, will be able to vote themselves the social, economic, and political equality they desire as quickly as they demand is another matter. It is at this stage, perhaps, that the "do-it-yourself-via-the-vote" theory of civil rights reform will face its severest test. To put the same point in different words: our analysis leads us to expect moderate increases in Negro registration and voting on the basis of social and economic change alone. If some or all of the political reforms mentioned above are realized, the rate of growth in the Negro vote may prove to be fairly substantial. Whether these votes then will be translated into a political power capable of altering Southern racial practices fast enough to satisfy the heightening expectations of the Southern Negro remains yet to be demonstrated.

1. This account has been reconstructed from the *New York Times,* Sept. 9, 1961, Sept. 21, 1961, Oct. 24, 1961; *Tylertown Times* (Miss.), Aug. 31, 1961, Sept. 7, 1961, Sept. 14, 1961, Sept. 21, 1961; the *Baltimore Afro-American,* Sept. 16, 1961; the *Pittsburgh Courier,* Sept. 30, 1961, Nov. 4, 1961, Nov. 25, 1961.

2. *New York Times,* Aug. 27, 1961; *Atlanta Journal,* Sept. 6, 1961, Sept. 7, 1961, Sept. 12, 1961; *Atlanta Daily World,* Sept. 14, 1961, Sept. 23, 1961; *Baltimore Afro-American,* Oct. 7, 1961, Oct. 14, 1961.

3. *New York Times,* Jan. 7, 1962. See also H. L. Moon, *Balance of Power: The Negro Vote* (Garden City, N. Y.: Doubleday and Company, 1949), p. 7 and *passim.*

4. *New York Times,* Jan. 7, 1962; Louis E. Lomax, "The Kennedys Move in on Dixie," *Harper's Magazine,* CCXXIV (May, 1962), 27–33.

5. *Baltimore Afro-American*, Oct. 7, 1961; *New York Times*, Aug. 17, 1961, July 2, 1962.

6. The 1962 Atlanta, Georgia, national convention of the NAACP had the "Battle of the Ballots" as its theme. *Raleigh News and Observer* (N. C.), June 24, 1962.

7. *New York Times*, March 29, 1962; Lomax, *op. cit.*

8. The registration figures used in this analysis are from U. S. Commission on Civil Rights, *1959 Report* (1959 Commission on Civil Rights Report) (Washington, 1959) and U. S. Commission on Civil Rights, *Voting* (1961 Commission on Civil Rights Report) (Washington, 1961).

9. A complete list of sources used to obtain county frequencies for the independent variables used in this analysis would be too lengthy to reproduce here. A mimeographed list will be supplied by the authors upon request.

There are 1,136 counties in the eleven Southern states (counting Virginia's independent cities as counties), of which 1,105 had populations containing at least 1 per cent Negroes in 1950. Negro registration figures are available on 997 of these counties.

We are indebted to the following research assistants for their help in collecting these data: Lawton Bennett, Lewis Bowman, Barbara Bright, Jack Fleer, Donald Freeman, Douglas Gatlin, and Richard Sutton. All told, the collection and coding of these data took one man-year of work.

10. The 1958 registration data, contained in U. S. Commission on Civil Rights, *1959 Report*, are more complete and were used for all states except Tennessee. The 1960 figures, printed in U. S. Commission on Civil Rights, *Voting* (1961), are the only ones available for Tennessee.

All computations were made on the University of North Carolina's UNIVAC 1105 high-speed digital computer.

11. For an extreme statement of this position see E. Franklin Frazier, *Black Bourgeoisie: The Rise of a New Middle Class in the United States* (Glencoe: The Free Press, 1957). Less exaggerated statements to the same effect may be found in the literature cited in note 12, below.

12. V. O. Key, Jr., *Southern Politics* (New York: Alfred A. Knopf, 1949) gives little attention to Negro voting since it was of little importance at the time he wrote (see, however, p. 518). His stress upon the overriding importance of Negro concentration for all aspects of Southern politics makes his study highly relevant, nonetheless. Other works specifically on Negro voting which stress the importance of Negro concentration include James F. Barnes, "Negro Voting in Mississippi," unpublished M.A. thesis, University of Mississippi, Oxford, 1955; Angus Campbell *et al.*, *The American Voter* (New York: Wiley, 1960); Margaret Price, *The Negro and the Ballot in the South* (Atlanta: Southern Regional Council, 1959); H. D. Price, *The Negro and Southern Politics: A Chapter of Florida History* (New York: New York University Press, 1957); Donald S. Strong, "The Future of the Negro Voter in the South," *Journal of Negro Education*, XXVI (Summer, 1957), 400–407; U. S. Commission on Civil Rights, *Voting* (1961).

13. See especially, U. S. Commission on Civil Rights, *Voting* (1961), pp. 143–199.

14. On Negro voting in urban settings, see Charles D. Farris, "Effects of Negro Voting Upon the Politics of a Southern City: An Intensive Study, 1946–48," unpublished Ph.D. dissertation, University of Chicago, Chicago, 1953; Cleo Roberts, "Some Correlates of Registration and Voting Among Negroes in the 1953 Municipal Election of Atlanta," unpublished M.A. thesis, Atlanta University, Atlanta, 1954; Harry J. Walker, "Changes in Race Accommodation in a Southern Community," unpublished Ph.D. dissertation, University of Chicago, Chicago, 1945; Bradbury Seasholes, "Negro Political Participation in Two North Carolina Cities," unpublished Ph.D. dissertation, University of North Carolina, Chapel Hill, 1962.

15. Samuel A. Stouffer, *Communism, Conformity, and Civil Liberties* (Garden City, N. Y.: Doubleday and Company, 1955).

16. Allan P. Sindler, *Huey Long's Louisiana: State Politics, 1920–1952* (Baltimore: The Johns Hopkins Press, 1956); V. O. Key, Jr., *Southern Politics*, chap. viii; John H. Fenton and Kenneth N. Vines, "Negro Registration in Louisiana," *American Political Science Review*, LI (Sept., 1957), 704–713.

17. The classification of states along the one dominant faction, two competitive factions, multifactionalism dimension follows the procedure employed by Key, *Southern Politics*, pp. 17–18. The median per cent of the total vote polled jointly by the two highest candidates for governor in the first Democratic primary, 1950–1960, was:

Virginia	100.0	Texas	69.3
Tennessee	95.8	Florida	60.5
Georgia	94.7	Louisiana	58.6
South Carolina	89.8	Alabama	58.1
Arkansas	81.5	Mississippi	44.4
North Carolina	77.9		

Unopposed candidates and contests in Arkansas and Texas involving incumbents were omitted. All those ranking below North Carolina were classified as multifactional states.

In order to distinguish between competitive and non-competitive factional arrangements, the median per cent of the total vote polled by the leading candidate for governor in the first Democratic primary, 1950–1960, was obtained. The percentages are:

Virginia	65.8	Texas	39.9
South Carolina	61.3	Florida	34.7
Tennessee	55.6	Alabama	34.1
Georgia	49.3	Louisiana	33.1
Arkansas	47.7	Mississippi	28.1
North Carolina	46.7		

Factional strife seems unusually uneven in Virginia and South Carolina and they were classified as "One Dominant Faction" states.

The classification of states according to whether or not one or more major candidates were favorable to the Negro cause was based on our subjective evaluation of newspaper accounts.

18. Martin Luther King in a speech at the 1962 NAACP annual convention. *New York Times*, July 6, 1962.

Robert J. Steamer

Southern Disaffection with the
National Democratic Party

A decade ago that sage old British academician D. W. Brogan, who had been observing the American political scene with tea and sympathy for many years, declared that the South was not even a one-party system. It was, he said, "a one-label system for whose possession individuals, families, oligarchies, pressure-groups, great interest blocs fight,"[1] and he suggested that in order to get one real party it is probably necessary to have two. It would be folly for anyone to suggest that the South has today, ten years later, one real party or even a weak two-party system, but some of the uncontrollable currents of history are sweeping the South into the mainstream of American politics and it is safe to predict that in a generation at most, the South, for better or for worse, will be politically nationalized.

Already in presidential elections the term "solid South" is an anachronism. The eleven states of the Old Confederacy have not been unanimously Democratic since the 1944 election. In the past three presidential elections Louisiana has cast its electoral votes for Republican candidates once, Texas has done so twice, and Virginia, Tennessee, and Florida have not gone Democratic since 1948. The most Republican of the Southern states are the "rim" states or the outer South, but this does not obscure the fact that in 1960 the Kennedy forces could not count on holding even the "inner" or Deep South states. South Carolina was touch and go all the way with Mr. Kennedy ultimately capturing slightly better than 51 per cent of the state's popular vote, and in Mississippi the Nixon vote was some 13,000 greater than the Eisenhower vote in 1956. National Democrats might write off the Southern defections to Mr. Eisenhower in 1952 and 1956 as a temporary enchantment with a glamorous war hero, but the Nixon gains in Dixie made it clear that the roots of Southern Republicanism were embedded in something more substantial than charisma, a father image, and military generalship. As encouraging as these trends in presidential elections may be to the

Republican party, they are a misleading index of over-all Republican strength in the South. Only one of the region's twenty-two senators, John Tower of Texas, bears the Republican label and a mere 11 seats of the 106 alloted to the states of the South in the House of Representatives are held (as of 1963) by Republicans. In the Southern state legislatures Republicans are equally scarce. At last count there were only 61 of them among the 1,794 members and they were concentrated, in the manner of the Southern Republican seats in the national House, in Florida, Tennessee, Virginia, and North Carolina.[2] These four states have nine of the eleven Southern Republican congressmen; Texas has the remaining two.

If large numbers of Southern voters desert the Democratic party every four years and cast their lot with the Republican presidential candidate, there is yet another group of voters in the South who receive no Southern comfort from the national Democrats but who cannot abide the Grand Old Party. Their only recourse has been to vote for electors pledged to a third-party candidate or for unpledged electors who stand for white supremacy and states' rights. Whether these choices of action will be made available to the voters of a state depends mostly on the decisions of professional politicians who must organize and secure the financing of such movements of defection. Almost intuitively, if not through a familiarity with American political history, the professional politicians are aware of the handicaps to even short-term third-party movements. It is difficult enough to shake the voter out of his ingrained habits in strong two-party states, but the task is even more formidable in one-party states. The South's commitment to one-partyism has been durable and intense. It systematically fights its political battles in the primary, the state central committee, or the convention—all within the Democratic party, of course. In the full-fledged third-party movement of 1948, the Dixiecrats managed to capture the electoral vote of four states, but then only by listing their candidates as the "official candidates" of the state Democratic party. Although the Dixiecrats received 1,169,312 votes, over half of these were cast in the four states which had captured the Democratic party label. In the remaining Southern states this third party could not even draw enough votes away from Truman to throw the state to the Republicans. Third-party rumblings have since remained on the periphery of presidential elections in the South, although in 1960 unpledged electors were victorious in half of Alabama and all of Mississippi, and they ultimately voted for Senator Harry F.

Byrd of Virginia. Louisiana was the only other Southern state which gave a substantial vote to a slate of unpledged electors (169,572), but they ran a poor third to those pledged to Mr. Kennedy (407,339) and to Mr. Nixon (230,980).

Since four presidential elections in a row are three too many to be classed as temporary aberrations, it may be concluded that the Democratic party can no longer count on a solid bloc of electoral votes from the eleven states of the Old Confederacy. Now the question presses: What has caused the disaffection of Southern voters from the party of their traditional allegiance? Although so complex in detail as to defy perfect analysis, four main factors, in most respects beyond control of the individual voter, have brought the South to the threshold of a new political era. They are: (1) the technological revolution and its resultant urbanization; (2) the restless migration of a rootless society manifested in its Southern form by the Negro going out and the Yankee coming in; (3) the changing political and economic status of the Negro, North and South, and (4) the emergence of a national Democratic party as a party of the ideological left committed to national regulation of the economy, the welfare state, civil rights, and now even "medicare." All four factors are interrelated, and an analysis of one necessarily involves allusions to the others. We shall attempt, nevertheless, to look selectively at each in turn.

Industrial growth with all its concomitant goods and evils came late to the Southland, but its coming has brought about what is probably the greatest revolution in the South's history. Industry has moved to the South from all over the nation, initially seeking cheap labor, tax benefits, and non-unionized workmen, latterly to be near expanding markets and raw materials for production. The economic revolution of the past thirty years has transformed the region from one of poverty and deprivation to one of material adequacy for most, abundance for many, and downright luxury for some. Going hand in hand with rapid industrialization is a great farm revolution, including diversification of crops and a changeover from cotton to cattle. Between 1940 and 1958 the South cut cotton production by ten million acres and thereby propelled five million farm laborers into cities in and outside of the region. The effect on politics aside, our aesthetic natures are hardly ennobled as smokestacks replace live oaks and magnolias. Or in the words of Jonathan Daniels, it is "probably not all gain that the drag race has taken the place of the coon hunt."[3]

The startling effects of the new technology and consequent urbanization on voting behavior in the Southern states have been carefully documented elsewhere.[4] All point to an increasing presidential Republicanism, and the pattern is the same whether in Atlanta, Birmingham, Nashville, Baton Rouge, or Durham. These cities are populated by a large and growing respectable middle class plus, in varying proportions, wealthy oilmen and cattlemen, bankers, stockbrokers, and managers of the Southern industrial complex. In the composite this group thinks and acts like its counterpart in New York or Denver; it would feel more secure with Mr. Nixon in the White House than it does with Mr. Kennedy, and it would prefer Senator Goldwater to either one. On its fringe are those who send their contributions secretly to Robert Welch, leader of the John Birch extremists.

In part, at least, this new Southern urbanite is the "organization man" who appears wherever industry appears. This executive servant of the managerial society is, as Francis Pickens Miller has pointed out, something new to the South.[5] In the past the usual white Southerner had been no man's servant. He had been rooted in his community and family life and in his Southern heritage, but now he is a rootless nomad whose primary, and sometimes only, loyalty is to business. His political ideas are substantively barren, because at bottom, materialism is his life philosophy, but translating his thoughts into political maxims we get free enterprise, fiscal sanity, balanced budgets, states' rights, and racial integrity. These are, of course, not so much political principles as political clichés, but they have a broad and popular following.

Then there is the top echelon of management, the representatives of national corporations, sometimes natives but more often Yankee importees who exploit regional concepts that favor their economic predilections. These corporate executives identify their branch plants with states' rights, a commitment that manifests itself in support of right-to-work laws and opposition to increased minimum wages and to any increase in funds for the public sector. Such ideas in recent years have found more fertile soil for growth in the Republican party, although the leaders of the local Democrats are more often than not willing allies for these industrial merchants of the new prosperity. It would not be accurate to characterize the political behavior of this urban white-collar class as homogeneous, for its views range the conservative political spectrum from moderate stand-patism to the reactionary right. The more responsible elements of this managerial class support candidates of the type characterized by Professors William

Havard and Loren Beth as the "urban business conservative," a politician representative of a new trend in Southern statewide politics who "comes much closer to a manifestation of the economic and social spirit of the times than does the stump-speaking cracker-barrel wit of the piney flats."[6] Since it is no longer unfashionable in Southern middle-class society to admit that one is a Republican—the Junior Chambers of Commerce are filled with men who are Republican in outlook and who are proud to be so acknowledged—those who think Republican will move into the Republican party. They are now in the transitional state in which they assume the appellations Democrats for Eisenhower or Democrats for Nixon, but the final break is not far off. Unquestionably the organization men, often bright, articulate, and able, can reorganize the Republicans in the South into an effective instrument for serving the legitimate interests of the business community.

Set over against the challenge of the new conservatives is a conglomeration of disparate elements which, if they can co-operate in a good old-fashioned American political coalition, may produce in the South a Democratic party which more closely parallels its national parent. Comprising this group are, first, the academic and intellectual liberals who have a strong tradition in the South going back to Thomas Jefferson. Although relatively small in numbers, they have a long-run impact on the region through the newspapers, the literary media, particularly the novel, and through the university and college communities. Second are the have-nots in labor and agriculture, both black and white, whose racial distinctions have been exploited locally but who see their economic interests better satisfied by the Democrats nationally than by the Republicans. Making up the final component of the coalition are the traditional Democrats, mostly agrarians, who have followed the Democratic party blindly in the past. Many of them voted Dixiecratic in 1948, some might jump to a third party given proper persuasion, and some might eventually move to the Republicans even though the name is still anathema to them. Given the advent of two real parties, this latter group might wield the balance of power in any given election depending upon the candidates and upon the exploitable emotional issues.

We have already alluded to the migration of our rootless society in terms of Yankee emigrés who are Republican by nature, by family, or by pocketbook and who are disturbing the old pattern of Southern presidential voting. Another and in some ways more crucial aspect of this phenomenon is the out-migration of the Negro. The mid-twentieth-century Negro has for a couple of decades manifested a restless displeasure over the place assigned to him by the white man, and he has been getting out of it, making what to many of us seems the unwise choice of a city slum over the country shack. It is, nevertheless, a free choice in a nation which emphasizes the individual's right to make such decisions, wise or unwise. In 1910 only 7 per cent of American Negroes lived in cities. The number tripled to 21 per cent in 1940 and doubled again to 41 per cent in 1960. The Negro population in Dallas and Houston went up 2½ times from 1940 to 1960 and in Atlanta and Miami it rose 75 per cent. In 1910, 80 per cent of the Negro population lived in the eleven states of the Old Confederacy, but between 1940 and 1960 the Negro population outside the South increased 125 per cent while increasing by 9 per cent in the South, thus placing almost half of the American Negroes in the North, East, and West. More important, 65 per cent of the non-Southern Negroes are concentrated in twelve of America's largest cities (New York, Los Angeles, Chicago, Philadelphia, San Francisco, Detroit, Boston, Pittsburgh, St. Louis, Washington, Cleveland, and Baltimore). If Negroes cast their votes predominantly for one party in national elections, and indications are that they do, they hold a neat balance of power in presidential elections. This simple political arithmetic underlies Jonathan Daniels' observation that "Negroes have greater political power in America than the Southern politicians."[7]

Industrialization and urbanization of the South have tended to make the region more like the North, and the emigration of the Negro to other parts of the country has tended to make the non-Southern part of the nation more like the South. Because of the differences in the intellectual and political environment, overt manifestations of Negrophobia are socially less acceptable outside the South and votes are sought without regard to race by both parties within the framework of healthy bi-party systems. The non-Southern regions deserve no special credit for this greater racial tolerance. Historical accident has until very recently kept the size of the Negro population well below the point of being a threat to the social, political, and economic supremacy of the Northern white community. Now with the radical change in the Negro-white population ratio over most of the country it is too late, even if many non-Southern whites desired it, to alter political and social patterns in the direction of racial repression. Domestic considerations aside, America's world position does not merely prohibit us from acting officially on the race question as South Africa acts officially, but requires that we demonstrate persistent progress in the other direction in our handling of the race problem. This broadened and deepened support of the Negroes' cause is one of the most crucial elements in American politics today.

Mark Hanna once boasted that he carried the Negro vote around in his vest pocket, and in his day it would have fitted comfortably into a vest pocket, possibly reaching 75,000 at the outside. What is significant about Hanna's remark is that the Negro vote, what there was of it, was solidly Republican and the party leadership did little about increasing it. In fact, since roughly the end of the Taft Administration, the Republican party has largely ignored the Negro whereas the Democrats, at least on the local level in cities like Chicago and New York, have actively sought his vote. Prior to 1936 no Negro delegate had attended a Democratic national convention but Southern Negroes were in attendance in the Republic convention of 1868 and in all subsequent Republican conventions thereafter, with Northern Negroes in evidence after 1916. It was not until 1936 that the Negro vote began to take on meaningful proportions both North and South, and it was in that year that the majority of American Negroes voted for a Democrat for president for the first time. The motivation for the intensified Negro interest and for the switch to the Democrats was primarily economic, for it was the party of Franklin Roosevelt that literally had put bread and butter on the table. One prominent Negro leader, Bishop R. R. Wright, Jr., of the African Methodist Episcopal Church, urged Negroes to support Mr. Roosevelt because the Republicans, in his view, had been responsible for breadlines, loss of life savings, inability of the people to pay for their children's schooling, the difficulty of obtaining homes to live in, the difficulty in borrowing money from banks, and the virtual Negro reenslavement through conditions of peonage of tenant farmers and sharecroppers.[8] True or false, such charges persuaded the Negro, like a majority of his fellow Americans, to turn to the only available alternative to Republicanism—FDR and the New Deal. Roosevelt, the WPA, public housing, and the welfare state reversed overnight several generations of a solid racial allegiance.

From the latter New Deal period to 1956 about 80 per cent of the Negro vote went to Democratic candidates in presidential elections, but in part, after 1944, it was for the added reason that the national Democrats, and President Truman in particular, became identified with the new educated, urban Negro's struggle to attain political and legal equality. Mr. Truman carried Illinois by 33,612 votes, California by 17,865, and Ohio by 7,107. A switch of less than 15 per cent of the Negro vote in these states would have put Mr. Dewey in the White House. Unswerving loyalty of the Negro voter to the Democrats was manifested in 1952 when the 80 per cent figure held, although it was not enough to deliver the large Eastern states to Mr. Stevenson. In 1956 Negro support for the Democrats dropped to 64 per cent. Many Negroes were doubtless infected with the Eisenhower charm but more likely the desegregation decisions rendered by a Supreme Court led by a Republican Chief Justice, appointed by a Republican President, had some effect on Negro voting behavior. In 1960 Mr. Kennedy's ability to recapture about 10 per cent of the white and nearly all of the Negro defectors of 1956 was not without importance in his narrow victory. Mr. Eisenhower's reluctance to support desegregation actively in day-to-day actions and his official neutrality on the merits of the Supreme Court's decision in *Brown v. Board of Education* were not compensated by his later precipitate action in the Little Rock crisis. On the other hand, the firm, relentless pressure of the Kennedy Administration for desegregation in education, transportation, and employment might well raise the Negro support for the Democratic party above the 80 per cent level in 1964.

A glance at Congress reveals a similar pattern. Prior to the 1962 elections only one (Los Angeles) of the ninety-six congressional districts with a Negro population of 20 per cent or more sent a Republican to Congress. In 1962 a Negro Democrat, A. F. Hawkins, defeated that Republican in the newly created 21st district in the Los Angeles area, and thereby became the first member of his race elected to the Congress from west of the Mississippi. Each of the other four Negroes in the House of Representatives is also a Democrat, and each has been elected from a district which contains a majority or near-majority of Negro residents: Dawson of Illinois, Powell of New York, Nix of Pennsylvania, and Diggs of Michigan. The Southern Negro, in terms of his impact on all but presidential elections, is as yet a relatively weak political force. Less than a third of eligible Negroes are registered voters compared to two-thirds of the eligible whites. Negroes make up 19 per cent of the total voting-age population in the Southern states but comprise only 10.6 per cent of all registered voters of the region. This situation is bound to change radically, possibly by as early as 1964. The Kennedy Administration is working on it through active enforcement of the Civil Rights Acts of 1957 and 1960, and the Voter Education Project of the Southern Regional Council will result in increased Negro registration, virtually all Democratic.

Politics does make strange bedfellows, but the marriage of the Southern white supremacist and the Negro is one of the strangest of all time. In fact, it is outright political miscegenation and no white Southern racist can long tolerate that! Yet it is not so easy for Americans to vote for racial discrimination under a Constitution which frowns upon it and under a two-party system in which both parties are dedicated to its abolition. Although the wholesale transfer of allegiance by the Negroes from the Republicans to the Democrats is a powerful factor in alienating the Southern whites from the party of their forebears, whether they will play musical chairs with the Negro and go over to the Republicans depends to some extent on the Republican national leadership. In high Republican councils there is no unanimity on the question of writing off the Negro vote. The liberal wing would continue to court it, whereas the conservatives tend to regard it as a hopeless cause and prefer to concentrate on the unhappy Southern whites. What will happen finally is anyone's guess, but it seems unlikely, given the political climate of present-day America, that the Republican leadership will willingly choose to create the political monstrosity that would result from surgically removing what Jasper Shannon calls the rump of the jackass and grafting it on to the back of the jumbo. If the Republicans cannot afford to ignore the Negro vote, then the South will have to eschew white supremacy or create a permanent third party in its own image.

The final reason for the disenchantment of the South with the Democratic party is its rise as the party of the ideological left. From 1865 until 1936, and particularly after the compromise of 1896 when the Southern Bourbons agreed to give up the quest for national power in return for a non-intervention pledge in local politics by the Republicans, the Democratic party did what the Southern political leadership wanted it to do. It gave the upper-class white minority of the South control of the state governments, a control maintained in part by systematic disfranchisement of Negroes and poor whites. Protection from interference by the national government was sustained through the seniority system in Congress and by the two-thirds rule at the Democratic national conventions, devices which gave the South a virtual veto over hostile presidential candidates and unacceptable public policies.

The origin of the 1948 revolt and subsequent disaffection of Southern Democrats with the national party goes back to the Roosevelt era. When the South acquiesced in the abolition of the two-thirds rule in the presidential nominating convention of 1936, it relinquished its first bastion of defense. When the Roosevelt coalition began to crack under the stresses and strains of the political wars, the South no longer held a trump card at the Democratic national nominating conventions. Had it not been for World War II the Southern move away from the Democratic party might have begun earlier. Much of the New Deal had worried the Southern political leadership from the beginning, particularly the economic gains of labor and its growing political influence within the Democratic party. Minimum wages, maximum hours, and guarantees of collective bargaining were especially menacing to the South's favorable situation in the labor market, and even the Supreme Court, after the 1937 crisis, no longer held that such legislative innovations were out of line with the Constitution. Another irritant to Southern sensibilities was the attempt by President Roosevelt to purge the party of all save 100 per cent New Dealers, particularly those of the Southern variety. Thus, a combination of personal and ideological discontent produced an estrangement, one result of which was the emergence of the conservative congressional alliance of Republicans and Southern Democrats.

Although Southern dissatisfaction with the party has manifested itself in every Democratic national convention for the past twenty years, the diminishing influence of the Southern delegations and the growing power of the liberals in national party councils has been particularly marked since 1948.[9] During the twilight of the Roosevelt years Southern political leadership read correctly the vote-getting power of the old master, and had they bolted the party in any of the years of his candidacy, he would have won without them. In 1948 conditions, men, and events combined to present the ideal moment for an open break. It appeared that the Democrats would lose the presidency, and in this event the South would lose its strategic chairmanships as well as presidential patronage. But all analyses of the Dixiecrat movement indicate that the ideological position of the Democratic party as the home of labor, liberals, and welfare staters was as much the goad to rebellion as the fear of civil rights legislation.

At the 1952 Democratic convention the party's sectional liberals attempted to bar from the party's deliberations those Dixiecrats who would not take an oath to support the convention's nominees. The ensuing bitterness eventually produced a compromise that remained in effect through the 1956 and 1960 conventions. It was clear after each of these conventions, however, that control of the presidential nominating machinery would remain with the moderate left, and the faction that controls the convention most assuredly dominates the presidential wing of the party. Now that Mr. Kennedy's political architecture has emerged, the ideological line from the New Frontier to the Fair Deal to the New Deal seems straighter than ever.

The generalizations we have made so far are applicable to the South as a regional entity, but it would be a gross inaccuracy to assume that the factors we have emphasized affect all Southern states to the same degree or even in precisely the same way. In some respects the individual states of the South differ in their politics from each other as much as they differ collectively from the rest of the nation. However, our general comprehension of past events and what they portend for the future might be enhanced by focusing our attention on the politics of a single Southern state.

Among the states of the Deep South, Louisiana, as a result of the rise of Huey Long, developed the most successful substitute for genuine two-party politics. Like the other Southern states, Louisiana became the victim of the Bourbon-Republican post-Reconstruction arrangement whereby the Negro was politically neutralized in return for Southern acquiescence in Republican leadership nationally. Until recent years the offhand characterization of Huey Long as a home-grown political dictator and just another Southern demagogue obscured the fact that Long and Longism represented the triumph of the previously submerged but incipiently rebellious forces whose earlier attempts to overthrow the domination of the planter-merchant alliance aborted in either Populist or Socialist movements. The politics which emerged from the rise of Longism roughly paralleled the conservative-liberal dichotomy that characterizes American politics elsewhere, although it was not and cannot be precisely identical to a healthy two-party system. Professor Allan P. Sindler gave Louisiana politics its most descriptive and accurate label when he called the system "cohesive bifactionalism."[10]

From 1928, when Huey Long was elected governor, to the time of the death of his brother, Earl, in 1960, Louisiana politics was practiced in terms of the Long and anti-Long factions. Although the system now appears to be in a state of disintegration, it might yet be pulled together by any one of several surviving Longs in politics, the most prominent being Huey's son, Russell, United States Senator from Louisiana since 1948. The fact that the old Louisiana system needs the name Long to perpetuate it suggests its greatest weakness— the personalized rather than institutionalized nature of the arrangement. But in spite of this, Louisiana voters in the past have had some choice between liberal and conservative policies and candidates and they exercised it by alternating between the Longs and the anti-Longs. The Long faction's support was derived in large measure from the economic have-nots: the farmers of the non-plantation rural areas, the industrial workers, a small group of liberal intellectuals and the Negro, who, after the Supreme Court decision in the White Primary Case (*Smith v. Allwright*) in 1944, began to register in far greater numbers. The Longs, from Huey to Earl, had never been race baiters and more important, actually included the Negro in their public policy plans. One of the results of Longism was the establishment of one of the most pervasive welfare states in the Union, and the Negro has been a prominent recipient of the state's largesse. Although the anti-Long faction in Louisiana has been less clear-cut either in its leadership or in its policies, its prime movers are the old business-planter element, now joined by the industrial managers and the oil and cattle interests.

In terms of presidential politics these factions provide the key to an adequate understanding of the past thirty years as well as to any prognosis of new political alignments. The Long faction was fairly consistent in maintaining either an overt or *sub rosa* alliance with the national Democratic party, in part because of its agreement with the latter's ideology. It is important to recall that Huey Long was a strong supporter of FDR's nomination in 1932, that his own program as Governor of Louisiana from 1928 to 1930 anticipated the New Deal to some extent, and that Long's break with the Roosevelt Administration was motivated in part by the conviction that the President was moving too slowly and on too narrow a front. It was Earl Long in 1948 who, after dissociating himself from the state Democratic committee's endorsement of the Dixiecratic candidates, was instrumental in obtaining legislation that enabled the Truman-Barkley ticket to appear on the ballot as an independent slate. In 1952 and 1956 the organized support which Louisiana produced for Stevenson, meager though it was, was led by Earl and Russell Long.

On the other hand the conservative anti-Long coalition has found itself in an untenable position vis-à-vis the national Democratic party. Their dislike of Longist liberalism is equaled only by their distaste for the leftist policies of the national Democrats with whom they have attempted to negotiate a *modus operandi* every four years in order to retain a monopoly of Democratic party power in the state. However, two former governors, Sam Jones (1940–1944) and Robert Kennon (1952–1956) of the anti-Long faction, personify the struggle to identify the state Democratic party with a conservatism that better fits the Republican mold. Jones has been consistently associated with the states' rights movements that erupted into the Dixiecratic revolt of 1948 and into presidential Republicanism in the last three national elections. Kennon has been an open supporter of Republican presidential candidates, leading the Democrats for Eisenhower and Democrats for Nixon movements in 1952, 1956, and 1960.

The trend in voting behavior in Louisiana over the years portrays graphically the impact of social and economic change on the state. In the four presidential elections from 1932 to 1944 the Democratic party successively retained high, but after 1936, diminishing majorities, capturing respectively 88.6, 88.8, 85.9, and 80.6 per cent of the total vote cast. Only twelve times in these four elections and only twice prior to 1944 did any parish (county) deliver less than 70 per cent of its total vote to the Democrats. Although the Democratic vote in 1944 diminished only 5.3 percentage points over 1940, the central and northwest area of the state, which encompasses slightly over a third of the state's parishes, increased its Republicanism by 15 to 27 percentage points. This area, incidentally, is over two-thirds Protestant and has a Negro population incidence varying from a minimum of one-third to a high of 71 per cent in one parish. But as the state began to increase its over-all Republican allegiance, the southeastern part of the state, known as the "Sugar Bowl," which historically had displayed a mild Republican sentiment stemming from the days when the sugar growers had been sympathetic to high-tariff protectionism, increased its Democratic support by 5 percentage points. Over two-thirds of the population of this area professed the Roman Catholic faith and the Negro population was under 30 per cent.

In the 1944 Democratic national convention the Louisiana delegation revealed a sympathy for Senator Harry F. Byrd and ultimately five electors resigned rather than pledge themselves to the Roosevelt-Truman ticket. In the 1948 convention the Louisiana delegation did not walk out, but the sentiment of the conservative, and as it turned out, controlling forces in the state party organization was expressed by state senator Horace Wilkinson, who said, in a seconding speech for the nomination of Richard Russell of Georgia:

This convention has seen fit to trample ruthlessly underfoot all of the time-honored political philosophy of the bulwark of democracy, the Southern states of our nation. A line has been drawn. . . . there is only one side on which a self respecting Southerner can stand.[11]

On September 10, 1948 by a unanimous vote the state central committee of the Louisiana Democratic party placed the names of Thurmond and Wright on the ballot directly beneath the "rooster" symbol of the party. With the exception of three New Orleans assessors not a single elected public official in Louisiana would support the national Democratic party ticket. Even Governor Long, who attempted to hold some liaison with the national party by insisting that Truman and Barkley at least appear on the Louisiana ballot, would not endorse them. The closest the Governor dared come to an approval of the national nominees was a negative statement that he was not behind Thurmond and Wright. Such a situation painfully emphasizes the decentralized nature of the American party system in which a state party organization may go so far as to prevent the national party from securing a place for its candidates on the official ballot.

The States' Rights ticket received 49.1 per cent of the four-party vote compared to 32.7 per cent for Truman, 17.5 per cent for Dewey, and .7 per cent for the Wallace Progressives. Of twenty-three parishes with a Negro population of over 40 per cent, twenty were carried by the Dixiecrats. Equally significant is the fact that the area which had been moving gradually toward presidential Republicanism delivered a majority of its votes to the States' Rights ticket. In fact, in some of these northern parishes the Democrats ran third. The greatest Democratic support came from the six most urban parishes, which may suggest that racial appeals were somewhat less important to the urban than to the rural voter. Actually, the Truman-Barkley ticket benefited from undercover support by organized labor and the urban Negro vote, which, although small in total numbers, was strongly pro-Truman.

Anyone who reads the election statistics in this political debacle can see the glaring importance of the race question and the subtleties of economic conservatism that determined the result. What is never shown by statistics, however, is the nature and intensity of the campaign, which is an important but mathematically unmeasurable factor. We do know that campaigning is always taken seriously by candidates and parties in a competitive situation and that it does have *some* effect on the outcome of elections. In 1948 Louisiana's professionals campaigned for the Dixiecrats. Not a single politician of any stature nor any political action group raised a finger in behalf of the national party, and a state which had been giving a party 80 per cent of its support dropped it to 33 per cent. In 1952 and 1956 it appeared that the old 80 per cent Democratic majorities had been broken permanently as Eisenhower mustered 46.9 per cent, and four years later carried the state with a comfortable 53.3 per cent majority. In 1956 the same area of the state that had begun to move away from the Democrats in 1944 gave Eisenhower a whopping 65 per cent of the Republican votes cast in the state. Campaigning in behalf of the Democratic ticket in 1952 and 1956 was again sparse and unenthusiastic.

The 1960 presidential election in Louisiana is not susceptible of any simple analysis since (1) a state with an unusually high percentage of Catholics had a chance to support a Catholic nominee for the first time in over thirty years; (2) the Long forces were in a state of disarray after the demise of Earl, and Jimmie Davis, the new governor and leader of the state's Democrats, had displayed a coolness bordering on hostility to the Kennedy-Johnson ticket; and (3) the election was held at the height of the school desegregation crisis in New Orleans, during which the legislature meeting in its first of five special sessions had created the distinct impression that the real enemy of the people of Louisiana was the government of the United States. The Democratic party of the state was badly split between the party regulars, primarily south-Louisiana French Catholics, and those, predominantly from the northern part of the state, who would prefer a third-party movement. Paradoxically, the embittered leader of the anti-national party forces was Leander H. Perez, a south Louisiana Catholic, whose status in the Church has since been altered by an excommunication decree.

After meeting for three-and-one-half hours the state central committee by a vote of fifty-one to forty-nine decided to place the Kennedy-Johnson ticket under the traditional party "rooster." The vote was an accurate barometer of the election results. In twenty-five of the twenty-six parishes whose delegates backed the national ticket in the meeting of the central committee heavy majorities were delivered to Mr. Kennedy, and all but two of these parishes contain a Catholic majority. In only three of the twenty-five do Negroes constitute as much as a third of the population. The thirty-eight parish committeemen who supported an unpledged slate of electors were for the most part from northern Protestant parishes with a high Negro-white population ratio, including those parishes that had been moving away from the national Democrats since 1944. These dissidents ultimately placed a slate of unpledged electors on the ballot, based solely on a segregationist appeal, thus giving the voters three choices. For the first time in several presidential elections the Democrats conducted a well-organized campaign shrewdly concentrated in the southern parishes, the area of the party's greatest potential strength. The States' Rights group, in contrast, had no effective party organization, no candidates, and no issues save one. All influential Democrats in the state spoke vigorously on behalf of the national ticket, including Senators Long and Ellender and some members of the Louisiana delegation in the House of Representatives. It became clear early in the campaign that Kennedy had a chance to win, and were he to do so, it was also clear that disloyal Southern Democrats might have serious trouble in maintaining their seats of power in Congress. The Democrats received 50.4 per cent of the state's vote, the Republicans 28.6 per cent, and the States' Rights group 21.0 per cent.

While the north-south, Catholic-Protestant schism with its racial overtones stands out boldly in the political ecology of the state, the lasting base of Republicanism is located in the urban-industrial parishes, which now cast approximately half the state's total vote in a presidential election. Since 1948 the seven most urban-industrial parishes have contributed consistently about 58 per cent of the total statewide Republican vote while declining in their Democratic support.[12] Furthermore, this urban Republican vote tends to be concentrated in the wealthier parts of cities, coming from the business community, lawyers, physicians, and industrial managers, many of whom are migrants from the North. At the same time the working-class and Negro precincts have been giving the Democrats strong support. In an analysis of the voting demography of Baton Rouge, a not atypical urban center in Louisiana, it was found that Kennedy carried the predominantly working-class precincts and all of the Negro precincts regardless of economic status, whereas the higher-income precincts of business, lawyer, physician, and managerial groups showed the highest percentage of Republican votes.

The trend to presidential Republicanism in the cities, and toward a healthy two-partyism has been remarkable and has been marred only by the intrusion of the states' rights movements. With the States' Rights party in the picture in 1948 Louisiana voters increased their Republican support over 1944 by slightly more than 1 percentage point, but the Republican vote in 1952, when the States' Rights movement was dormant, swelled by some 18 percentage points over 1948.[13] In 1960 the combined Republican–States' Rights vote was 49.6 per cent of the total, almost identical to the Republican vote of 49.2 per cent in 1952. This is not to suggest that a slate of electors pledged to support a States' Rights candidate draws votes only from potential Republicans. Unquestionably a Southern party based on local traditions in opposition to both major parties will diminish the vote of both. However, the Louisiana voter—and the Southern voter generally—is often more sophisticated than he appears to the rest of the nation, and today as in 1948, many who vote for a States' Rights platform are aware that they are espousing a strong economic conservatism as well as white supremacy. If a States' Rights political movement lacks the impetus of an immediate racial crisis, as was the case in 1956, large numbers of States' Righters will support the Republicans nationally. Of the seventeen Louisiana parishes that gave the States' Rights ticket a plurality or a majority in 1960, nine had gone Republican in 1956. Of the remaining eight, five had turned in Democratic pluralities, but only three had chosen States' Rights electors in preference to the major parties.

The large, concentrated Catholic population in Louisiana gives the state a political uniqueness in comparison to the other Southern states, particularly when a candidate for office is of the Catholic faith. Four predominantly Catholic parishes in south Louisiana—Cameron, Evangeline, St. James, and St. John the Baptist—delivered majorities of better than 80 per cent to Mr. Kennedy, but in 1956 the latter two parishes were in the Eisenhower column, and Cameron and Evangeline gave the Democrats majorities of 58.2 per cent and 60.5 per cent, respectively. Even more startling is the case of St. Mary parish, also predominantly Catholic, whose voters shifted from 61.4 per cent for Mr. Eisenhower in 1956 to 61.6 per cent for Mr. Kennedy in 1960. Clearly Mr. Kennedy's Catholicism was the strongest motivation for large numbers of southern Louisiana voters, a factor that makes it difficult to predict future political alignments in the state. The fact that the race issue is not of primary importance in the southern parishes is not solely the result of the relatively low incidence of Negroes in the population. The strong moral stand of the Roman Catholic church against segregation combined with the tolerance of the Franco-Americans of the area produce a public attitude somewhat different from that in north Louisiana, where the status of the Negro is the dominant political issue. Moreover, south Louisiana (defined by political observers generally as the thirty-five parishes encompassed by the 1st, 2nd, 3rd, 6th, and 7th Congressional Districts) contains 73.4 per cent of the state's registered vote. If three-fourths of the state's electorate exhibits a reasonable solidarity in a given election, which it did in 1960, it can determine which party will receive the state's ten electoral votes. It seems reasonable to assume, however, that since the barrier of Catholicism in the presidency has been surmounted, the saliency of the religious issue to Louisianans will not again be as high as it was in the Kennedy-Nixon contest. The race issue, by contrast, may be expected to continue to cut deeply across the political culture of the state.

For many years Louisiana voters tended, as a result of Longist political leadership, to vote along class lines, and bread-and-butter issues to a great extent pre-empted the questions of race and religion. After the Supreme Court ruled against segregation in the public schools in 1954 it became increasingly difficult for Earl Long to continue to ignore the segregation issue. In terms of sheer political expediency, white supremacy agitation had taken a new lease on life. When Governor Long suffered a mental breakdown in 1959, a collapse precipitated in part by his truly heroic effort in behalf of Negro rights against the onslaught of the state's extreme racists, the disruption of old voter loyalties was inevitable. In the first Democratic gubernatorial primary held in December, 1959, there were five serious contenders among the eleven hopefuls, including two former governors. The latter were James A. Noe, who headed the traditional Long ticket, which included Earl as the candidate for lieutenant governor, and Jimmie H. Davis, the ultimate victor, whose views on public policy were then and are now virtually unknown. The other three serious entrants were Mayor of New Orleans de Lesseps S. Morrison, an urbane and wealthy Catholic; Willie Rainach, a primitive white supremacist; and State Comptroller William Dodd, a veteran Long supporter and ideologically close to the national Democrats. Since none of the candidates received the required majority, a runoff primary was held in January, 1960, in which Davis, polling 54.1 per cent of the vote cast, handily defeated Morrison.

Apparent in both primaries was a pattern of north versus south Louisiana, a novel alignment wholly unlike that underlying the Long versus anti-Long politics of the past. The multiplicity of variables in a wide-open primary race of this kind makes it hazardous to compare the gubernatorial to the presidential race, even though both contests were held in the same year. While Mayor Morrison and Mr. Kennedy appealed to the same elements among the voters and ran well in roughly the same geographic areas of the state, Kennedy won narrowly (50.4 per cent), whereas Morrison lost. It is worth noting that because of a larger turnout in the gubernatorial primary, Morrison actually polled more votes (414,110) than Kennedy (407,515). Contributing to the Davis victory were (1) Earl Long's support of Davis in the runoff because, as speculation had it, Earl wanted to run for governor in 1964 and he feared four years as governor would enable Morrison to build a formidable state–New Orleans machine; (2) the extreme segregationists managed to pin the label "nigger lover" on Morrison, who probably received the lion's share of the Negro vote in the first primary; and (3) the urban "business class" vote, which would have supported a Republican under a two-party system. The votes of the white working class are an unknown quantity but indications are that Kennedy was the recipient of a greater share of its support than Morrison, since the latter's vote totals in parishes where wage earners are numerous were less than Kennedy's. Of the seven most urban parishes Morrison carried only two: Orleans and Lafayette, the latter located in the heart of French Catholic territory. The voting statistics of the governor's race and the presidential election in 1960 thus suggest that in the former, with the breakdown of the Long–anti-Long bifactional system, the race question cut through all other political issues, whereas in the latter, unusually large numbers of Roman Catholics placed the issue of a man in the White House of their own faith above all other considerations.

Although there is a great deal of evidence to support the contention that Louisiana is moving toward presidential two-partyism, the anemia of the Republic party organization has been a major barrier to development of two-partyism in state politics. Prior to 1952 state Republicanism was organized to the extent of 1 parish committee out of a potential 64 and a state central committee consisting of 40 members out of a possible 101. By 1957 there were 22 parish committees in existence and a central committee with a full membership. Since 1952 eight congressional district committees have been organized as well as several municipal committees, although only Shreveport has a truly active Republican organization.[14] But gradually the Republicans are beginning to compete for office in state and local elections and the vitality of Republicanism and a two-party system in Louisiana may, in the final analysis, hinge on the party's ability to organize solidly down to the precinct level. The 1962 congressional elections provide mixed evidence on the point. The willingness of Republicans to contest the general election in two congressional districts and in the re-election bid of Senator Russell Long indicates that the party is at least beginning to build at the grass roots. On the other hand, since each of the Democratic candidates secured better than two-thirds of the vote cast, it may still be concluded that Republican organizational strength remains feeble in contests other than presidential elections.

On July 21, 1962, the Louisiana Republican Platform Committee issued a report that presumably reflects a consensus of Republican thinking in the state. It is instructive to note some quotations taken at random from the nineteen-page document. Louisiana's Republicans are "unalterably opposed to the United Nations as it is presently constituted" and "unequivocally oppose the admission of Communist China to the United Nations."[15] They "oppose any and all attempts to repeal the Connally amendment"[16] and characterize the American foreign aid program as one "of profligate waste, extravagance, graft and corruption," particularly when used to aid "Communist Yugoslavia, and Poland and 'Neutralist' India."[17] They urge that "positive action must be taken to destroy the Communist government of Cuba,"[18] stating that "the primary goal of United States foreign policy must be absolute victory over Communism."[19] They "deplore the tendency of some administrative officials to minimize the Communist menace within the United States" and "support the work of the House Committee on Un-American Activities and the Senate Internal Security Sub-Committee."[20] In the domestic arena the party is "against regimentation and higher taxes and restriction of socialistic Medicare with forced participation under Social Security."[21] It believes that unemployment can be eliminated only by private industry, which "freed of punitive tax rates and with assurance of reasonable profits can more effectively create new and permanent employment opportunity."[22] They urge that "all encroachments by the federal government in the field of so-called 'civil rights' in the past several years because of the United States Supreme Court's decisions should be abolished by constitutional amendment,"[23] and they advocate "the continuance of our Southern tradition of the separation of the races."[24]

Such is the tone of Louisiana Republicanism. Its basic conservatism, the race issue aside, fits well with the right wing of the national Republican party. If the local Democrats were to accept their inheritance as the rightful heirs to the liberal Longist tradition, the voters of Louisiana would be given honest alternatives on public questions on the state as well as on the national level. The liberal and conservative viewpoints are as tenaciously held in the South as they are in other parts of the nation, but a combination of historical accident and stubborn, shortsighted, selfish leadership have for too long virtually closed off the political channels for protest, dissent, and social change.

What then is the future of Southern politics in terms of national elections? For many years the American political parties, in Clinton Rossiter's words, "have acted as skillful brokers of sectional interests,"[25] and the Democratic party in particular has held together two powerful sections in recent years seemingly by divine intervention. Prior to 1932 the Democratic party in the South remained the great bulwark of white supremacy, and nationally it deviated little in its economic predilections, excepting the protectionist tariff, from the Republican concept of laissez faire. But in the 1940's it was evident that the Democratic party was no longer performing its function in the South. A world in which the national Democrats indulged in high taxes, unbalanced budgets, and Robin Hood welfare programs, and in which Negroes were voting in larger numbers, not only in the North but in Southern Democratic primaries, was a world turned bottom side up. The party of the New Deal—the party of the urban masses, union labor, Negroes, civil rights, and social reform—became an affront to the conservative, rural-minded, and rural-dominated, if no longer rural, South. The old system was bound to crack up, and so it has, but a new institutionalized system has yet to emerge.

After a generation of backing and filling the South faces three reasonably clear-cut choices. First, it may pursue its present course of retaining local control by attempting to hold a monopoly of political power in each state, pressuring the Democratic national convention every four years with threats of walk-outs, unpledged delegates, and half-hearted third-partyism. This policy of drift is the easiest since it invokes no long-range strategy but merely a year-to-year tactical reaction to national developments. It fits the older political grooves and satisfies those Southerners who argue that it makes little sense to embrace an alien national party whose conservatism is uncertain and whose local organization is weak when they already have a conservative Democratic faction that runs the state regardless of which party wins nationally. Also, why should conservatives in the South vote against men like Harry Byrd, James Eastland, and Richard Russell?

The great weakness in this position is that the pressures of a dynamic society make it more and more difficult for the South to roll with the punch. Many voters in the South prefer the Republican party and still others would be happier with a liberalized Democratic party. Such groups have emerged as a result of the multifarious social changes discussed earlier. Furthermore, the Southern white Democrat has been frustrated by what seems to him to be a hostile federal judiciary. In 1944 he lost control of the Negro vote when the Supreme Court invalidated the white primary. Ten years later he was forced to relinquish his authority over the Negro's social status when the Court ordered desegregation of the schools. And in 1962 he appears to be losing his power to perpetuate a rural-conservative gerrymander as a result of the Court's turnabout on the question of apportionment of state legislatures.

What about the deliberate creation of a third party to serve the South's sectional interests? Theoretically, the South might use its 128 electoral votes as a power lever in order to throw presidential elections into the House of Representatives in which the South could demand concessions from a candidate before casting its vote. This would be a hard road for at least two major reasons. First, assuming a healthy two-party system elsewhere in the nation, the Southern contingent in Congress would be forced into hard bargaining on every vital issue with both the Republican and Democratic parties since they could no longer occupy committee chairmanships and the power attached thereto. Second, they would face rebellion in their own back yards as a liberal, Negro-white coalition increased in numbers, as it surely will. Only if it were possible to extend a party of white supremacy, and this is what it would be, to the suburban areas over the nation which are attempting to maintain the Negro in a residentially segregated ghetto, would such a party have a reasonable chance of permanency. Either of these alternatives assumes a much greater political solidarity among the Southern states than actually exists.

The final possibility is intensified presidential Republicanism and eventually an institutionalized two-party system at the state levels. Such an outcome presupposes several critical assumptions.[26] The first assumption is that the Democratic party nationally will remain primarily the home of the liberals. A second assumption is that Democratic parties in the Southern states will contain a liberal faction that can occasionally win and hold power, driving conservatives in meaningful numbers into Republican organizations. The final assumptions are that the national Republicans will actively work at the task of constructing and guiding local organizations and that the national Democrats will politically punish defectors when and where they can—in the nominating conventions, in Congress, and through presidential patronage. The obstacles to a bona fide Southern Republicanism and a healthy bi-party system are many, varied, and tough. But even the best of politicians can shape events only within the framework of the moving currents of history, and the lesser lights among them merely ride the crest of the waves. It is possible that the Southern electorate will move its political leadership in the direction of two parties that approximate the aspirations and beliefs of their national parents. Once the civil rights issue settles down, even the Negro, as he moves up the economic ladder, will divide his vote more evenly between the two parties.

Almost a generation ago Wilbur J. Cash suggested the South might be compared to a "tree with many age rings, with its limbs and trunk bent and twisted by all the winds of the years, but with its tap root in the Old South."[27] Today it appears that the "tree" is moribund and that the old autocracies of class and race are destined for oblivion as the social, economic, and political currents converge upon the Southland and press with unyielding intensity. We cannot perceive the new system perfectly, but the outlines are clearly marked, and they include equality of economic opportunity, equality of political condition, and reasonably clear choices between candidates and public policies. In short, the South is becoming a democracy.

Bibliographical Note

In addition to the references cited in the footnotes the following books provided the indispensable background material: V. O. Key, Jr., *Southern Politics* (New York: Alfred A. Knopf, 1949); Alexander Heard, *A Two-Party South?* (Chapel Hill: University of North Carolina Press, 1952); Samuel Lubell, *The Future of American Politics* (New York: Harper, 1951); and Jasper Shannon, *Toward a New Politics in the South* (Knoxville: University of Tennessee Press, 1949).

I am particularly grateful for permission to draw on current research in Louisiana politics by my former colleagues at Louisiana State University: William C. Havard, Rudolf Heberle, Perry Howard, and A. Wright Elliott.

Basic statistical information was obtained from *The World Almanac, Congressional Quarterly Weekly Reports,* and the bulletins of The Public Affairs Research Council of Louisiana, Inc.

1. D. W. Brogan, "The American Party System, 1952 Model," *Political Studies*, I (Feb., 1953), 19.

2. *The World Almanac* (New York: New York World Telegram Corp., 1962), pp. 70–74.

3. Jonathan Daniels, "Political Arithmetic for the South," *South Atlantic Quarterly*, LIX (Summer, 1960), 348.

4. See particularly the writings on Southern party politics of Donald S. Strong, James W. Prothro, O. Douglas Weeks, and William C. Havard.

5. See Francis Pickens Miller, "The Democratic Party in the South," *Christianity and Crisis*, XXI (May 1, 1961), 63.

6. See William C. Havard and Loren P. Beth, *Politics of Mis-Representation* (Baton Rouge: Louisiana State University Press, 1962), p. 113.

7. See Daniels, *op. cit.*, p. 343.

8. See Elbert Lee Tatum, *The Changed Political Thought of the Negro, 1915–1940* (New York: Exposition, 1951), p. 156.

9. For a careful analysis of the sectional conflicts at the past four Democratic national nominating conventions, with particular emphasis on 1948 and 1952, see Allan P. Sindler, "The Unsolid South," in Alan F. Westin, ed., *The Uses of Power* (New York: Harcourt, Brace and World, 1962), pp. 229–283.

10. See Allan P. Sindler, *Huey Long's Louisiana: State Politics 1920–1952* (Baltimore: The Johns Hopkins Press, 1956).

11. New Orleans *Times Picayune*, July 15, 1948.

12. See Rudolf Heberle and Perry Howard, "The Presidential Elections of 1960 in Louisiana." Unpublished manuscript.

13. *Ibid.*

14. See Kenneth N. Vines, "Two Parties for Shreveport," Case Studies in Practical Politics Series (New York: Holt, Rinehart and Winston, 1959).

15. *Report of the Louisiana Republican Platform Committee*, July 21, 1962, p. 1.

16. *Ibid.*

17. *Ibid.*, p. 2.

18. *Ibid.*, p. 3.

19. *Ibid.*, p. 4.

20. *Ibid.*

21. *Ibid.*, p. 6.

22. *Ibid.*, p. 7.

23. *Ibid.*, p. 11.

24. *Ibid.*, p. 19.

25. Clinton Rossiter, *Parties and Politics in America* (Ithaca: Cornell University Press, 1960), p. 55.

26. Sindler, "The Unsolid South," pp. 279–280.

27. Wilbur J. Cash, *The Mind of the South* (Garden City, N. Y.: Doubleday Anchor, 1954), p. 14.

Donald S. Strong

Durable Republicanism in the South

Everything seemed to be reasonably stable in the solid Democratic South in the presidential election of 1944. Voters did what was expected of them and went overwhelmingly for Franklin Roosevelt. A close look at the situation would have revealed the appearance in Texas of an anti-New Deal group describing themselves as the "Texas Regulars." They polled 135,000 votes. A curious observer might have commented on the attempted electoral-college revolts in Alabama and Mississippi. Yet none of these events could have led anyone to prophesy that in the four postwar presidential elections only three of the eleven states of the late Confederacy would have an unblemished record of loyalty to the party of their forefathers. The other eight states would one or more times wander off either to the Republicans or to third parties. Indeed, Florida, Tennessee, and Virginia were in the Republican column for three consecutive elections beginning in 1952. Although it may be incautious to classify these states as safe Republican territory in the future, they certainly supply strong evidence that the Solid South has come apart at the seams.

The historic Solid South was an artificial device designed to assure white supremacy. The plot was fairly simple. No Southern Negroes were to vote. All Northern Negroes were presumed to be Republicans. From the viewpoint of white Southerners, Northern Democrats might be somewhat obnoxious allies and not even 100 per cent Anglo-Saxon, but they were certainly white and not the kinds of men who would have any motive for using the powers of the national government to improve the status of the Negro. No such trust could be placed in the Republican party. As late as the presidential campaign of 1928 a small central-Alabama newspaper editorialized in favor of support of Al Smith in the following language:

The reason that the Force-Bill, anti-lynch laws and federal bayonets at the polling places have not been visited upon this section in the recent past is because the South has remained Democratically solid.

It is a real peril that confronts us—not an imaginary one.

The Republican part is aiming an arrow straight at the heart of the white men's civilization in the South, and it is distressing to know that we have in our midst good men and women who are apparently lending aid and comfort to a common enemy.[1]

In retrospect there is a certain charm about the thought of the Republican party under Herbert Hoover taking aggressive steps against segregation. Yet only twenty years later the Democratic party was doing just this and ceasing to be the party of white supremacy. It is the thesis of this paper that when the Democratic party ceased to be the champion of white supremacy Southern whites began to act like other Americans and vote in harmony with what they perceived to be their economic interest.

Prior to 1936 an estimated three-quarters of Northern Negroes were Republicans. A sudden and remarkable change in their party preferences occurred in the presidential election of 1936, in which Negroes switched parties until the proportion was more nearly three-quarters Democratic. This movement of Northern Negroes into the Democratic party does not seem to have been a result of a party strategy designed to lure them there, but rather a by-product of other policies. A cardinal point of the New Deal policy was prompt and direct relief for the unemployed and the destitute. Probably no group in the population had so many beneficiaries of this policy as the Negroes. Reasonable Negroes could understand the contrast between this and Republican policy toward them, the latter consisting in the preceding half-century chiefly of favorable references to the Great Emancipator during each presidential election. Other factors probably contributed to this change. The Roosevelts were much more prone to entertain Negroes socially at the White House than their Republican predecessors had been; Mrs. Roosevelt went out of her way to be courteous to Negroes; Secretary of the Interior Harold Ickes abolished segregation in his department; and the party machinery occasionally passed out a responsible job to a Negro. All these matters were duly reported on page one of the Negro press. More earthy considerations were doubtless involved. When the Chicago city government passed out of Republican hands in 1931, it ceased to be prudent for Negroes to be loyal to the party that seemed likely to be out of office for a long time. Only once in the presidency of Franklin Roosevelt did he take an official step that was specifically designed to improve the Negro's status, and he did this only after considerable pressure had been brought to bear upon him. Although the prewar defense effort was rapidly lessening unemployment, Negroes were always the last to be hired. There arose a very real threat of a march by 50,000 Negroes on Washington to protest this situation. Under these circumstances FDR finally by executive order created the wartime FEPC.

In the seven years following 1941, Negroes became of increased importance to the Democratic party in presidential politics. The great migration of Negroes from the South to Northern metropolitan centers, a migration that had begun in World War I, was greatly accelerated during World War II and the immediate postwar years. The census of 1950 was to discover that 37.5 per cent of Negroes lived outside the South, an increase of nearly 10 percentage points since the 1940 census. Never before in American history had so large a proportion of the Negro population lived in areas where there was no hindrance to their voting. These areas were also pivotal states in the electoral college. Negroes were now in a position to make greater demands of the party that they had been supporting, and it became sound politics for that party to make responsive gestures. To be sure, anti-lynching and anti-poll tax bills had been debated in Congress, but the full power of the presidency had not been exerted on their behalf. It was truly newsworthy, when in February, 1948, President Truman proposed to Congress the enactment of a ten-point civil rights program. The features of direct applicability to Negroes included the use of the powers of Congress to create a permanent FEPC, abolish segregation in interstate commerce, eliminate poll taxes in federal elections, and make lynching a federal crime. The fact that these proposals stood little chance of enactment by Congress is immaterial. The significant fact is that a Democratic President proposed to Congress the enactment of laws to improve the status of the Negro. This was heresy; the whole logic of the South's loyalty to the Democratic party was the assumption that the party was pledged to leave race relations in the hands of the states. When the Democratic party ceased to be the party of white supremacy, the deepest basis of Southern solidarity had been destroyed.

Those who had the greatest stake in the Democratic party being the party of white supremacy reacted violently. A States' Rights party broke away from the Democrats and nominated Governor Thurmond of South Carolina for President and Governor Wright of Mississippi for Vice President. Thurmond campaigned vigorously throughout the South. Nor was he the only nominee to appear in the region.

President Truman spent two days in Texas, during which time he made campaign addresses in the four largest cities and paid a ceremonial visit to John Nance Garner. It had been many years since a presidential candidate had appeared in a Southern state and made an appeal for the voters' support.

Although the Republicans put on no particularly serious campaign in the South, they emerged with 26 per cent of the popular vote, and in this respect they bettered the States' Righters, who received only 22 per cent. However, the Republican votes were widely scattered, whereas the Dixiecrats were able to concentrate their strength in a manner to carry the electoral votes of the states of Mississippi, South Carolina, Louisiana, and Alabama. One should note that the four states do not represent a random sample of the eleven former Confederate states; they are the four states with the highest per cent Negro population. Although there was not a statistically precise relationship between the per cent Negro in each state and the per cent of the vote for Thurmond, there was in most cases a general relationship. Thus, in Texas with less than 13 per cent Negro, Thurmond secured less than 10 per cent of the total vote.

In the states of the Deep South it is assumed that few Negroes were voting in 1948 and that the vote was cast by a largely white electorate. Substantially this pattern of voting appeared at the county level also. Southwide throughout most of the black-belt, plantation counties, Thurmond showed impressive strength. In counties with few Negroes, his support was trifling. In East Tennessee few counties gave Thurmond as much as 5 per cent of the vote. In Texas, Thurmond's strength was concentrated almost wholly in the eastern third of the state, the home of most of the state's colored population. Other analyses of this election by counties failed to produce any interesting results. If Negro percentage of total population is held constant, Dixiecrats were found to be no more numerous in cities than in rural areas, save only in North Carolina. A single isolated datum suggests that Dixiecrats appeared uniformly in all income levels. This datum comes from a study in which Jacksonville, Florida, all-white precincts are separated according to three income levels—upper-income, middle-income, and lower-income. Although there was an appreciable difference in the strength of the two major parties among the three income levels, the support for Thurmond varied less than 2 percentage points among the three income levels.[2]

And this is about all that an analysis is likely to squeeze out of the

1948 election. The real emphasis was on racial rather than on economic anxieties. White Southerners with many Negro neighbors expressed, by their support of a third party, their sense of outrage at the Democratic party's ceasing to be the party of white supremacy. These people had formerly been the backbone of the South's one-party system; the black-belt areas in which they lived had remained loyal to Al Smith in 1928 when people elsewhere in the region wandered off to Herbert Hoover. Since few of these defecting whites could bring themselves to vote for the party of the ancient enemy, the Republican party's 26 per cent of the region's popular vote in 1948 was about par for the course. However, the location of Republican strength provided interesting clues for the future. Dewey polled 37 per cent of the vote in Houston and ran strongly in Richmond and Dallas. Similarly interesting was the vote split in the Jacksonville precincts mentioned above. In the low-income precincts Dewey won only 12 per cent of the vote, but in the middle-income precincts he polled 25 per cent, and his support in the higher-income precincts rose to 41 per cent.[3]

In 1952 any newspaper reader was aware long before November that the year's presidential campaign would produce more than a ripple in the South. The South played a spectacular and pivotal role in the Republican convention. Thousands of Southerners manifested a desire in the spring of 1952 to help nominate Eisenhower, thereby putting a considerable strain on the rusty machinery of Southern Republican organizations. Once nominated, Eisenhower did not disappoint his Southern supporters. He made at least one campaign appearance in nine Southern states, and in Texas he spoke in six cities. While Stevenson did not equal this record, he made campaign addresses in four Texas cities and spoke in three other Southern states. It was history-making for major-party presidential nominees to campaign systematically in Southern states. When the votes were counted, Eisenhower had secured a remarkable 48 per cent of the Southwide popular vote and had carried the electoral votes of Texas, Florida, Tennessee, and Virginia. In 1956 his share of the region's popular vote rose to almost 49 per cent (a plurality, incidentally), and he repeated his victory in the four states he had carried in 1952 and added Louisiana to the list as well.

Eisenhower in both elections drew his support from different areas of the South from those that had supported Thurmond. To be sure, there must be many voters who supported Thurmond in 1948 and Eisenhower in 1952 and 1956. However, anyone examining the aggregate election returns cannot but be impressed by the fact that the high points of Dixiecrat and Eisenhower strength rarely coincided. The most obvious contrast is in the states carried by Thurmond and Eisenhower. Thurmond carried Louisiana, Mississippi, Alabama, and South Carolina, all in the Deep South. Eisenhower carried Texas, Florida, Tennessee, and Virginia, all on the periphery of the South. The one instance of overlapping was Eisenhower's adding of Louisiana to his string of states in 1956. At the county level the absence of an overlap is even more apparent. One may compute the per cent of the vote for Thurmond for all counties in a state, rank the counties, and mark off the top quartile of these counties on a map. A similar procedure may be followed for Eisenhower's top quartile of counties in each state in 1956. An overlay of these two maps shows little coincidence in the high points of strength. Whereas Thurmond did best in the black-belt counties, Eisenhower did best in the mountain counties and in the cities. In both the 1948 and 1956 elections the South was discontented with the Democratic party, but there were two separate streams of discontent.

It is of little note that Eisenhower received considerable support in the Appalachian counties, since Republican presidential nominees have been securing substantial backing from those areas for the last three-quarters of a century. The important point is that Eisenhower secured new support, the nature of which may be gauged by the simple method of determining percentage-point gain, by counties, for the Republicans in 1952 as compared to 1944. For instance, if in the year 1944 a particular Alabama county had given Dewey 10 per cent of its vote and then in 1952 had supported Eisenhower to the tune of 50 per cent, one could refer to a gain of 40 percentage points in the support of Republican presidential nominees. In each Southern state the counties were ranked in terms of their Republican percentage-point gain. Since the mountain counties had traditionally registered a high per cent Republican, they did not appear in the top quartile. In each state in the year 1952 the counties in the top quartile of percentage-point gain included always the urban counties. In this context the expression "urban" is loosely used, but the real metropolitan centers always appeared in the top quartile, and quite generally counties with towns no larger than 10,000 were likely to appear there.

For the election of 1956 a somewhat more systematic presentation of the notion of urban—or metropolitan—Republicanism may be presented. Here the procedure is to use the census definition of a metropolitan area, that is, a county containing a city of at least 50,000 population. The procedure is to separate the counties of each state into metropolitan and non-metropolitan counties and compare the support for the Republican nominee in each group of counties. Thus, if a state with a total of sixty-seven counties has three metropolitan counties, one compares separately the per cent Republican of the three metropolitan counties with the per cent of the total vote Republican of the sixty-four non-metropolitan counties. If there is anything to this notion of metropolitan Republicanism, the metropolitan counties should register a higher support for Eisenhower. In 1956 in each of the eleven states the per cent Republican in the metropolitan counties exceeded the per cent Republican in all the remaining counties of the state. The percentage-point lead varied from 19 percentage points all the way down to a fraction of 1 percentage point. In the median state of the eleven Southern states the metropolitan counties showed a 7.2 percentage-point lead in Republican vote over the non-metropolitan counties.

The analysis of metropolitan areas confines the analysis rather arbitrarily to cities of 50,000 population or over and leaves unanswered the question concerning the Ike-liking tendencies of smaller centers. If one sets up a third category of counties with cities of 10,000 to 50,000 population, one finds that in 1956 they lean more to Eisenhower than counties with no cities of as much as 10,000. However, this preference for Eisenhower was of a lower order than that exhibited by the metropolitan counties.[4]

A limitation of the foregoing procedure is that there are several states with large areas of traditional, rural Republicanism. In Arkansas, Tennessee, and Virginia, the difference in per cent Republican between the metropolitan counties and non-metropolitan counties was small. It is possible to use another procedure to demonstrate the increasing degree of Republican sentiment in the South's growing urban areas. The procedure here is to see whether the greatest gain for Republican presidential nominees has taken place in the metropolitan areas. Specifically, a comparison is made between the years 1936 and 1956. The year 1936 is chosen as the low point of Republican fortune from which the only direction of movement is upward. For instance, if in 1936, 10 per cent of the total vote of the metropolitan counties of Alabama went for Landon and twenty years later 50 per cent of the vote of these metropolitan counties went for Eisenhower, one could say that Republican strength had recorded a gain of 40 percentage points. A comparable procedure for the non-metropolitan counties might reveal for them a gain of only 20 percentage points. The results of an eleven-state analysis show that metropolitan counties have registered a greater Republican percentage-point gain than the non-metropolitan counties in all the states except Florida. The median state of the eleven shows the metropolitan counties outgaining the rest of the state by almost 13 percentage points. The atypical behavior of Florida is in all probability due to the large number of Northern Republican immigrants, not all of whom take up residence in metropolitan centers. Without wishing to disparage the importance of this immigrant Republicanism, the present line of argument is that something truly significant is afoot only if large numbers of *native* Southerners change their voting behavior. If a Republican presidential nominee carries St. Petersburg, this is a curiosity; when he carries Memphis and Mobile, we may have a development worth examining.

A sharp-eyed critic may feel that the use of the year 1936 as the base year to demonstrate the greater increase in Republican strength in metropolitan counties is arbitrary. Actually, it can be demonstrated that the same results are achieved regardless of what earlier year is used as a basis of comparison. For example, if one substitutes the year 1924 for 1936, it still turns out that residents of metropolitan counties showed a greater increase in Republican enthusiasm than did their non-urban cousins.[5] In summary, then, the case for urban Republicanism emphasizes that Eisenhower strength in metropolitan counties exceeds that in counties housing cities of 10,000 to 50,000 population, and the GOP strength in the latter exceeds that in counties with no town of 10,000. Likewise, the gain in Republican strength in metropolitan centers in almost all cases exceeds that of the non-metropolitan counties of the state.

Yet this support for Eisenhower was not uniform among all classes of city dwellers. One needs to examine for any Southern city a breakdown of the party vote by precincts or boxes to grasp the wide variation in support for Eisenhower. In examining the returns of cities in the area between Richmond and Houston it was not hard to find voting boxes in 1952 that went for Eisenhower seven- or eight-to-one. At the other end of the spectrum some voting boxes went nine-to-one for Stevenson. A quick examination showed that the boxes with lopsided enthusiasm for Eisenhower were always in the most exclusive residential suburbs. The closer to the country club, the higher the percentage for Eisenhower. By contrast, the voting boxes in 1952 most top-heavy for Stevenson were the Negro boxes. (As will be indicated below, this latter situation changed somewhat in 1956.)

It is a great deal easier to generalize about the upper-income support for Eisenhower than to produce a systematic demonstration of it. City voting wards frequently do not coincide with the areas for which census data are available. Ward lines change from election to election. Suburban areas grow so rapidly that census data at ten-year intervals do not always supply reliable information for a given election. However, for 1956, an examination was made for at least one metropolitan area in nine Southern states. Precincts were classified by race and income. Income was measured in terms of median rental and median value of owner-occupied homes. Many precincts had to be excluded from the analysis because of their biracial character or other factors. It was the upper-income, all-white precincts that produced the most definite results. One could rank all precincts by per cent Eisenhower and then take a cut-off point at the top quartile. These were invariably all-white areas in the highest-rental and highest home-value section of the city. As one proceeded downward in home-value levels in all-white precincts, these precincts always showed a decline in enthusiasm for the Republican candidate. When with considerably more difficulty it was possible to locate an all-white precinct in the lowest quartile of home-value, it showed a further decline in support for Eisenhower. This is not to dismiss Southern Ike-likers as a strictly silk-stocking crowd. In 1956 Eisenhower carried the city of Mobile, Alabama, with 53.6 per cent of the city's vote. The least Republican of the city's nineteen wards gave him nearly 41 per cent. Not all of Eisenhower's supporters were wealthy, but enthusiasm for him was greatest among the most prosperous.

In 1952 Negro voters in city after city supported Stevenson by such overwhelming margins as nine to one. In 1956 an abrupt change occurred. For Jacksonville, Florida, a fairly precise comparison may be made. In both years we are comparing areas where the registrants are in excess of 98 per cent Negro and areas where the majority of the city's Negro population resides. In 1952 these nine precincts gave Eisenhower 10.6 per cent of the votes; in 1956 the figure was 51.2 per cent. The extent of this shift does not seem unrepresentative of other Southern cities. Certainly, the percentage-point gain for Eisenhower was in excess of any comparable gains in Negro wards outside the South.[6]

The tremendous upsurge in Southern support of the Republican presidential nominee in 1952 and 1956 was not accompanied by corresponding victories of Republican nominees for state and local offices. In fact, relatively few Republican nominees offered for these posts. In the Eisenhower years the Republicans picked up five Southern seats in the U. S. House of Representatives and retained their two traditional seats in East Tennessee. The seats picked up in either 1952 or 1954 and held today are: the First District of Florida (the St. Petersburg-Tampa area), the Fifth District of Texas (Dallas), the Tenth District of North Carolina, and the Sixth and Tenth Districts in Virginia. The First District of Florida and the Tenth Virginia District, which is largely suburban Washington, can both be explained largely on the basis of immigrant Republicanism. The remaining three districts need to be examined in terms of the argument that the emerging Southern Republicanism is essentially an urban phenomenon. The Dallas county, Texas, district needs no comment. North Carolina's Tenth District consisted at that time of six counties. Five of these have strong to moderate amounts of traditional Appalachian Republicanism. The sixth county contains the city of Charlotte, which traditionally provided the necessary Democratic margin to keep the district in the Democratic column. This margin grew perilously thin in 1950, and in 1952 the five rural counties performed as usual while urban Mecklenburg county (Charlotte) produced a large enough Republican vote to elect a Republican to Congress. Substantially the same thing occurred in Virginia's Sixth District, which includes some eight counties with considerable Appalachian Republicanism as well as the city of Roanoke, which has a population of around 100,000. The mountain Republicans have remained true to their faith while Roanoke has become progressively less Democratic. The result is that the drive toward urban Republicanism elected a third GOP Congressman.

A comprehensive story of Republican campaigning on the state and local level during the Eisenhower era would be too tedious to recount here. Moreover, the essential fact is that few Republican candidates stood for office. This is true even for the U. S. House of Representatives, which would have been a logical place for an assault from the standpoint of the party nationally. Of the 106 congressional districts in the eleven Southern states the largest number ever to be contested in the Eisenhower era was 42, and in 1958 the number dropped to 22. An examination of these contests indicates that they were most frequently made in congressional districts containing a metropolitan area, and the nominees tended to run rather stronger races in these districts than in non-metropolitan districts. Yet many districts housing a standard metropolitan area were never contested.

Before proceeding to the 1960 election let us ponder the meaning of the developments just recounted. The use of the terms "Republican" and "Eisenhower" interchangeably may have caused confusion. There can be no doubt that the immense popularity of a distinguished military hero at the head of the GOP ticket facilitated breaking the conditioned reflex of many Southerners to vote Democratic. The basic question is whether we are about to witness the development of a full-fledged two-party system in which the Republican party will offer candidates from governor down to sheriff or whether we can dismiss Eisenhower's two impressive sweeps as merely a "vote for the man." This vote-for-the-man concept apparently implies that if a person had to indicate his party affiliation he would still say "Democratic," and he would also indicate that he would not feel constrained to support Republican nominees other than Eisenhower.

The infrequency of contests by Republicans for state and local offices should lead one to be extremely cautious about any sudden evolution of a full-fledged, grassroots Republican party. Yet the dismissal of Eisenhower's plurality victory in the South in 1956 as merely a "vote for the man" may be equally misleading. The relevant question is *which* Southerners "voted for the man"? If a voter's motivation is his admiration for a likable military hero, Eisenhower might have been expected to do equally well in the city and on the farm, in Texas and in Mississippi, in the slums and in the suburbs. But this randomness or uniformity of support simply did not exist. Eisenhower's strongest support came from prosperous city dwellers and suburbanites. Residents of suburban Birmingham voted strongly for Eisenhower just as did the residents of suburban Chicago. Since similarly situated people outside the South are most pronounced in their Republican loyalties, it must be concluded that in the elections of 1952 and 1956 prosperous Southern urbanites acted like Yankees.

Prior to the Eisenhower era the term "presidential Republicanism" was occasionally used in the South. This described the fact that for many years Republican presidential nominees secured a substantially larger percentage of the vote than did the occasional Republican nominee for governor. Apparently, prior to 1952 there were many thousands of people Southwide who had some favorable disposition toward the Republican party nationally but were uninterested in its fortunes locally. In a sense the Eisenhower successes in the South may be regarded as presidential Republicanism on a grand scale. Moreover, after the 1956 election even a cautious observer might have predicted that this vastly expanded presidential Republicanism was here to stay. Prosperous Southerners were backing Republican presidential nominees just like their similarly situated Yankee cousins. And like their Yankee cousins more Southerners are moving to the cities. Presidential Republicanism is growing most rapidly where the population is growing most rapidly. The population shift appears to be on the side of the Republicans.

The most obvious test of the vote-for-the-man hypothesis was the 1960 election. If Nixon's strength had fallen far below Ike's or if it had been distributed significantly differently, this theory might be substantiated. At the outset it might be noted that in 1960 neither of the presidential nominees accepted the vote-for-the-man hypothesis, or assumed that Southern voters would return to the pre-Eisenhower status quo. Nixon made at least one campaign appearance in each of the Southern states. Kennedy visited six Southern states, including a two-day tour of Texas during which he spoke in ten different cities. For Lyndon Johnson's whistle-stop tour there is no precedent in Southern campaigning. In the course of a week his campaign train traveled 2,500 miles through eight states to give Johnson an opportunity to make sixty speeches.

The election results showed that Nixon had secured a shade over 46 per cent of the region's total popular vote, only 2 or 3 percentage points below the record set by his chief. He carried Florida, Tennessee, and Virginia, three of the four states carried by Eisenhower in 1952. Professor Cosman provides some evidence of a shift among Negro voters in Dallas and in Columbia and Charleston, South Carolina, back to something approximating their 1952 degree of support for the Democratic party.[7] In Dallas the Nixon vote dropped from Eisenhower's 65 per cent to a mere 62.2 per cent! Even after this trifling decline of Republican strength, Dallas turned in the highest

Republican percentage among cities of its size in the nation. Nixon carried Memphis and he improved on Eisenhower's percentage in Birmingham. He did well in Shreveport, Houston, and just about everywhere else in the metropolitan South. Cosman's analysis of the two South Carolina cities and Dallas shows the same vote distribution on an income basis demonstrated for a larger group of cities in 1952 and 1956. Whereas in 1956 Eisenhower secured 78 per cent of the vote in ten upper-income precincts in Dallas, Nixon's support in those precincts slipped only to 76 per cent.

The impact of the religious issue seems to have had no profoundly disrupting effect on the political pattern of the Eisenhower era. The fact that Nixon did almost as well as Ike is no proof that religion was not a factor; different supporters of each candidate could produce the same total. Yet a reasonable assumption is that if the two men had greatly differing constituencies the ranking of counties would vary substantially between the two elections. Thus, counties which had been in Eisenhower's top quartile might be expected to appear in Nixon's third quartile while counties where Ike received little support might show up in Nixon's top quartile. By and large the ranking of the counties by quartiles remained remarkably similar. The religious shifts appear rather in the Catholic-loyalty direction. Professor Cosman has isolated some parishes in Louisiana and some counties in other states that are overwhelmingly Catholic, and all of these showed a substantial gain for the Democrats over 1956.[8]

The number of Republican nominees whose name appeared below Nixon's on Southern ballots showed no substantial increase over the Eisenhower era. Forty-two candidates ran for the U.S. House of Representatives. Seven of these were elected. These included the five seats picked up in the Eisenhower era plus the usual First and Second Congressional Districts in East Tennessee.

The results of the 1960 presidential election leave no doubt in the writer's mind that presidential Republicanism has come to the South to stay. It will be an enduring phenomenon, not a transient one associated with the personality of Dwight Eisenhower. This means that the South has permanently rejoined the nation insofar as presidential politics is concerned. Many Southern states are going to be in the doubtful column for the predictable future—that is, unless one wants to argue that Virginia and Florida are safely Republican. All this must be considered in the context of the closeness of the 1960 election. Democrat Franklin Roosevelt would have won all four times had he not secured a single electoral vote in the South. Future Democratic nominees can look forward to no such happy situation.

If presidential two-partyism in the South is now a reality, can we then look forward to the emergence of a full two-party system in which the GOP will make a practice of contesting most offices from governor to sheriff? It would be useful first to speculate on the reasons for the rather small number of GOP state and local candidates down through the 1960 election. Then, notice will be taken of the rather surprising proliferation of Republican state and local nominees since the 1960 defeat.

Any speculation about why presidential Republicanism has not been speedily converted into the grassroots variety must begin by attributing some motives to the presidential Republicans. Since, as has been demonstrated above, their ranks included many people of wealth and substance it may be presumed that this element viewed the national Democratic party with misgivings because of the latter's generally liberal economic orientation. Terms like "this socialistic nonsense coming out of Washington" fall easily from the lips of these folk, many of whose prosperity is of recent origin. The timing of their sensitivity to this "liberal menace" is related to the demise of the Democratic party as the party of white supremacy. Once the cross-pressure of an appeal for white solidarity was removed, large numbers of Southerners were free to vote in line with their perceived economic interests. However, the attitude that leads one to vote against the more liberal of the presidential nominees does not necessarily require that one begin building a grassroots conservative party in the South. Although the spectrum of opinion in the South includes a substantial degree of economic liberalism, it is still true that one cannot easily compile a long list of Southern governors and local officials whose economic liberalism is such as to occasion great insecurity among the well-to-do. Stated differently, it would seem that the greatest stimulus to a grassroots Republican party in the South would be a succession of truly liberal governors—a highly unlikely development. Since the majority of Southern officials are "good sound men" there is no need for a second conservative party on a state level.

A second and related notion takes notice of the large number of Southern congressmen who are committee chairmen. Not all of these individuals are conservatives, but the spectrum is heavy in the conservative direction. The reasoning proceeds to the effect that Southern conservatives should take advantage of the many strategic committee chairmanships to block the enactment of any "unsound, crackpot, and socialistic schemes."

A third reason for slow growth of a grassroots GOP is the self-interest of state and local Democratic officeholders. To be sure some have flirted with presidential Republicanism, as witness the classic example of Democratic Governors Shivers of Texas and Kennon of Louisiana in 1952 working openly for Eisenhower's election. Yet all this is based on the assumption that the Republicans will be too gentlemanly to run candidates against them in state and local races. Southwide, several thousand state and local Democratic officials have a vested interest in confining Republicanism to the presidential level. Likewise, countless presidential Republicans have influence with Democratic local officials. If one has good relations with a Democratic sheriff or a Democratic tax assessor, why should one encourage or support a Republican to run against him?

Finally, there was little evidence during the Eisenhower years that the GOP national organization gave more than token attention to their Southern converts. In fact, some evidence suggests that the national organization was blind to the possibilities in the Southern situation. In Dallas, Congressman Bruce Alger was elected entirely on his own effort and to the surprise of the national organization. In 1960 the press reported surprise on the part of Nixon and his advisors at the tremendous crowds and enthusiastic welcome that they received in Atlanta. Many natives had converted themselves before the missionaries arrived.

One might have assumed that the Kennedy victory of 1960 would leave the Southern Republicans in a state of discouragement and inactivity. Far from it. The Southern Republicans seem stimulated by the defeat. Particularly in the tier of states from Texas east to South Carolina there has been a spurt of grassroots activity, including several victories, for which there was no counterpart in the entire Eisenhower era. Without making any pretense at completeness, let us examine some of the instances of Republican activities since November, 1960. The most important office won by Republicans was the U. S. Senate seat won by John Tower in Texas. Tower had run against Lyndon Johnson in November when Johnson was running for both the Vice Presidency and the Senate. Tower ran the senior senator a close race and apparently was able to keep his campaign organization in shape for the race in the following spring. Also in Texas in 1961, Republicans contested congressional seats in two districts that had not seen party contests in many years. One of these districts included San Antonio, the other the city of Wichita Falls. Both were special elections, and the GOP candidate in San Antonio ran a close race. In Louisiana in December, 1961, a Republican entered the special election for the House of Representatives from the Fourth Congressional District. He lost, but polled some 28,000 votes to the Democratic victor's 33,000. In the spring of 1962 a Republican ran for mayor of New Orleans on a platform of being a tougher segregationist than his opponent, and he polled 20 per cent of the vote. In Meridian, Mississippi, a Republican candidate ran for mayor in June of 1961 and attracted 28 per cent of the vote. Three Republican candidates for council secured about the same degree of support. In December, 1961, a Republican candidate for public prosecutor of Lowndes County (Columbus) defeated a Democratic opponent to become the first GOP officeholder in Mississippi in a century. In Alabama in October, 1961, a Republican was elected mayor of Mobile. Technically the election was on a non-partisan basis and the victor asserted, "I did not unfurl the banner of Republicanism in this race. . . ." A few months earlier another Republican in Mobile narrowly lost a special election for the state legislature. In Georgia, two Republicans have been elected alderman in Atlanta. In South Carolina, Republicans have won two special elections to the state legislature. One was elected from Columbia in August, 1961, the other from Charleston in February, 1962.

In the 1962 congressional campaign the GOP showed the same aggressive spirit. A record-breaking number of fifty-six House seats were contested; there were fifty-four in 1948 and forty-two in 1960. In Texas, eighteen of the twenty-three seats were contested; in Florida, ten out of twelve. More important, the GOP won eleven of these races. It will be recalled that in the five elections from 1952 through 1960, only five seats were gained; now four new seats were picked up in this one election of 1962. The eleven Republican victories included the five seats won in the Eisenhower era, the two traditional East Tennessee districts, and one additional seat in Texas, Florida, North Carolina, and Tennessee. In three contests the GOP losers polled 49-plus per cent of the vote—in Memphis, Richmond, and in Virginia's Seventh District. The returns may be sliced another way to reveal Republican strength. Of the fifty-three contests in which GOP nominees ran in single-member-districts (in Alabama their three nominees ran statewide against no particular one of the eight

Democrats) their candidates polled less than 20 per cent of the vote in only three instances. In twenty-six races they polled from 20 to 40 per cent, and in twenty-four races, including their eleven victories, they took more than 40 per cent of the vote.[9] The strongest GOP race for the Senate was run in Alabama, where James Martin polled 49.1 per cent of the vote. It might also be noted that the Alabama Republicans contested no less than eighteen seats in the state legislature—an unheard of number for Alabama—and captured two.

Several characteristics of these recent campaigns should be noted. In many instances these were special elections, in which the GOP was shrewdly taking advantage of low turnout. Another characteristic was the minimum party emphasis in these campaigns. The nominees for the most part did not flaunt their Republicanism. It was acknowledged but de-emphasized, and the campaign appeal was made to the "independents, Republicans, and disaffected Democrats." Moreover, much evidence points to the development of a substantial amount of Republican precinct organization, more elaborate than anything on the Democratic side in the Deep South. Greatest evidences of it appeared in Alabama and Texas but this may have been region-wide as well.

One isolated datum may be significant. A representative of the national organization asked leaders of the Alabama Republicans at their state convention whether they planned to meet their annual financial quota for the national organization. They replied firmly that they did not and that they intended to keep all the money in the state to spend on state races. Moreover, they requested that the national organization send them three field men. This appears to be the first time in Alabama experience when the missions have not been willing to contribute to the support of the parent church. Clearly, refusal to do this is the first step toward a substantial grassroots party in the state. One will never elect Republicans in Alabama if Alabama Republican money is used to finance GOP nominees in Ohio and California.

In explanation of this contemporary spurt of party activity, it would appear that defeat was a great spur to the Southern Republicans. The presence of Eisenhower in the White House had a soothing effect upon them. By contrast, Kennedy is perceived as a menace. The reaction is one of alarm; one must act. Hence, there is considerable campaigning in terms of an ideology that evokes in an older generation nostalgic memories of the 1936 campaign in the Middle

West. Defeat is helpful also in that the Democrats will have to bear the onus of all federal force used to implement integration. It should be recalled that Eisenhower's use of troops in the Little Rock crisis was a serious but temporary blow to Southern Republicans. It was probably most injurious to the hopes of GOP nominee Theodore Roosevelt Dalton, who seemed otherwise to have a fighting chance for the governorship of Virginia in November, 1957. Yet this incident was forgotten even before 1960. So when the Kennedy administration used federal marshals to uphold order in Montgomery during the Freedom Rider incident, there was substantial Southern criticism of Kennedy's action and muttering to the effect that Nixon would have handled the matter differently, an allegation that doubtless does Mr. Nixon an injustice. Due to the shortness of public memory, the Republicans are now in a position to capitalize on any integration incident in which it is necessary to use federal force to uphold public order in the South.

This increase in zeal and activity among Republican candidates calls for a reconsideration of the explanation offered earlier of why so few GOP local candidates appeared in the Eisenhower years. The most vulnerable of the several explanations may be the notion that the South will remain Democratic on the state and local level because of the value of congressional committee seniority. This fight-within-the-party approach is entirely rational and logical. From the writer's standpoint it would appear to be the most effective way to maintain the status quo. However, we may not be dealing with a completely logical situation. Ambitious and enthusiastic Republican leaders do occasionally thrust themselves up, and they may succeed in appealing to an electorate that does not grasp the importance of the seniority rule.

The 1960 campaign may have brought about a new relationship between presidential Republicanism and the grassroots variety. Eisenhower's victories in the South were merely frosting on his cake. He won the election outside the South, as had most presidents before him. The 1960 campaign was different. Its closeness emphasizes the importance of the Southern states to both parties. It is difficult to see how the Republican party can fail to campaign vigorously in each and every Southern state in future presidential years. If one sets up an organization in a state to carry it in the electoral college every four years, is it efficient or even sensible to allow this organization to go to pieces at the finish of each presidential campaign? And how can one better keep these organizations in vigorous condition than to give them the motivation of contesting for state and local offices? Republican organizations in the Southern states were not essential to the party in the Eisenhower era. In future elections they may be crucial.

The Solid South was always a somewhat artificial entity that tended to repress conflict along economic lines. It was held together by the tradition of the Democratic party being the party of white supremacy. When it became apparent that the Democratic party had abandoned its historic role, many Southerners began to vote what they regarded as their economic interest. The immense popularity of a distinguished military hero at the head of the Republican ticket doubtless facilitated the breaking of the conditioned reflex to vote Democratic. But the reflex has been broken. The last four presidential elections were not unique events which will be followed in 1964 by a return to the pattern of normal Democratic supremacy that last manifested itself in 1944. Much of the South of 1944 is no longer with us. There is a housing subdivision where that cotton field used to be. Moreover, since 1960 there have been some surprising manifestations of Republican state and local activity. Now that the South has rejoined the Union in terms of presidential elections the national GOP can no longer afford to ignore its Southern converts. Instead, it will have a real motive for keeping its Southern organizations vigorous through grassroots activity. The result may be a much more rapid growth of a real two-party system than occurred in the Eisenhower years.

A Note on Method and Findings

Professor Converse, in his paper in this volume, chides me—quite gently as academic disputes sometimes go—for compressing political change into too short a time and for unwillingness to see the South as participating in national trends and therefore offering too uniquely Southern an explanation for the changes. Our differences will continue because we cannot agree on an index for political change. Although reliance on election returns can be misleading, I cannot accept his concept of party identification, particularly when it is projected backward.

Professor Converse's persuasive argument that party identification means the same thing North and South does not quite overcome my prejudice that in the ex-Confederate states there is a greater reluctance to disavow Democratic identification by persons who have often supported GOP nominees. This situation is recognized by Southern GOP candidates. John Tower was elected to the Senate from Texas with a minimum emphasis on the fact that he was a Republican, and James Martin, who nearly unseated Lister Hill in Alabama in 1962, was so completely silent on his Republicanism that Hill eventually needled him about being "ashamed of his party." While isolated instances of this practice may be cited outside the South, it is certainly not standard procedure. Although future studies employing a larger Southern sample could persuade me as to the validity of the party identification concept in a Southern context, the projection backward of this concept to define basic loyalties in earlier elections will always appear to me hazardous in the extreme. The notion is ingenious but has nothing about it to convince a skeptic.

Since this paper has focused on the postwar South, my remarks about earlier years were kept to a minimum. This should not be interpreted as meaning that the prewar South was politically monolithic. Certainly the fortunes of the Southern Republicans at that time paralleled national trends although at a much lower level. Figure 2 in Professor Converse's paper emphasizes this parallelism but might convey the impression that the parallel lines run closer together than the actually do. Moreover, if one charts the per cent for GOP presidential candidates in the eleven-state South, 1920–1960, there is little visual support for the concept of the slow upward trend. The GOP vote actually dropped between 1920 and 1924. It zoomed upward in 1928 to nearly 44 per cent, then plummeted sickeningly to 13 per cent in 1932. From that year to 1948 there was indeed a gradual rise to 26 per cent. Between 1948 and 1952 there was a precipitate rise in per cent Republican to 48 per cent, and the GOP line on the graph runs horizontally at this level for 1956 and 1960. Since graph lines of GOP fortunes nationwide and in the South do rise and fall together, part of any rise in the South must be attributed to the national trend; the region is not insulated from national political tides. Yet there is no national parallel for the enormous rise in Southern GOP strength from 26 per cent in 1948 to 48 per cent in 1952. The largest part of this change is to be accounted for by uniquely Southern factors.

The notion of the importance of race is least convincing when applied to the growth of Southern urban Republicanism in the pre-war years. Dr. Bernard Cosman finds that in every year, 1920–1956, the Republican percentage of the urban South is higher than that of the non-urban South. The graph lines for the two types of areas run parallel but with the urban line always at a higher level. Moreover, he demonstrates that the urban South was moving in the GOP direction at a more rapid rate. Taking 1956 as his base year and then comparing it with 1920 and each succeeding presidential year, he finds that, considering the South as a whole, urban gains exceeded non-urban gains whatever year is compared with 1956.[10] This evidence of prewar Republican stirrings in the urban South suggests that my thesis on the importance of race needs restatement in more general terms. The impact of race created an artificial Democratic solidarity. As cities and industry grew, a diversity of interest appeared. Southern businessmen, while remaining orthodox on race, felt the cross-pressure of economic issues, and the more hardy among them turned to the GOP in the prewar years. After the war the Democratic party's abandonment of white supremacy removed the historic prop of Democratic loyalty and made it easy for thousands of the less hardy to vote their pocketbooks.

1. *The Watchman* (Greensboro, Ala.), Oct. 25, 1928.

2. Charles D. Farris, "Effects of Negro Voting on the Politics of a Southern City," unpublished Ph.D. dissertation, University of Chicago, 1953, p. 399.

3. *Ibid.*, p. 399.

4. Bernard Cosman, "Republicanism in the Metropolitan South," unpublished Ph.D. dissertation, University of Alabama, 1960, pp. 17–18. Dr. Cosman creates a separate category of "traditional Republican counties" and excludes these from his analysis of the several urban categories.

5. *Ibid.*, p. 40.

6. A more detailed analysis of voting within cities appears in the author's *Urban Republicanism in the South* (University, Ala.: Bureau of Public Administration, University of Alabama, 1960), chap. ii.

7. Bernard Cosman, "Presidential Republicanism in the South, 1960," *Journal of Politics*, XXIV (May, 1962), 310.

8. *Ibid.*, pp. 317–319.

9. See Strong, *op. cit.*, p. 42 for a table which carries this type of analysis back through the election of 1946. The 1962 figures are based on unofficial returns appearing in the *Congressional Quarterly*.

10. Cosman, "Republicanism in the Metropolitan South," pp. 35, 40.

Philip E. Converse

A Major Political Realignment
in the South?*

In the several decades since Herbert Hoover first cracked the Solid South in a resounding way, observers have awaited with notable impatience a collapse of the Democratic grip upon the region. For some time, the collapse has seemed "just around the corner." Yet while the signs of impending change persist, the South has yet to see anything like the major partisan realignment which appeared so imminent fifteen years ago.

No one would quarrel with the proposition that the South is undergoing a real and rapid change on many important fronts. Fundamental shifts in the technological and economic base of the region have begun to have observable impact on legal and political institutions, aspects of which are the focus of attention of several of the other chapters in this volume. Nevertheless, the fact of change itself—even change as fundamental as this—does not guarantee that changes will follow in all other sectors of Southern life. Quite to the contrary, it seems reasonable to suppose at this point that members of human societies are rather adept at muffling and hedging in such change as cannot be avoided. Man seems to respond to change as slowly and narrowly as the situation permits, and what the situation permits is often surprising.

This paper is limited not only to political change, but to a particular type of political change involving the basic party loyalties of the mass Southern electorate. It is our purpose here to take survey of those signs of change in mass partisanship that have been visible over the past decade, and to judge what these signs may mean for the partisan future of the South. Since there are a number of distinctive outcomes—including that of no change—that are logically possible for the South, it would be useful to take stock of the major possibilities at the outset.

The most dramatic outcome, of course, would be that of a shift of

* The able assistance of Aage Clausen is gratefully recognized.

the South from the Democratic to the Republican camp. We shall call this the *realignment* outcome. It has long been obvious that the historical link between the South and the Democratic national party has become quite implausible from an ideological point of view. The marriage has remained tolerable to each partner only on rather expedient grounds, such as easy presidential votes for the Northern wing, and congressional seniority for the Southern. On most other counts, however, the grounds for divorce have become overwhelming. Hence it has not been unreasonable to look for the development of a South as solidly Republican as it once was Democratic, thereby joining the rural and small-town conservatism of the South to that so clearly represented by Republicanism in much of the rest of the nation.

Yet the most salient features of current Southern change might suggest a much milder outcome. The effects of growing industrialization and urbanization are wearing away at the regional distinctiveness of the South. Regionalism elsewhere in the United States has been waning for decades, and the South is its last prime bastion. Politically, these changes might suggest less a realignment outcome than a *convergence* outcome, whereby the South might slip more directly into the mainstream of American political life. Such an outcome would not require that the South become Republican or even, for that matter, lose its Democratic majority. But it would mean several important political changes at the mass level: some growth in Republicanism, sufficient to maintain a more vigorous party competition; voting trends in national elections that parallel more clearly those elsewhere in the country; the development of political divisions of the vote based more on social class and urban-rural distinctions than upon the older regional questions, and the like.

A third broad outcome, the development of a more permanent third party in the South, could stem from Southern disaffection with both national parties on the race question. Such a development, contrary to the convergence outcome, would be a step in the direction of greater rather than less regionalism.

There are, of course, other possible outcomes involving combinations of these three basic types of change. For example, one of these changes might arise at one level of office—the presidential perhaps—without comparable change at other levels. In this paper, however, we choose to focus on the outcomes which involve at least some increase of Republican allegiances among voters in the South, which means either the convergence or the realignment outcomes. We have two reasons for such a choice.

First, as a matter of practical politics, these two outcomes seem to be the primary *stable* rather than transitional ones. There may be spates of Dixiecrat-style protest, but there seems to be little stomach among Southern politicians for developing a truly independent third party, and there are many forces operative in American politics to counter the durability of such a development. Combined outcomes, such as presidential Republicanism but maintenance of Democratic supremacy at other levels of office, seem intrinsically unstable in the long term as well.

Second, we shall focus upon the growth of some stable Republicanism because we are much better equipped conceptually and empirically to handle such change. For many years now we have studied the characteristics of basic party loyalties, where the choice lies between the two major parties. However, we have had little experience with the dynamics of voting when a third-party alternative is offered, especially when that alternative is only poorly dissociated from that presented by one of the existing parties, as tends to be true of Dixiecrat-type movements that make use of the state Democratic label.

In sum, then, we address ourselves specifically here to an assessment of the likelihood that the number of Republican loyalists in the South will grow sufficiently either to bring Southern voting patterns more in line with those elsewhere in the nation, or to create a truly Republican South.

Long-Term Party Loyalty vs. Short-Term Voting Choice

One other distinction should be clarified before we undertake this assessment. A common phenomenon in current American voting behavior is that of the momentary party defection, either in a particular election or, more narrowly still, in casting one vote for a specific office in a given election. The defection is momentary in a sense that can be very clearly defined: the voter himself does not consider that he has changed his party loyalty in any way as a result of the defection, and he is no more likely to defect again in an ensuing election marked by a new configuration of forces than is someone else of the same party who had not defected.

The distinction between the short-term defection and what we call "party identification" seems to be a rather crucial one, for at times these defections become large and systematic in a particular vote. Thus the Eisenhower victories in 1952 and 1956, handsome though they were, did not turn out to be the harbingers of basic partisan realignment that most observers took them to be at the time. Rather, they involved momentary defections on the part of masses of people who continued to consider themselves Democrats, who voted Democratic in the off-year elections of 1954 and 1958, and who even voted Democratic at other levels of office in the Eisenhower elections themselves. Similarly, some remarkable new voting patterns appeared in the South in 1960, with some of the traditional "Bible-belt" strongholds of the Democratic party shifting markedly in a Republican direction. These changes probably represented once again momentary defection among fundamentalist Protestants in the South, touched off by the religious question surrounding the 1960 Democratic candidate, rather than change in basic party loyalty in these areas.[1]

Short-term phenomena of this sort, while interesting in themselves, have little to do with our central question regarding the development of stable Republican loyalties in the South. The ever-present possibility of defection means simply that one cannot be sure, in any given election, that the party enjoying the underlying majority of loyalties will win. But rather special circumstances are required to prevent it from winning, and it has every right to expect to capture the majority of any lengthy sequence of elections. It is in these terms that knowledge of the distribution of underlying party identifications is critical.

Hence we shall not rest our analysis upon any recent vote in the South, but rather upon trends in the expression of party loyalties given us by the Southern portions of our national samples in the past decade. (In view of the sampling base on which our studies are constituted, we are obliged in any analyses to define the South somewhat broadly. Fifteen states are included, with Maryland, West Virginia, Kentucky, and Oklahoma added to the eleven states of the Confederacy.) Such a strategy requires further explanation, however, because it presumes implicitly that expressions of identification with the Democratic party have the same meaning and the same predictive value in the South as in the rest of the nation. We frequently receive the complaint that this is not the case: a self-styled "strong Democrat" from Mississippi, it is said, does not respond to the national parties in the same way as a "strong Democrat" from Illinois. More specifically, it is often contended that there is in the South a substantial contingent of voters who see themselves as Democrats because of state and local party offerings yet who are addicted to voting Republican in presidential races.

This argument is so credible that we have invested a good deal of time in evaluating it. However, we have thus far been unable to find any support for it. This is not to say that there are no self-styled Democrats in the South who have preferred to vote Republican at a presidential level over quite a sequence of elections. But it is to say that such people are so extremely rare in the total Southern electorate that they cannot be identified as a meaningful proportion through a sample survey, and hence can contribute little to the general flavor of Southern voting.

While the evidence against the argument is varied, we shall present here two of the most definitive proofs. First, for a decade we have asked our respondents this question: " [In the elections since you have been old enough to vote] have you always voted for the same party or have you voted for different parties for president?" (If 'same') "Which party was that?" Coded answers include "always" having voted for the same party, "mostly" having voted for the same party, and having voted for "different parties." If responses to our standard party identification question had a different meaning South and non-South, we should find a lower proportion of strong Democrats in the South who have always voted for the same party for president than among strong Democrats elsewhere. Similarly, one would expect a visibly higher proportion of strong Democrats in the South who indicate that they have voted "mostly" Republican at the presidential level. While one finds less party fidelity among weaker partisans everywhere in the nation, we should still expect parallel discrepancies to arise between North and South for "weak Democrats," if these responses have different regional meaning for partisan behavior.

Table 1 gives little support to such expectations. The table is somewhat awkward from an analytic point of view, as it combines data from three quadrennial samples during which the general cast of responses showed some secular shift, and two of the component samples have a large overlap in personnel interviewed. However, the combination was made to secure sufficient cases outside of the two Democratic categories in the South to permit at least loose examination. The secular trend in party fidelity responses that the table masks follows in the most natural way from political realities of the period. That is to say, the 1952 election was the first major "deviating" election (an

Table 1. Reports of Past Party Fidelity in Presidential Voting by Party Identification Category, South and Non-South[a]

Report of past presidential voting choices:		Party identification						
		Strong Dem.	Weak Dem.	Ind. Dem.	Ind. Ind.	Ind. Rep.	Weak Rep.	Strong Rep.
Non-South	Always Dem.	81%	56%	29%	6%	4%	3%	1%
	Mostly Dem.	3	5	3	1	1	1	*
	Different	15	37	65	87	65	42	21
	Mostly Rep.	0	*	0	0	0	3	6
	Always Rep.	1	2	3	6	30	51	72
		100%	100%	100%	100%	100%	100%	100%
	Number of Cases[a]	557	628	234	246	259	530	586
South	Always Dem.	83%	55%	26%	5%	14%	2%	1%
	Mostly Dem.	6	5	14	2	0	1	1
	Different	10	38	50	75	57	33	21
	Mostly Rep.	0	0	0	0	0	1	9
	Always Rep.	1	2	10	18	29	63	68
		100%	100%	100%	100%	100%	100%	100%
	Number of Cases[a]	324	349	42	56	35	96	101

[a] The table includes only white respondents in the two regions who had voted sufficiently to respond to the question, and is based on a combination of samples from 1952, 1956, and 1960. Since a large number of the same respondents were reinterviewed in 1956 and 1960, the numbers of cases indicated cannot be taken as totally independent observations, although the question was posed anew in 1960 and reports were shifted to take account of more recent voting behavior.

* Indicates less than half of 1 per cent.

election in which defections to the minority party are sufficiently large to put it in power) since the realignment of party loyalties due to the Great Depression, and it was rapidly followed by another massive defection to Eisenhower in 1956. The election of 1960 brought a new and relatively independent wave of defections on the religious question. Hence reports of past party fidelity (particularly among Democrats) were weaker in 1960 than they had been in 1956, and weaker in 1956 than in 1952. Similarly, Southern Democrats who had reported slightly greater party fidelity in 1952 and 1956 than comparable non-Southern Democrats, slightly surpassed the non-Southern Democrats in reports of infidelity in 1960. However, this 1960 difference is a direct consequence of the far more numerous Protestant Democrats who avoided a Kennedy vote on religious grounds in the South; equally fervent Protestant Democrats *outside* the South show the same decline in reports of fidelity. All of these regional differences are rather weak at best, and the largest summation possible (Table 1) shows but slight and irregular differences over-all. (The regional differences which are largest in an absolute sense lie outside the two critical Democratic columns on the left, where most of the Southern cases fall. It must be remembered that where Southern cases are fewest in the central columns, sampling error is largest. The only striking differences here cast a rather mixed light on the hypothesis.)

A second test is equally convincing. In 1958, out of continued concern with the Southern problem, we asked respondents who had just told us their direction and degree of party identification in the usual way whether in making the response they had been thinking primarily of the national level or of the state or local level of political competition. Here again, the hypothesis of presidential Republicans in the South would lead one to anticipate an unusual proportion of Southerners who would confess after the fact that their stated Democratic allegiance had been given assuming a state and local context only.

We were surprised to discover that very few people in either North or South discriminated between national and state party allegiances. In the nation as a whole about 94 per cent of the respondents indicated that they would enter the same report of party identification indiscriminately for either level. Furthermore, of the 6 per cent who wanted to indicate some discrimination between levels, less than one-fifth (1 per cent of the total population) felt that they had different party loyalties at the two levels; the vast majority of discriminators simply felt that they were independent at one level and partisan at the other. There were slight regional differences in these figures which are nearly significant in a statistical sense: 95 per cent of non-Southerners failed to discriminate between levels, while the corresponding figure for the South was 91 per cent.

However, the item which is important for our purposes is not the fact of discrimination itself, but rather what statement of party identification had naturally been given in response to the party identification question before the novel probing. Here again the answer from the data is very clear: none of the respondents either North or South who had discriminated between levels had given their more-local response to our general question. In other words, all of the few (N of 6, out of 441 cases) Southern respondents who considered themselves Democrats in state politics but Republicans nationally had spontaneously labeled themselves "Republicans" in first indicating their party identification.

In short, the evidence lends no support to the claim that our measure of basic party loyalty has any notably different meaning in the South. Hence we may turn directly to the central problem of this paper, using as our key criterion not the result of any specific vote, but rather expressions of basic party identification. We want to know whether there are signs of any change in the South which would token a partisan realignment of the region or a convergence with political behavior in the rest of the nation.

Convergence in Voting Behavior, South and Non-South

There are several signs pointing to some slow convergence between critical facets of mass electoral behavior as they appear in the South and elsewhere in the nation. As perhaps the most important example, the great gulf between the strongly Democratic mass loyalties in the South and the more balanced but slightly Republican loyalties typical outside the South is in the process of narrowing. Figure 1 presents a portrait of this convergence from data collected between 1952 and 1961. For the purposes of this figure we have used a technique which permits a distribution of party identification to be reduced to a single proportion or an "expected" vote division, following norms established over the years for identifiers of different types.[2] The figure presents the trend in the difference between these proportions for South and non-South. Thus the declining slope reflects a decreasing difference in partisanship between South and non-South. (The actual observations in Figure 1 are somewhat irregular, with the short-term reversals of the trend. It should be kept in mind that each observation contains some sampling error. Nonetheless, there seems to be little question but that over-all, a convergence is under way.)

We have taken the liberty to add a straight line to Figure 1 to show the linear trend which best fits the data. (The linear function is estimated by the method of least squares.) This line, if extended, would arrive at the point of convergence (the baseline of zero difference) in the month of June, 1983. We cite such a precise figure facetiously, of course, since we know enough about the dynamics underlying the trend to be assured that the change could hardly be linear in any long term. Hence our point is figurative, not a literal prediction. But this extrapolation does serve to give a concrete sense of the current rate of change. The change which is occurring is proceeding at a snail's pace. It smacks more of a slow erosion of regional differences than of any dramatic partisan realignment, even in its early stages.

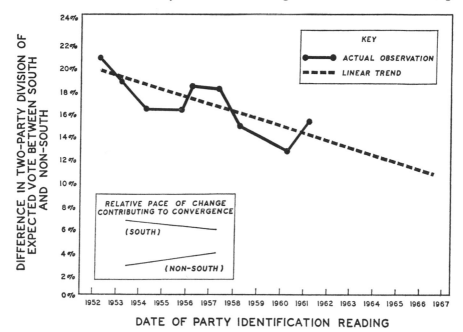

Figure 1. Declining Differences in Partisan Loyalties,
South and Non-South

This fact is further underscored where the South itself is concerned, for the North is contributing more to the convergence than is the South. The relevant data are presented in the box inserted in the lower left corner of Figure 1, where the slope changes which combine in the over-all convergence are isolated. The South in this period has been losing Democratic strength (at an average rate represented by the slope of −0.25 per cent per year), but Democratic strength outside the South has been increasing slightly more rapidly than this (slope of +0.35 per year). Perhaps if there had not been a mild motion toward the Democrats in the nation as a whole, the Southern shift toward the Republicans would have registered in an absolute sense as more rapid. However this may be, it is clear that partisan change within the South has been sufficiently feeble in the past decade as to render analyses of that change rather difficult. Nonetheless, Figure 1 will serve as a primary point of departure, for it sums up change in a rather vital statistic.

Convergence in class voting patterns. Other indicators of slow convergence are worth at least brief mention. One of these is the development of a class flavor to voting patterns in the South that is more akin

Table 2. Change in Status Polarization in the South, 1952–1960

Year	Rank-order correlation, party identification by occupation status
1952	− .06
1954	− .05
1956	− .04
1957	+ .02
1958	− .02
1960	+ .11

to those patterns familiar elsewhere. Up until very recently, it seems, the Democratic party had been the symbol of small-town, middle-class respectability quite generally in the South, much as the Republican party has maintained this image in the small towns outside the South. Indeed, in our earliest studies it appeared that middle-class voters were if anything more solidly committed to the Democratic party than were blue-collar workers in the South. This arrangement, anomalous from the point of view of national politics, may be expressed usefully as a *negative* coefficient of status polarization—in the terms which we have employed elsewhere[3]—that measure representing roughly the difference in proportions of partisans between status levels.*

It is interesting, therefore, that since 1952 there has been a fairly steady progression of this coefficient toward the positive non-Southern norm (Table 2). Two facts seem rather evident again. First, one can hardly doubt that this "normalization" of the class-party correlation in the South is a product of growing industrialization. Indeed, it can be shown that the new polarization is focused in areas of the South that have become most industrialized, and that the old negative correlation persists in more rural or economically stagnant counties of the South (Table 3). Second, the evidence seems to suggest once again a slow erosion of distinctive regional patterns and a drift toward the type of voting norms more characteristic of the rest of the country.

* The conceptual character of the coefficient depends to some degree upon the type of measure of partisanship employed. Thus the association of status and vote tells something of the short-term disposition of class political alignments, in the degree that it departs from the association between status and underlying party identification, which represents more a long-term description. See the distinction drawn in Angus Campbell *et al.*, *The American Voter* (New York: Wiley, 1960), pp. 365–368. Here our interest lies in the long-term loyalty component.

Table 3. Status Polarization and Industrialization, Southern Counties[a]

	Rural	*Intermediate*	*Industrialized*
1960 Status polarization, occupation by party identification	−.11	−.05	+.16
(Number of Cases)	62	158	168

[a] Counties are subdivided according to the relative proportions of agricultural and manufacturing workers.

Increased voting turnout. It seems likely that convergence is going on as well in regard to voting turnout rates. Low rates of Southern turnout in presidential elections appear to be on the wane. Such an assessment is a difficult one to make, for middle-term fluctuations in voting turnout are notoriously confusing. However, Professor Donald S. Strong has worked with aggregate data for a much longer term than those spanned by our studies, and feels there is evidence of genuine secular rise in Southern turnout.[4]

Later analyses of this turnout trend may illuminate an important facet of the decline of regionalism, for low Southern turnout, like many other regional peculiarities, may be seen partly as regional in a direct sense, and partly as regional only in a very indirect way. That is, two of the more distinctive Southern characteristics even in the current period are its low level of education and its relatively rural economy. Both of these factors are quite strongly associated with low voting turnout, not simply in the South but in virtually any area of the world for which satisfactory data are available. This may be seen as an indirect regional influence on turnout: turnout will increase "automatically" as Southern education is increased, but cannot be expected to converge fully upon figures typical of other areas until education levels have come to match those elsewhere. On the other hand, even when all of the factors known to be important in determining turnout (and here we include the problem of Negro franchise, to be sure) are held constant, the Southerner still typically votes less regularly in presidential elections than does his non-Southern counterpart. Until clearer causes may be located, this residual difference can be considered the result of a more direct regional influence.

The trends discussed in this section comprise some of the more notable signs of political change in the South, where mass voting patterns are concerned. Although they are a rather varied collection of symptoms, they all seem to hint in common at (1) change which is rather slow, and (2) change that is edging the South toward convergence with the mainstream of American political life, rather than toward a more dramatic political realignment.

Mechanisms Underlying Southern Political Change

Whenever change is at stake, we can improve our estimates of the shape of the future if we can arrive at an understanding of the mechanisms that are producing the change. While we often make the simple assumption that attitudinal changes in a population mean that people are changing their minds, this is not necessarily the case. If the drift away from purely Democratic allegiances in the South is taken as an example, it is true that such change could be produced through re-evaluations of the major parties by the existing Southern population. Such change we shall call individual partisan *conversion*. Nevertheless, the partisan drift in the South could also be produced by a change in the composition of the population, without any individual conversion whatever. A change in population composition can come about either through *replacement* of a dying generation by a new one of different partisan preferences, or through population exchanges with other regions (migration). With the aid of panel studies that we have recently conducted over a four-year period,[5] the contribution of each of these three sources of change (conversion, population replacement, migration) to the slight observed Republican drift can be roughly estimated. We must stress the crudity of such an estimate, for the observed drift is so slight that the change wrought over even a four-year period lies within our sampling error. Nonetheless, the relevant data have some general interest.

Partisan conversion of white Southerners. It is undoubtedly true that individual conversion is the most exciting type of change. Certainly conversion must be involved in any rapid and dramatic partisan realignment, for population turnover mechanisms can account for nothing more than slow change. Conversion is probably the type of change most pregnant with political meaning as well, since change stemming only from something as politically neutral as population turnover is likely to strike us as change by default.

Yet if individual partisan conversion is occurring in a manner that systematically favors one party over the other in the South, the phenomenon is so weak that it very nearly eludes any sample analysis for the 1956–1960 period. The portion of Table 4 dealing with the South

Table 4. 1956–1960 Change in Party Identification among Whites, South and Non-South

			Party identification pre-election, 1960			1956 Over-all
			Demo-crat	Inde-pen-dent	Repub-lican	
Southern White[a]	*Party ident.,* 1956	Democrat	62%[b]	3%	2%	67%
		Independent	3	11	2	15
		Republican	2	2	14	18
	1960 Over-all		67%	16%	17%	100% (N = 318)
Non-Southern White[a]	*Party ident.,* 1956	Democrat	31%	5%	*	36%
		Independent	9	16	5%	30
		Republican	2	5	27	34
	1960 Over-all		42%	25%	33%	100% (N = 901)

[a] Excluded from the table are those respondents who moved into or out of the South between the 1956 and 1960 interviews.

[b] The box of nine (three-by-three) percentages adds to 100%, as do the summary rows and columns, which give the "marginal" distributions for each year. Because of differences in rounding, occasional rows or columns forming the internal box fail to sum precisely to the marginal entry.

* Indicates less than half of 1 per cent.

shows a modest amout of *gross* change in partisanship in the interior of the table. However, most of this change is self-compensating: the marginals show almost no *net* change. If we reduce the 1956 and 1960 marginals from the South to precise "expected" votes, we do find that the 1960 distribution would generate a vote about 0.5 per cent more Republican than the 1956 distribution.

Nevertheless, the Southern half of the table stands in rather sharp contrast to the non-Southern portion, where there seems to be greater gross change and a very unmistakable net change favoring the Democrats. It is not our purpose here to explore this non-Southern change. However, this shift represents the non-Southern contribution to the convergence phenomenon noted earlier, and it is interesting that outside the South we capture this change quite clearly as individual conversion. The amount of change to be expected in the South is sufficiently slight, and our sampling error sufficiently large, that it would be impossible to claim that individual conversion toward the Republicans cannot account for all of the observed Republican drift. Nonetheless, the evidence that such is the case is weak indeed, and it behooves us to consider the other mechanisms as possible sources of the drift.

Population replacement: the younger generation of Southern whites. Since the younger generation often serves as the leading edge of change, we look with particular interest at recent trends in expressions of partisanship by Southern whites in their twenties.

A survey of these newer voters as they have been interviewed in our samples during the 1950's shows little of interest with respect to long-range change, however. We know from much past experience that the incoming generation of voters has somewhat less stable party loyalties, and hence shows some slight tendency to "float" with the momentary national tide in reports of party identification. This familiar phenomenon is visible if one compares the cohort of Southern voters in their twenties with their elders, and particularly the oldest generation which the new is replacing. That is, in 1956 when the Republican tide nationally was at its peak for the series, these young Southern white voters were slightly more Republican than their elders, and in 1958 when the Democratic tide was at its peak, they were slightly more Democratic. But these differences have been weak at best, and the total pattern is relatively meaningless: on balance over the years, the younger Southern white generation seems no more and no less Democratic than older generations. The inevitable population replacement seems to be contributing nothing toward long-range partisan change among whites in the South.

Migration. If persons moving from one area of the country to another adopted the partisan norms of their new habitat with fair speed, the regional redistribution of the mobile American population would do very little toward erasing the partisan distinctiveness of regions. This does not appear to be the case, however. It now seems that once an adult has developed relatively firm partisan loyalties—usually by the time he is thirty or thirty-five—migration has little effect in inducing partisan change. A Republican moving from a Republican area, for example, is little or no more likely to change his party identification over ensuing periods than is the Republican who remains.[6] Under such circumstances, migration can serve to reduce regional differences in partisanship in a notable way.

One can conclude with unusual certainty that migration has been playing a considerable role in some of the convergence phenomena noted between South and non-South. The effect has been particularly marked in the past ten years because of certain new characteristics of the interregional exchange in this period. While U. S. Census Bureau materials on this exchange are not very definitive, we can use our sample data to aid in a rough description of recent trends.

First, the relative size of the North-to-South and the South-to-North streams has been rather uneven over time. For several decades the South has exported substantial numbers of both white and Negro migrants seeking urban industrial jobs elsewhere. However, this stream reached a peak in the 1940's during World War II, and seems to have been tapering to a weaker flow during the 1950's. At the same time, the 1950's have seen a very rapid increase in the stream of movement into the South. Thus, for example, sample estimates in 1952 showed that over three-quarters (77 per cent) of the whites who were currently residing in the region other than that in which they had grown up were of the South-to-North, rather than the North-to-South, stream. By 1956 this figure had been cut to 61 per cent. The result is well summed up by Table 5, which shows the distribution of periods

Table 5. Period of Entry into State of Current Residence, for White and Negro Interregional Migrants

		White				Negro	
	Grew up: *Currently:*	*Non-South* *South*		*South* *Non-South*		*South* *Non-South*	
Period of entry into state of	1956–1960	41%	45%	10%	15%	10%	10%
current residence	1952–1955	23	25	15	22	19	21
	1948–1951	14	16	10	15	17	18
	1940–1947	13	14	31	48	47	51
			100%		100%		100%
	Prior to 1940	9		34		7	
		100%		100%		100%	
Number of Cases		56	51	60	40	42	39

It should be noted that the periods entered in Table 5 do not refer specifically to the dates at which the migrant changed region. Instead, they refer to the time at which the migrant reported that he had established residence in the state where he currently lives. There is thus some margin for error in deductions from the table, although by and large the times of entry into the state are likely to coincide with the times of movement from one region to the other.

reported for entry into the state of current residence as of 1960, on the part of people who had migrated from one region to the other since the period in which they grew up.

Prior to 1950, the steady exodus of Southerners (at first primarily white, but joined in increasing numbers by Negroes in the 1940's) contributed something to a regional convergence in partisanship, since the migrants were much more Democratic than the populations they joined outside the South. They have tended to remain so, and have thereby increased the Democratic partisanship of non-Southern areas into which they have moved. But the partisan effects of this migration were felt only outside the South. In general, the departing Southerners have had much the same partisan coloration as the non-migrants whom they have left behind: their departure has done little to change the over-all partisanship of the region.

The population redistribution since 1950 has had a much different influence upon the South, however. For the first time the South is not only losing Democrats, but is receiving a significant non-Southern population more Republican than the native South. Furthermore, unlike the South-to-North migration, the new North-to-South stream is selective along partisan lines: it turns out that the non-Southerners moving into the South are actually *more* Republican than the non-Southerners they leave behind. This fact means that interregional convergence in partisanship is correspondingly speeded, for the departure of these Republicans leaves the non-South more Democratic than it would otherwise be at the same time as the South becomes the more Republican.

The selectivity along partisan lines which operates in the North-to-South migration is an accident of the types of persons who are moving South. In the first place, the migration is a high-status migration, in marked contrast to the traditional South-to-North movement. As of 1956, for example, only about one-quarter of North-to-South white migrants were blue-collar workers, whereas almost two-thirds of South-to-North white migrants (and well over four-fifths of Negro migrants) were engaged in blue-collar occupations. Since, outside the South, higher-status persons have for a long period been more Republican than low-status persons, much of the explanation of the partisan selectivity lies in the status characteristics of the migrants. However, there are two social types particularly prominent in the North-to-South movement, and these two types are notably Republican even among higher-status non-Southerners: the young white-collar person whose move to the South is more or less directly associated with the growth of industry in the region (e.g., the junior executive transferred to a Southern subsidiary), and the retired non-Southerner of sufficient means to establish new residence for the remainder of his days in the sunnier Southern climate.

In short, then, peculiarities of migration to the South in the 1950's have been such as to maximize its impact both upon partisan change in the South and upon the more general phenomenon of partisan convergence between regions. At the same time, the fact that this migration has been biased rather sharply from a partisan point of view should not obscure the attendant truth that migration is normally a very limited mechanism of change, in the sense that relatively small proportions of the parent populations are involved. We are currently awaiting more refined 1960 census figures that will help establish just what these rates of transfer have been. Nonetheless, it does not seem likely that the number of non-Southerners who have taken up residence in the South in any given year in the 1950's could much exceed 1 per cent of the region's prior population. At such a rate of transfer, even a migration pattern strongly biased toward partisan change will produce only small shifts in any limited period, such as the four-year span between presidential elections.

Still, we must return to the fact that the amount of partisan change to be explained in the South in the 1950's is relatively small as well. Indeed, making a set of somewhat conservative assumptions on the basis of sample data, we can calculate roughly the partisan change which migration phenomena could be expected to have induced in the South in this period, and we find that the effects would easily account for the observed Republican drift.

From a Southern point of view, however, the effects of migration may appear more impressive on a number of counts. First, the emigration and immigration are geographically concentrated in ways that give them maximum visibility, and that in the long range may have maximal political implications. That is, the exodus from the South has been heaviest in the poor and backward interior uplands, and the new carpet-baggers of the 1950's have not, of course, been settling in these areas. Rather, they have moved either to the littoral or to burgeoning urban-industrial areas. Among Southern states, probably Florida is most clearly receiving both streams of non-Southerners at once— the retired and the young white-collar personnel. The population of Florida increased at a more rapid rate between 1950 and 1960 than did the population of California. Census figures show that of 1960 Floridians, 26 per cent had not been residing in Florida in 1955. While one could hardly consider all of this 26 per cent to have entered from outside the South, the figure remains a rather astonishing one. It is in such areas that the effects of migration patterns will be most clearly felt.

Second, the immigrants bring with them not only a more Republican coloration, but also voting habits quite unlike those of their Southern counterparts. Hence they contribute to the rising turnout in the South, and also have a somewhat higher partisan impact on voting patterns than could be expected if native Southerners were turning out at equal rates.

In the third place, the immigrants to the South are contributing in a clear fashion to the increase in status polarization of the Southern vote. They are of remarkably high status, and are much more Republican than their Southern high-status counterparts. The effects are obvious, and the clear localization of status polarization in urban and industrialized counties (Table 3) is in part a reflection of the areas which attract these migrants.

On the other hand, the increase in status polarization of partisanship in the South since 1952 cannot be entirely explained by immigration, for the change has been quite marked (Table 2). It involves many more people than the slight net drift toward Republican loyalties, and the numbers of high-status immigrants would simply be insufficient to account for all of the change. Hence we may return to see if some of the gross partisan conversions represented for the South between 1956 and 1960 (Table 4) conceal any differential change by social class. Table 6 shows this division, and it is clear that the two class groups among Southerners are evolving in differential, though largely self-compensating, partisan directions.

While these instances of "real" partisan conversion are few in terms of numbers of interviews, it has been instructive to read the interviews, spaced as they are over a four-year period, to get some flavor of the partisan perceptions which underlie the changes in loyalties. At an entirely clinical level, the interviews that create the increase in polarization fall in three rough classes of changers. The first group, made up of higher-status respondents, has shifted from Democratic to Republican in party identification between 1956 and 1960 out of indignation at the Democratic party for having nominated a Catholic. This is not to say that lower-status Southerners were not upset as well, but the few

Table 6. 1956–1960 Change in Party Identification among Southerners,* by Class

			Party identification pre-election, 1960			1956 Over-all
			Democrat	Inde-pendent	Repub-lican	
South: Blue-collar[a]	Party ident., 1956	Democrat	65%[b]	3%	0%	68%
		Independent	2	10	2	14
		Republican	2	4	12	18
	1960 Over-all		69%	17%	14%	100% (N = 107)
South: White-collar[a]	Party ident., 1956	Democrat	57%	7%	5%	68%
		Independent	3	11	1	15
		Republican	3	1	12	17
	1960 Over-all		63%	18½%	18½%	100% (N = 103)

* Exceptionally, this table includes both Negroes and whites, although the polarization shown is not primarily a Negro phenomenon.

[a] Excluded from the table are those respondents who moved into or out of the South between the 1956 and 1960 interviews.

[b] The box of nine (three-by-three) percentages adds to 100%, as do the summary rows and columns, which give the "marginal" distributions for each year. Because of differences in rounding, occasional rows or columns forming the internal box fail to u m precisely to the marginal entry.

instances in which party identification as well as 1960 vote was shifted on such grounds turn out to have come from devout middle-class Protestants. From our experience in these matters we would highly suspect that these changes are transient. However, these interviews contribute to the rather sudden leap which the polarization coefficient takes between 1958 and 1960 (Table 2). We suspect that the underlying evolution is more regular than this leap would suggest.

The second group of interviews are those from lower-status Southerners who defend their shifting allegiance on the ground that the Democratic party is "the party of the common man," the archetype of the working-class reaction. The third group is made up of higher-status Southerners who are concerned about the economic liberalism of the Democratic party at a national level. These people talk in typically conservative fiscal terms, and mourn the lack of national power of the Southern conservative Democrats. Their shifts are equally class shifts, and are indicative of increasing weight placed on politics at the national level.

Most surprising among the white contributors to the second and third group of interviews, however, is the integral role which partisan perceptions concerning desegregation and the Negro problem play in the accounts of change. By and large, the Negro question seems *as* salient if not *more* salient in the partisan shift than do the socio-economic perceptions. The fact that the question is salient is not surprising, as this is true of many Southern interviews. But the interesting fact is that lower-status Southerners who have been Republican blame the Republicans for desegregation pressure and thereby help to justify a shift to the Democrats, while the higher-status changers justify their shift by precisely the inverse perceptions. It is not at all clear whether this perceptual difference is merely a rationalization after socio-economic pressures have led to the shift, or whether it springs from more genuine differences in attention to national events. Where the latter hypothesis is concerned, the flavor of some interviews suggests that possibly the flamboyant events at Little Rock, associated with Eisenhower and hence the Republicans, had greater weight in the minds of the relatively uninformed lower-status Southerners, while the higher-status Southerners were seeing the forest and not the trees, perceiving the national Democratic party as a more radical long-term threat on the race question. One crucial fact is clear, however: the competition of both national parties to become associated with a strong stand on civil rights creates an ambiguous situation which Southern voters can interpret to justify partisan shifts in either direction.

The Southern Negro and partisan change. We have left the Southern Negro apart from most of our analyses up to this point. The subject is a difficult one to treat, in part because there is such a considerable discrepancy between the total number of Southern Negroes in our sample and the number who are actually in a position to vote. The latter cases are too few for much direct analysis. The subject is difficult as well because our panel materials make clear that in the current period the reports of party identification on the part of Southern Negroes as a total group are extremely labile, showing much gross change from one interview to the next. This lability, while rather typical of very poorly educated and relatively apolitical populations, makes any reasonable prognosis almost impossible. Change among

Table 7. 1956–1960 Change in Party Identification among Southern Negroes[a]

		Party identification pre-election, 1960			1956 Over-all
		Democrat	*Indepen-dent*	*Republican*	
Party ident., 1956	Democrat	52%[b]	0%	18%	70%
	Independent	4	9	0	13
	Republican	4	2	11	17
1960 Over-all		61%	11%	28%	100% (N = 46)
		Party identification post-election, 1960			
Party ident., 1956	Democrat	56%	2%	10%	69%
	Independent	10	0	5	14
	Republican	10	5	2	17
1960 Over-all		76%	7%	17%	100% (N = 42)

[a] Excluded from the table are those respondents who moved into or out of the South between the 1956 and 1960 interviews. Excluded from the table also are numerous Negroes who gave "apolitical" responses on one or the other of the readings.

[b] The box of nine (three-by-three) percentages adds to 100%, as do the summary rows and columns, which give the "marginal" distributions for each year. Because of differences in rounding, occasional rows or columns forming the internal box fail to sum precisely to the marginal entry.

Southern Negroes at the time of the 1960 election serves as an excellent case in point. The matrix showing changes in party identification between 1956 and the pre-election report in 1960 seems to show a marked swing toward the Republicans among Southern Negroes as a whole, and upon seeing this table alone one would rapidly conclude that the Negro was making a visible contribution to the net Republican drift in Southern partisanship (see top portion, Table 7). However, the second report in 1960, taken after the election, not only fails to reproduce this 1956–1960 swing, but actually shows a swing toward the Democrats! (See bottom portion, Table 7. This second table is particularly curious since, of forty-two Negroes who gave some party identification at both of the readings, only one considered himself a Republican both times.) Uninformed and labile citizens are particularly susceptible to bandwagon effects, and it is likely that this singular performance represents a reaction to Kennedy's election victory.

A scanning of the Southern Negro interviews over time suggests that we should distinguish two types of changeability in party loyalties. The first is lability properly speaking, and could be applied to the very great majority of the Negro interviews. Most of these respondents are extremely ignorant, disoriented, and in the most utter confusion about politics. However, a handful of interviews are politically quite articulate. They come without fail from relatively young Negroes into whose life a fair amount of education has crept: a schoolteacher in Louisiana, a young man in Alabama trying to finish high school at night, and the like. These latter Negroes figure prominently among those whose party identifications have changed over the course of our interviewing. However, this change is not the lability of ignorance; rather, the respondents are attempting to adjust their party choice to a civil rights calculus, and that assessment is apparently difficult enough that choices shift rather readily over time. Whereas the older and more ignorant Southern Negroes change parties without any apparent coherence or rationale, indicating in one interview that they are "strong Democrats" and a few weeks later that they are "strong Republicans," the interviews from these younger Negroes tend to show a coherent evolution of party perceptions and party loyalties over time, passing from one party through periods of doubt to the opposing party, etc. What is striking here, exactly as in the case of the Southern white changers, is that one set of these coherent Negro respondents moves from Republican identification in 1956 to Democratic identification in 1960, justified on civil rights grounds, while the other set, attempting the same calculus for the same reasons and with the same information in the form of broad national political events, moves from Democratic identification in 1956 to Republican identification in 1960. Once again, the ambiguity of the major party positions in the civil rights debate leads to the same aggregate diffusion of voting strength as is apparent among Southern whites concerned with the problem.

Summary and Perspectives for the Future

In many ways our data and our interpretations are of the same cloth as those of Professor Strong elsewhere in this volume. This is particularly true when it comes to political changes in industrializing areas of the South. Our accounts diverge quite widely, however, in terms of the *rate* of change that is presumed. We see a very slow trend, one that probably was under way not too long after the turn of the century, and that is likely to continue its slow evolution to the turn of the next, barring dramatic and unforeseeable interventions. Professor Strong sees much the same political ground as being covered in a relatively short time—in the twenty-four years from 1936 to 1960, and perhaps more especially in the sixteen years from 1944 to 1960.

It would seem that these differences spring in large measure from the different indexes of political change that have been chosen. Professor Strong focuses his attention upon vote trends for selected areas in the South, whereas our emphasis has been upon trends in the underlying division of party loyalties for the South as a whole. The rough sketches in Figure 2 represent much of our conceptions of the divergence in view. The dashed line, representing the presidential voting for the fifteen Southern states treated in this paper and for the remainder of the country, is a matter of public record (because of occasional incursions of third parties in one region or another, some portions of the curve must represent reasonable estimation). The more stable heavy line is intended to represent the basic division of party loyalties. For the period since 1952, this heavy line is faithful to existing data; prior to that time it is entirely putative, for no comparable measures exist. The most controversial assumption that has been made is the following: since the relationship of party loyalties to actual vote has been very similar in the South to those for the nation as a whole, 1952–1960, they probably were similar before this period as well, within such confines as the slightly different "pitch" which the voting curves suggest.

In view of the presumptive nature of part of the data, the reader should not put too much emphasis on early portions of the figure. In particular, the timing of the sharp and rapid realignment of basic loyalties connected with the Great Depression is quite imaginary, although there is a great deal of consensus that such occurred roughly in this time period. What the figure is primarily intended to portray is the likelihood that Republican candidates in the 1920's were receiving slightly more than their "fair share" of votes (as defined by party loyalties); that Roosevelt started the 1930's by receiving greatly more than a Democrat's "fair share" of votes; that in the 1950's Eisenhower received greatly more than a Republican's "fair share" of the

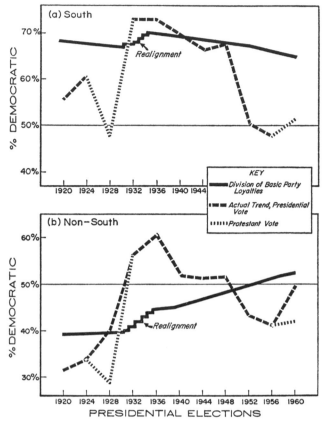

Figure 2. Trends in Voting and Party Loyalties, 1920–1960

votes, and Nixon slightly more in 1960, although among Protestants this pro-Republican increment remained large. All of these facts were common to both South and North, as the voting trends show, and hence are not likely to be explained by factors unique to the South. This is particularly true when the Protestant South is matched with the Protestant contribution to the national vote in the two elections involving a Catholic candidate. These departures of the actual vote from the baseline set by party loyalties are attributable to what we have called "short-term forces" associated with transient political objects like Roosevelt, Eisenhower, and the religious question in 1928 and 1960.

Our view of the recent history of the "Solid South" (as measured by electoral votes) is therefore as follows. From 1880 through 1916 the South was perfectly solid, save for McKinley's capture of the border state of Kentucky in one of the stronger pro-Republican swings of the period. We presume that considerably prior to 1920 some gradual convergence phenomenon had begun, however. In 1904, the last strong pro-Republican swing from the baseline prior to 1920, the South was still behaving quite like a region apart, even where short-term forces were concerned, and certainly was distinctive in the division of its underlying party loyalties. In 1912 voting patterns were confused by the Bull Moose party, and 1916 brought a pro-Democratic swing. By 1920, however, convergence was far enough along that a strong pro-Republican swing nation-wide was able to snare for Harding two of the more marginally Democratic states of the region. This Republican surge subsided somewhat in 1924, but Coolidge still captured Kentucky. Then came 1928, with its strong pro-Republican forces on devout Protestants, and the South actually gave Hoover the bulk of its electoral vote.

In the Roosevelt years, it appeared that the South was as solid as ever. One can presume that the South did share in some measure in the genuine realignments of the period. However, it seems clear that most of the "re-solidifying" of the South was attributable to short-term forces associated with Roosevelt: had a sharp pro-Republican swing occurred at a national level in this period, a Republican candidate could have won some Southern electoral votes, for the "center of gravity" of Southern partisanship was very nearly as within reach as it had been in the 1920's.

Once beyond the Roosevelt years, national trends moved back toward the central ground and, with Eisenhower, deep to the Republican side, thus exaggerating the apparent speed of partisan change in the South. It is this trend which Professor Strong is examining. When he compares 1924 with 1956 or 1960, the proportion of observed movement attributable to change in basic loyalties in the South (and not mirrored elsewhere in the nation) is substantial, although it still is much less than 100 per cent of such change. But when 1936 or 1944 is compared with 1956 or 1960, a large proportion of the change captured has to do neither with basic loyalties nor with the South *qua* South. For much of this change has occurred *outside* the South in the same way at the same time. We would certainly not care to use the decline of the white supremacy doctrine as a factor accounting for the motion toward the Republicans over this period in typical Protestant counties of Minnesota or upstate New York.

There is no doubt that Southern partisanship is in the process of change. As various Southern constituencies drift more nearly within reach of the opposition, Republican politicians begin to run candidates where interparty contests have been rare in the past. In the deeper Confederate South, for example, the number of national House seats contested in 1962 was almost three times as great as the number contested in 1958, and of course with this increase in the possibility for Republican minorities to vote Republican, the proportion of the Republican vote in this period nearly doubled. Nonetheless, even in 1962 the vote division at this level was more Democratic than the "expected" vote for the area, and will remain so until all or most of the remaining seats are contested. Below the presidential level on the ballot, then, the Republican party will be able by increasing its numbers of candidates to strike a new high-water mark in the popular vote every other election (or two elections out of every three) for some time to come, as has been true in the recent past. However, its successes are likely to be most impressive in narrower locales where there is a wave of discontent and, as Professor Strong intimates, with Republican candidates who make as little as possible of their party affiliation (as with John Tower and James Martin), for the Southern Democrat is still far from ready to receive Republicans with open arms. Finally, as Figure 2 suggests, voting at the presidential level is not likely to show any further Republican trend in the next few elections. Indeed, once the religious issue fades, the presidential vote division in the South is likely to move back to a more Democratic position.

*　　*　　*

It is in this sense that it does not seem reasonable to suppose that the South is about to become a reliably Republican region in its presidential voting, as might be suggested were we to extend the general 1936–1960 voting trend of the South in the same direction (Figure 2) for as little as two more elections. This is not to question the tremendous importance of the racial question in the South. Indeed, of current issues on the American scene, the Negro problem comes closest (in the South, but not elsewhere) to showing those characteristics necessary if a political issue is to form the springboard for large-scale partisan realignment. That is, unlike the stuff of many great historical debates on tariffs, fiscal standards, foreign policy, the scope of government, or domestic Communism, the culture patterns at stake in the racial issue involve the immediate daily experience of the quasi-totality of the Southern electorate. History suggests that this kind of immediacy is the first critical ingredient for large partisan realignments.

Yet such realignment requires something more as well. It requires that the alternatives offered by the parties be clearcut in the public eye. Each of the antagonistic elements must be left in no doubt as to which party is the champion and which the enemy of its interests. This condition is clearly not fulfilled at present, whether judged by our voter interviews or by an examination of party positions. The Southern wing of the Democratic party has, in forty years, been obliged to temper slightly its rabid antagonism to the uplifting of the Negro. The national Democratic party, in the same period, has moved from a position of occasional flashes of embarrassment about Southern Democrats to a position of increasing intransigence. What has not happened, of course, is that the Republicans have come forth to champion the Southern white. Instead, their gestures toward the Southern Negro have come close to matching those of the Northern Democrats. If we doubt that partisan realignment is likely to occur, it is to say that we expect no dramatic change in this state of affairs.

On the other hand, the slow partisan drift that marks the convergence outcome seems very nearly as inevitable as the realignment outcome is dubious. Convergence is under way, and there is nothing in the underlying mechanisms that would tempt us to predict that it will stop in the immediate future. Certainly in recent years migration from the North has contributed something to the phenomenon, and there is no reason to expect such migration to wither away.

There are, however, reasons to expect that the change will slow down before anything like full convergence is achieved. That is, the convergence process will lead to a more vital Republican party in larger urban areas, and a reshaping of the Southern political map quite generally, with a new kind of political differentiation setting city apart from exclusive suburb, and both apart from rural counties fifty miles distant, in the manner that has become familiar in the North. We would, however, hazard a guess that it will *not* lead to widespread party competition in portions of the South that remain rural. For the foreseeable future, we would anticipate that the rural Southern hinterland will remain largely a fief of the Democratic party, just as more rural areas in New England and the Midwest have remained Republican fiefs. There are precedents for such arrangements in Europe, where through historical accident one rural region has crystallized as leftist and another as rightist, even though to the observer the demands of the two areas upon the polity seem entirely similar.

Nonetheless, increased convergence will have the important consequence of reducing the probability of any partisan realignment of the region as region. While we have not labored the point in the course of this paper, in many senses the convergence outcome and the partisan realignment outcome are intrinsically incompatible. The South will inevitably participate in future partisan realignments, but it will do so as part of the nation, demonstrating internal patterns akin to those shown elsewhere, rather than moving *en bloc* by itself as a distinctive region. A decade or two ago the Democratic alignment of the small-town and agrarian South was highly anomalous next to the Republican alignment of non-Southern small towns and rural areas. As urbanization and industrialization have progressed in the South, the two parties have been developing Southern clienteles that are more appropriate to their national policy positions. From this point of view, the likelihood that the South as a region will undergo any distinctive and major party realignment is probably less in 1962 than it was in 1948, and is continuing to decline.

1. See Philip E. Converse, Angus Campbell, Warren E. Miller, and Donald E. Stokes, "Stability and Change in 1960: A Reinstating Election," *American Political Science Review*, LV (June, 1961), 269–280.

2. For a detailed explanation of this technique, see Philip E. Converse, *The Construct of a "Normal Vote" Cast by a Population Grouping* (Ann Arbor: Survey Research Center, University of Michigan, 1962).

3. See Philip E. Converse, "The Shifting Role of Class in Political Attitudes and Behavior," in Eleanor Maccoby *et al.*, eds., *Readings in Social Psychology* (3rd ed.; New York: Henry Holt, 1958), pp. 388–399.

4. Personal communication, July, 1961.

5. Respondents first interviewed at the time of the 1956 presidential election were reinterviewed again in 1958 and in 1960. The sequence of interviews was carried out with the aid of grants from the Rockefeller Foundation and the Social Science Research Council.

6. Angus Campbell, Philip E. Converse, Warren E. Miller, and Donald E. Stokes, *The American Voter* (New York: Wiley, 1960), chap. xvi.

Allan P. Sindler

Editor's Epilogue: Some Trends, Judgments, and Questions

In keeping with the conception of this volume, the editor's epilogue selectively comments on some themes advanced by the contributors and makes no pretense of any full recapitulation or synthesis of those themes. What follows, then, attempts to be neither overly repetitious nor overly independent of the preceding essays, but to relate back to them with an eye to raising some pertinent questions.

The Currents of Change

Each contributor, in dealing with his aspect of contemporary trends, has made clear that "the South" is not of one piece in its reaction to the forces of change. Whether the focus be effectuation of the law, economic development, the evolution of race relations, or the shaping of new political patterns, emphasis has properly been placed on the variations of response within the South, and on some of the important factors associated with such variation. Similarly, the preceding essays have given explicit attention to aspects of continuity as well as of change, particularly since much of what is considered change is less an innovation than a development, perhaps accentuated, based on discernible pre-existing patterns. Acknowledgment of these complex dimensions of change undoubtedly hampers the ease with which analysis can be undertaken and judgments can be formed, but any simplistic account of change is likely to be self-defeating for obvious reasons.

Discussions of significant currents of change in the South abound in the essays in this volume. By way of example, take the critical area of race relations and attitudes, factors that serve importantly to differentiate the Southern region from the rest of the nation. Professor Thompson entitles his chapter "The South and the Second Emancipation," thereby emphasizing that an ongoing revolution in the racial base of status relationships is aimed at reshaping the region's social structure in as fundamental a manner as possible. "Reaction to change," comments Professor Thompson, "brought the idea of race into existence as part of the Southern 'way of life' in the first place; reaction to change is dramatically altering that way of life and the idea of race implicit in it today." As another illustration, consider the broad assertion by Professor Clark, one that implies the inevitability of durable and irreversible changes in the region: ". . . the modern South cannot accept the advantages offered by industrialism without adapting many of its social and political ideas and forms."

To say that the winds of change are blowing lustily throughout the South—at times seemingly with hurricane proportions—is not necessarily to say that the South as a distinctive community is in the process of vanishing, of being fully absorbed into the mainstream of American life. (Although the question of whether such full absorption would be a good or a bad thing for the region and for the nation is a most enticing one, the editor refrains from exploring it since all the contributors chose not to examine that phase of the problem.) It is to be expected that speculation on this point often differs, not merely because it is difficult to appraise contemporary trends with perspective, but also because different aspects of change frequently are being looked at and different benchmarks for assessing rates of change are being employed. Such diverse speculation characterizes the judgments evident in this book.

Of the several essays on political affairs, Professor Steamer's is the most sanguine in predicting a rapid restructuring of Southern politics along lines characteristic of the rest of the country. He urges that "some of the uncontrollable currents of history are sweeping the South into the mainstream of American politics and it is safe to predict that in a generation at most, the South, for better or for worse, will be politically nationalized." At the risk of attributing to Professor Strong a position more unqualified than that to which he would ascribe, the direction of his analysis may be said to be broadly supportive of the viewpoint just quoted. Professor Converse, however, using materials other than election data and a measure other than actual voter preference at the polls, is markedly less optimistic concerning the scope of Republicanism in the South, its depth of penetration to state-local levels, and the speed with which the region is likely to achieve the durable reality of two-partyism. Some additional commentary on these different estimates of the political future of the region will be offered in a later section of this epilogue.

In regard to economic developments, Professor Clark acknowledges that "industrial community environment tends to submerge regional traditions and distinctions," but he hopes—as for example in the area of literary traditions—that the unusual richness of the Southern contribution to American letters will not be a casualty of advancing industrialization of the region. Professor Spengler, for his part, urges that the South's rate of economic advance is more impressive when viewed against the backdrop of its own past than against that of developments in the nation at large. While the South's turn to industrialism, therefore, points the region in a direction shared by the rest of the economy, Professor Spengler's analysis stresses that the nature and rate of Southern economic progress prevents a full convergence of regional and national economies in the foreseeable future. The South, in this view, will remain nationally distinctive in the relative underdevelopment of its economic resources, both human and material.

On matters of race, making allowance for the fact that non-Southern practice often violates preachment in important ways, it may safely be concluded that the South will remain the region most laggard in adjusting to the behavior patterns consistent with contemporary majority attitudes on race relations. Without minimizing the significance of the forces making for changed relationships between whites and Negroes, Professor Thompson nonetheless soberly suggests in his concluding section that "it is likely that the idea of race and the deeper social structure that supports it will be with us for a very long time to come." Mr. Frank's endorsement of those doctrinal developments in law that have greatly contributed to the current advance of the Negro does not blind him to the obstacles to uniform and meaningful implementation of those legal doctrines. The critical factor, in Mr. Frank's view, is whether influential elements of the community proffer their support for implementation of the law. In Mr. Frank's own words:

> . . . to borrow a military analogy, the law is the landing force. It makes the beachhead. But the breakthrough, if it is to be significant, is broadened by forces from behind, which take advantage of the opening to go the rest of the way. Where these forces are present, significant alterations of social practices result. Where they do not exist, the law has been unable to hold its beachheads and the legal action becomes a kind of military monument on which is only recorded, "We were here."

In their examination of factors associated with variable Negro registration levels in the Southern states and counties, Professors Matthews and Prothro clearly demonstrate that legal protection of the right to vote, however much a precondition of enfranchising the mass of

Negro citizens in the South, does not in itself necessarily lead to practical achievement of the goal of high rates of Negro registration. The explanatory factors they stress relate in a rather direct way to themes present in several of the other chapters and already briefly noted here, namely, the economic context, also examined by Professor Spengler, and the attitudes of the white community, also commented on by Professor Thompson and Mr. Frank.

Even this cursory review of some of the positions taken by the contributors to this book suggests something of the variety of change-inducing forces at work and the differences among these forces in their depth of penetration of the underlying regional structure and in the degree to which they may provoke counteraction by Southerners to resist or delay change. These forces, considered logically, doubtless all push in a common direction, but even if one allows for their interdependent and cumulative interaction, there remains room for considerable differences of view as to the certainty and speed with which nationalizing changes will be made effective in the South.

Whatever the analyst, from his distant perspective, may conclude about the scope and depth of change in the South, the Southern resident is intimately aware on a day-to-day basis of important alterations in the region's way of life. To many a Southerner, change seems omnipresent and overly demanding, particularly with respect to the pressures for new race relationships. Those who have viewed such currents of change primarily with distaste and unease would do well to ponder the insight in Professor Thompson's observation that "the problems presented the South by the status advance of the Negro count as practically nothing compared with the problems that would be presented by his failure to advance both in status and material change."

Economic-Based Political Change

Most of the essays in this volume underscore the capacity of economic developments to set in motion forces productive of enduring change in non-economic areas. Professor Clark, for example, comments that "no doubt the development of a modern industrial society, along with increased urbanization, promises a new regional political posture." In a similar vein Professor Steamer cites, as the first of four main factors that "have brought the South to the threshold of a new political era . . . , the technological revolution and its resultant urbanization." Concerning the ability of Negroes to become an accepted part of an "integrated American community," Mr. Frank heavily stresses the "economic advance" of the Negro and the development of a Negro middle class as central to that social acceptance. Professor Thompson likewise associates urbanizing trends with the emergence of a Negro middle class, and considers that Negro class element as providing the leading edge of the ongoing quest for racial equality.

While the broad change-inducing potential of economic trends may be readily acknowledged, the more extreme formulations of this approach should be guarded against. It is only a short step from the moderate position noted to the assertion that economic conditions constitute the primary set of factors and, in turn, to the conclusion that *only* economic change can bring about lasting significant changes in the South. The companion assertion often is that when meaningful economic changes occur, they *must* lead to various specified changes in non-economic areas as well. The encouragement such an approach gives to single-cause arguments and to panacea prescriptions needs no belaboring, but the pointed comment of Professor Converse on the limits of purely logical analyses of change merits reminder: ". . . members of human societies are rather adept at muffling and hedging in such change as cannot be avoided. Man seems to respond to change as slowly and narrowly as the situation permits, and what the situation permits is often surprising."

Applying these observations to the matter of Southern political response to regional industrialization, it may be noted that the Southern argument is but one aspect of a currently popular view of the displacement of sectionalism by "nationalizing forces" in American national politics. Invariably stressed in any listing of such forces is the factor of the diffusion of industry, urbanization, and unionization throughout the nation. This trend, in combination with others, is used as supportive evidence for the proposition that a more homogenized and less sectionalized pattern of national politics is in the making. As the states and districts become more similar in the mix of economic and other politically relevant interests contained within their borders, so the argument goes, the political behavior of all areas, wherever located in the continental United States, will tend away from distinctiveness and toward greater uniformity. The South, having been the most conspicuous example of political sectionalism in national politics, is in this view merely an accentuated example of a trend observable in all states and regions.

Although the general drift of this argument is plausible, even attractive, several caveats should be noted in addition to the observations made earlier in this section. In the first place, to say that the older forms of sectionalism may be declining is not necessarily to say that a nationalized politics is the only alternative. If it be true that the disparities in the economic capacity of such states, say, as South Carolina, Vermont, and Illinois have been decreasing over the past several decades, it is not less true that the differences that remain, and that can be expected to remain in the foreseeable future, could easily sustain sectional-like responses to important policy issues. Second, the political consequences of an increasing diversification of interests within the states may be nowhere as complete or as rapid as the argument implies. It is instructive to note that Professor Clark, who leans to the view that industrialization-induced changes in non-economic matters are inevitable even though their exact nature may be somewhat unpredictable, nonetheless observes that "the effects of this era of change are yet to be meaningfully reflected in the political reactions of the Southerners in attitudes toward current issues and partisan behavior." Nor should it be assumed that it is only a matter of time before such a political "lag" is corrected. What appears to many an analyst as an anomalous situation that history must be in the process of rectifying often exhibits impressive stability over time, as for example the durability of the federate nature of national party organization, notwithstanding the centralizing tendencies of government since the 1930's. Finally, and most importantly, the argument is misleading in its easy assumption that the term "industrialization" is a meaningful analytic category by means of which uniform political changes can be predicted.

Not the least of the virtues of Professor Spengler's chapter is his implicit demonstration that "manufacturing" is too undifferentiated a term for satisfactory economic analysis. For example, the economic implications of expansion of manufacturing relating to the processing of agricultural materials differ greatly from those relating to the production of steel. The labor-force implications of rural-based industry are not the same as those of metropolitan-based industry. Extending the same point to politics, it may fairly be suggested that the political consequences of various types of manufacturing also differ in important ways, and that greater research effort might profitably be expended on exploring those different consequences. If such information were available, the diverse political impacts of varying economic changes could be more precisely gauged for economic sub-regions within the South, and a deeper understanding of the results of economic-based change could be had in place of the cruder formulation that the nationalizing force of Southern industrialization will erode the political distinctiveness of the region.

The Negro, The Immigrant, and Political Rights

Is it reasonable to suppose that the progress of Negro integration into the larger community will follow-the pattern set by the assimilation experiences of post-Civil War European immigrants to America? Two of the essays in this volume touch on this question, and both tend to an affirmative answer to it. In Mr. Frank's view, the Negro adjustment pattern must follow that of the earlier immigrant model if a comparable acceptance of the Negro into the national life is to take place. In keeping with this position, one lesson Mr. Frank draws from the history of immigrant assimilation is that the critical need of the Negro is for economic opportunity and advancement that will produce a substantial Negro middle class. Professor Thompson develops the theme that the aspirations of Negroes closely resemble those of the early generations of immigrants, and he finds it useful to conceive of Negroes "as a sort of belated immigrant group." He, too, assigns great importance to the emergence of an influential Negro middle class as a precondition for effective advancement of Negro equality in the region and the nation.

The Negro-immigrant analogy is helpful in providing an historical perspective on the contemporary effort of Negroes to realize equal treatment. Instructive parallels between Negro and immigrant developments might readily be elaborated, thereby serving to remind that much of what passes for the Negro problem was evident in the struggles of earlier immigrant groups as well, and hence is not in itself unique to the Negro. Since the end of the immigrant story is, from the standpoint of cultural integration, mostly a happy one, the viewpoint under discussion has the additional attractiveness of optimism as to the ultimate resolution of the ongoing Negro quest for racial advancement.

Nonetheless, the fit of the analogy between Negroes and immigrants, as Professor Thompson has shown, is far from perfect. The problem invites further commentary, though mostly in the form of speculations and questions because of the incompleteness of the available evidence. The "belated" character of Negro group assertiveness, to make use of Professor Thompson's term, raises problems of timing which may make the immigrant model less than apt for the case of the Negro. Now that Negro pursuit of equitable community treatment is under way in enduring earnestness, will the Negro accommodate himself to the timetable of progress worked out by the trigenerational evolution of immigrant groups earlier? It might also be surmised that the assertion of rights will outpace the short-run ability of Negroes to exploit those rights effectively, with resultant tension not merely for the Negro community and its leadership but for white supporters of the Negro cause as well. Will whites now sympathetic to Negro objectives remain sympathetic during the coming decades as Negroes pursue the goal of acceptance as full Americans by applying their strength as a unified separate subcommunity of Negro Americans? Since such a Negro development would parallel that of the immigrants, to suggest that it might alienate white support is simply to speculate that the climate of expectations on the point is not the same in the latter half of the twentieth century as it was in the first half. And since the prevailing attitudes of the white community will continue to play a crucial role in the rate and thoroughness of Negro assimilation, it could be argued that the Negro may fail in his goal if his essential strategy is to emulate the pattern by which immigrants achieved their comparable goal.

The Negro-ethnic analogy can be questioned more frontally than on the matter of the different historical time periods in which each has come of age. Few would deny that the position of the Negro in America has differed from that of the immigrant in respect to durability, scope, and intensity of social repression of the minority group. No other sizable group has had to contend with a heritage of slavery in America or with a caste system based on the highly visible badge of color. If it be inferred from this special history of the Negro that his is merely an extreme example of immigrant trends, one differing in degree but not in kind, then the analogy under examination may appear fully valid. But if one infers that the unique treatment of the Negro locates that group not on the same continuum with immigrants, then reliance on the model of immigrant assimilation as a predictor of racial things to come could be seriously misleading.

These observations can be applied to raise questions about the popular and official view that the most critical of all Negro rights is the right to vote, the guarantee of which will provide the lever by which the Negro can secure broad racial equality in many areas of activity. This commitment to the centrality of political rights is shared by the Department of Justice and the NAACP, and underlies the federal civil rights legislation of 1957 and 1960. Southern inability to prevent passage of those acts testifies, not to a different assessment by Southerners of the likely importance of a Negro mass vote in Southern states, but to the existence of a firm national consensus on the incompatability of denial of the right to vote with democratic values. From the standpoint of tactics; then, there can be little quarrel with the wisdom of emphasizing the protection of Negro political rights, since that is a more realizable short-term goal than other categories of important rights might be. We are not here concerned, however, with appraising the voting rights proposition in the tactical terms of which rights enjoy what degree of popular support so as to facilitate enactment of federal protective legislation for Negroes. Rather, the point under consideration is the assumption that, since the vote of all men is of equal weight and colorlessness, Negro possession of the power of the ballot will inevitably lead to the same degree of group benefits and group acceptance as that enjoyed by ethnics through the exercise of their political influence.

Although Southern Negroes will not be able to muster full voting strength in the near future for reasons amply documented in the chapter of Professors Matthews and Prothro, let us waive that point by assuming the development of maximum Negro registration and turnout in the long run. Further, even though systematic research on a broad canvas on the relationship between Southern Negro voting power and favorable white treatment of Negroes is not available, let us assume that the relationship has been demonstrated. Thus, such things as token Negro representation on a city council and a lessening of police brutality toward Negroes would be expected to be associated with the presence of a sizable Negro vote. Without belittling the importance of these types of gains to the Negro, the question is still unresolved as to whether the more sensitive and far-reaching components of the goal of Negro equality can be wrested from less-than-sympathetic whites through the avenue of Negro political power.

We thus are led back to the initial question of whether, given the special disability of the Negro in terms of adverse white attitudes, it is reasonable to expect the Negro to realize the goals achieved by immigrants, and if so, whether by the same developmental patterns.

Since the Southern Negro has barely begun on the process of amassing and applying his political influence, it is of course much too early to attempt an answer with respect to the voting rights facet of the Negro-immigrant analogy. It may serve to relieve future frustration, however, to acknowledge at the outset the possibility that voting power may take the Negro considerably less along the way to community integration than it did the immigrant generations. There still would remain, under this view, every good reason to encourage a maximization of Negro voter registration and turnout, but the role of political rights would certainly be stripped of its panacea implications and perhaps of its alleged centrality as well.

Southern Republicanism

The capacity of the race issue to disrupt pre-existing molds of voter behavior, as evidenced by Professor Steamer's account of Louisiana events, cannot be denied. The unpredictability of the appearance of the race issue in politics makes it impossible, however, to accommodate that factor in any rational estimate of the immediate political future of the South. Intervention by Eisenhower at Little Rock, Arkansas, and that by Kennedy at Oxford, Mississippi, will temporarily depress the appeal, respectively, of national Republicans and Democrats, and who can predict when such incidents might recur? The race issue may be additionally neutralized, for forecasting purposes, by making the reasonable assumption that neither major national party can tactically afford to accede to the demands of segregationist white Southerners. Since the parties' common endorsement of Negro goals will probably continue to overshadow whatever slight differences exist between them on the implementation of those goals, the race-oriented white Southerner will have little opportunity to choose between the parties on that basis. Hence discussion of Southern political alignments can proceed with the race issue excluded from consideration.

For a combination of the same and somewhat different reasons, no great amount of effort need be expended on exploring third-party options as part of the political choices facing the South. Insofar as such third-party efforts constitute intermittent outbreaks of white racial anxieties, as was in part the case in 1948 and 1960, the argument made in the preceding paragraph would apply here as well. In addition, if

Democratic defection expressed through third-party channels ever did succeed in throwing a presidential election into the House of Representatives, it is probable that one result would be basic change in the method by which we elect a president, the consequences of which for the South would vary with the nature of the new arrangements adopted. Finally, support of a third party by Democratic leaders exposes them to possible party retaliation at a national convention and within the Congress, and hence is not likely to be resorted to with any frequency. In estimating Southern behavior in presidential politics, then, attention may be concentrated entirely on the major national parties.

The question of a changing Southern pattern in regard to alignments in presidential elections is, therefore, the question of Southern Republicanism, a topic which may be explored appropriately by reference to the essays in this volume by Professors Strong and Converse. The main outlines of Professor Strong's interpretation of Southern presidential Republicanism may be capsuled as follows. From the late New Deal period and on, and particularly since 1945, the national Democratic party abandoned its support of racial policy favored by the South, on the basis of which an historic tie between the region and the party had been forged since Reconstruction. As a consequence, Southerners were given the opportunity to react to presidential politics without the one-party commitment imposed by racial anxieties. Many white Southerners took advantage of that opportunity by supporting Republican presidential candidates, for economic and other reasons which made the axes of presidential choicemaking in the South quite similar to those structuring party alignment in the rest of the nation. The new sources of presidential Republican strength were and are associated with higher-status sections within metropolitan, urban, and suburban areas, a pattern as evident in the Nixon candidacy of 1960 as in the Eisenhower elections of 1952 and 1956. Hence, while the presence of Eisenhower doubtless spurred the rate of development of presidential Republicanism, the latter's dependence on his personal appeal was in no sense complete, so that Eisenhower's departure from the political scene did not put an end to the trend. Quite the contrary. Presidential Republicanism will be a durable pattern; with reference to presidential elections, the Solid South is no more.

If I read the Strong and Converse essays rightly, including their interchange of views on their disagreement, their positions seem more supportive than opposed, though some important differences remain.

This judgment applies particularly to Professor Converse's analysis of the actual election behavior of the South, as distinguished from his discussion of trends in the underlying party identification distributions of the Southern electorate.

Some distance separates the views of the two authors on the rate of partisan change in the South. As compared to Professor Strong's position on the matter, Professor Converse suggests that the party convergence trend has been and will continue to be more gradual, that it was under way before the late New Deal period, and that the convergence trend has been less a function of unique Southern responses and more of regional participation in national election patterns. Professor Strong's clarification, in the concluding portion of his essay, in which some part of the Republican trend is seen to antedate the New Deal and to be related to economic motives rather than to the national party's shift on racial matters, brings the position of the two analysts that much closer. There is agreement on the relationship between increasing Republicanism and industrialization, with the evidence of the more rapid rate of partisan change in the cities, as noted by Professor Strong, being supportive of Professor Converse's view that Southern urban areas will approximate national political norms more closely and sooner than will Southern rural areas. Both endorse the view that the Solid South in presidential politics is a thing of the past, but Professor Converse's estimate of the level of Southern presidential Republican voting in the near future is notably lower than that of Professor Strong, and for reasons which reflect an important difference in findings and interpretation.

Comparing the 1956 and 1960 presidential elections in the South in terms of election statistics for counties and various cities, Professor Strong concludes that the similarity in the level of support accorded Eisenhower and Nixon derived basically from the support of the same voters, i.e., there was considerable overlap between Eisenhower and Nixon voters, from which the inference was drawn as to the durability of the presidential Republican trend and its probable high level of mass appeal in the foreseeable future. In examining the same problem through sample survey data, Professor Converse concludes that while 1956 voting behavior was quite similar to that of 1952, the overlap between the 1952–1956 set of Democratic defectors to Eisenhower and the 1960 set of Democratic defectors to Nixon was little better than a chance distribution; i.e., the voting support base of presidential Republicanism shifted from 1956 to 1960, most of the shift being accounted for by the injection of the Catholic issue into the 1960 campaign. If it is assumed, then, that President Kennedy will run again in 1964 and that the Catholic issue will continue to structure Southern voting response, one would predict that the overlap between 1960 and 1964 Democratic defectors would be high. By the same token, the question of the durability of a high level of presidential Republicanism could not be adequately tested until 1968 at the earliest, assuming at that time the absence of any other cause of short-term defection comparable to an Eisenhower or a Catholic issue. And, in view of the near-independence of the 1952–1956 and 1960–1964 sets and their characterization as short-run defections, Professor Converse concludes that, other things being equal, the 1968 level of presidential Republicanism is likely to be lower than that exhibited from 1952 through 1964.

Much of the rest of the seeming differences between the essays of Professors Strong and Converse would appear to be related to the measures of change used. The party identification factor has long been an important conceptual and empirical tool in the political analyses undertaken by the Survey Research Center at the University of Michigan. The Center's evidence from sample surveys of recent presidential elections indicates, broadly, that party identification tends to be impressively durable, to the extent that only crisis-like events could bring about a mass shift in party attachments. As Professor Converse acknowledges, the race issue in the South contains the ingredients of crisis events, but as he then makes clear, the capacity of race orientations to dictate party choice requires also that the parties can be differentiated unambiguously with respect to their race policies. The current national Republican and Democratic parties do not meet this condition, nor, as earlier noted in this section, is there much reason to suppose they will in the immediate future. In view, then, of the nature of the measure used and the political circumstances facing the contemporary South, it is not surprising to learn that the change in actual Republican vote strength in the region far exceeds the shift in the same pro-Republican direction of underlying partisan identifications. Since the issue is clearly joined between the authors as to whether party identification means the same thing in the South as it does in the rest of the nation, the reader must make his own evaluation of the matter.

The concept of partisan change perhaps can be viewed in terms not of a change in self-designated party identification from Democratic to

Republican, but rather more moderately as a greatly increased probability that a Democrat, having defected in one or more presidential elections, will again defect in the immediate future. Here again, since the Center's data lead to the finding that the 1952–1956 and 1960 sets of Democratic defectors were more independent than overlapping, the conclusion from these data would be that most of the voters who, during the 1952–1956 period, continued to identify themselves as Democrats even as they defected to vote for Eisenhower, then returned to greater consistency in 1960 to vote for Kennedy. Whether the 1960–1964 Democratic defectors, assuming again that the President runs for re-election and the Catholic issue remains of importance to the South, will exhibit the same pattern of short-term dissociation cannot be known until data on subsequent elections are available, but the drift of Professor Converse's views suggests that a similar pattern of temporary defection and return would be expected.

Now that the South has freed itself from its one-party blinders in presidential contests, is it only a matter of time before two-partyism supplants the Democratic monopoly of state and local politics in the region? On the assumption that the former *must* produce the latter, many a publicist has argued in the affirmative. Although the judgments on this point by Professors Steamer and Strong are more cautious and qualified, both tend to be optimistic with respect to a strengthened Republicanism at the state-local level. One or both urge that the same impersonal and irresistible forces remaking the regional map of presidential politics tend to push in the same direction for state-local politics, that the maintenance of a vital national Republican organization in the South rests upon an intensification of Republican activity in state and local races in the lengthy interim between presidential campaigns, and that Republican leaders emerging initially in presidential elections will turn to state and local politics to satisfy their ambitions.

For the foregoing and other reasons, it may confidently be predicted that Republican contests for state-local public offices will increase in scope and frequency and, since the opportunities to vote Republican are thereby multiplied, that the level of voter support for state-local Republicanism also will increase. But this is *not* necessarily to say that state-local Republicanism has a high probability of becoming anywhere near as competitive in many areas of the South as presidential Republicanism will be.

The critical difference in the alleged parallel is that the supporters of presidential Republicanism are dissatisfied with the national Democratic party but are often quite satisfied with a continuance of Democratic control of state and local governments. Since, broadly speaking, it is the economic conservatives who must constitute the new support for a rejuvenated state-local Republicanism, it follows that a precondition of their willingness to desert the Democratic party *locally* is their dissatisfaction with the policy complexion of the Democratic faction controlling politics in the particular state involved. An unbroken succession of economically liberal Democratic administrations in a Southern state would do much to drive unhappy "Democrats who vote for Republican presidential candidates" to the camp of state-local Republicanism, including perhaps an open change in their party identification as well. But is there any so headstrong as to predict with assurance that such a condition is likely to be met in many Southern states, if any?

The same reasoning would obtain for the related matter of the reluctance of Southern Democratic national legislators opposed to the presidential wing of their party to consider shifting to the Republican party. As matters now stand, after all, the conservative Democratic congressman can have his cake and eat it too, enjoying all of the advantages of retaining the Democratic label while supporting the opposition party in legislative voting and in presidential elections. There is no reason to believe that leaders so advantageously placed will voluntarily relinquish their position. If the situation were altered so that their pro-Republican activities jeopardized their Democratic standing, then the possibility of coercing some of these nominal Democrats into an open embrace of Republicanism would be enhanced. Specifically, if such defecting Democrats were stripped of their posts of power in the chamber by their fellow Democrats, then a good part of their advantage in retaining the Democratic label would be taken away from them. Similarly, disaffected Democratic voters in the South would have greater incentive to support outright Republicans, rather than Republican-leaning Democrats, once the power of the latter group within the Congress was curtailed. Once again, though, who would care to argue that such developments within the congressional party are clearly discernible, much less imminent?

In the absence of the facilitative conditions noted, it is not likely that competitive two-partyism in state-local politics will follow soon on the heels of an ongoing developed party competition in presidential politics. The varied forces of change loose in the South would sustain state-local two-partyism in a natural way, but the necessary impetus rests with devising practicable ways of decreasing the attractiveness to economic conservatives of adhering to the pattern of presidential Republicanism complemented by Democratic loyalty in state-local politics.

Index

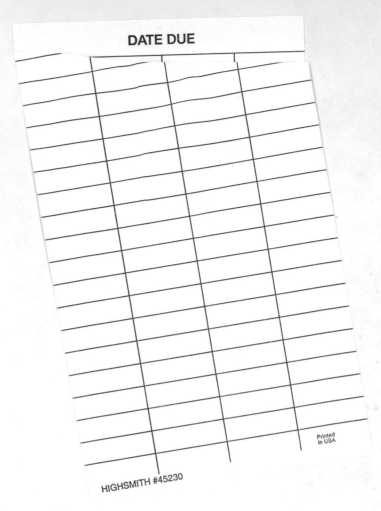

DATE DUE

HIGHSMITH #45230

Printed
in USA